FINANCIAL PERFORMANCE IN SOFTWARE INDUSTRY

By

Dr. S. Kalaiselvi

Vellalar College for Women
Erode
Tamil Nadu
(India)

DISCOVERY PUBLISHING HOUSE PVT. LTD.
NEW DELHI-110 002

First Published-2009

ISBN 978-81-8356-428-1

Published by:

DISCOVERY PUBLISHING HOUSE PVT. LTD.
4831/24, Ansari Road, Prahlad Street
Darya Ganj, New Delhi-110002 (India)
Phone: 23279245 • Fax: 91-11-23253475
E-mail: dphbooks@rediffmail.com
dphtemp@indiatimes.com
web: www.discoverypublishinghouse.com

Printed at:

Sachin Printers
Delhi

DEDICATED
TO
LORD SHIVA

PREFACE

Building an appropriate capital structure of a company is a most difficult task and it cannot be decided in isolation. Components like cost of capital, earnings available to owners and investment decisions are considered to be the pertinent aspects for taking appropriate Capital Structure decisions. By considering the different nature of the cost of Capital of each source, finance Manager has to plan that type of Capital Structure which Minimizes the overall cost of Capital and gives the Maximum benefits to the owners of the business.

Shareholders Value creation is considered important these days among the corporates. The twin measures of wealth creation are Economic Value Added (EVA) and Market Value Added (MVA). The Indian Software industry is the highest foreign Exchange earner. Hence, A study of Shareholder value creation of the Indian Software industry becomes necessary.

In keeping with the aim of this study, an earned effort was made to examine the capital structure and the EVA and MVA performance of the select Indian Software Companies.

During the course of this study, I have taken the help of several scholars and have claimed on the results done by several research scholars in India as well as abroad. The selected bibliography given at the end will bear testimony to my indebtedness to all of them.

I am very much thankful to my guide Dr. Mrs. D. Kamalaveni, Reader in Commerce, Vellalar College for Women, Erode,

Tamil Nadu, who has been a source of perennial motivation in making me to understand the complicacies of this work. Infact, no words would suffice to express my deep sense of gratitude to her. She has been the source of inspiration and continued encouragement throughout my work and without her co-operation, the study would not have been possible.

I am thankful to Mr. B. Sivakumar, PSG Institute of Management, for making me available the companies Annual Reports and the required data.

No work emerges without a great amount of 'behind the scenes' efforts on the part of many well-wishers. A special debt of gratitude is due to all of them.

This in-depth study is mainly directed towards examining, in real life situation of the Indian Corporate World, the pertinent aspects of Capital Structure and the Concept Of Wealth Maximization. As such, the book will be very much useful to the practicing Finance Managers of the corporate world, Students, Scholars, policy framers and the general Readers.

—S. Kalaiselvi

ACKNOWLEDGEMENT

I am indebted to many personalities from the early stages to the final write up of this thesis for the help, ideas and suggestions.

All praise and thanks are due to Lord Shiva for bestowing me with health, knowledge and patience to complete this work.

My greatest debt is to my guide and supervisor *Dr. (Mrs.) D.KAMALAVENI, M.Com., Ph.D., PGDCA.,* Reader in Commerce, PG and Research Department of Commerce, Vellalar College for Women, Erode, whose most creative and original thinking has been a great source of inspiration for me. I am greatly indebted to her for awakening my mind and soul to undergo the research work more energetically. Her blessings, valuable guidance, involvement have induced me to take up challenging assignments and to achieve success in this endeavour.

I express my deep sense of gratitude to *Thiru. S.D. CHANDRASEKAR, B.A.,* the Secretary and Correspondent, Vellalar College for Women, Erode, for having given me an opportunity to do my doctoral research in this prestigious institution and his blessings for the successful completion of my thesis.

It is a great pleasure for me to acknowledge my gratitude and warmest thanks to *Dr. (Mrs.) R. GANGA, M.A., M.Phil., Ph.D., the Principal and Prof. (Mrs.) CHANDRA THANGAVEL, M.Sc., M.Phil.,* Dean, Vellalar Educational Trust, Erode, for having provided me the opportunity and the support rendered to avail the facilities in this college to undergo Ph.D. (Part-time) course.

I feel privileged to record my sincere thanks to *Dr. (Mrs.) LEELAMMA KURUVILLA,* the Head, PG and Research Department of Commerce, Vellalar College for Women, Erode, for her encouragement during the course of my research work. I thank all the faculty members of this department for their support in completing this research work successfully.

I wish to thank *Mrs. V.SANTHI, M.Com. M.Phil., B.Ed., PGDCA.,* the Head and all the staff members of PG Department of Commerce (F & C), Vellalar College for Women, Erode, for their timely help.

I am benefited from the interactions with *Mr. SIVAKUMAR,* Librarian, *Mr. CHANDRASEKAR* and *Mrs. GEETHA,* PSG Institute of Management, Coimbatore. I sincerely thank them for their continuous encouragement and support to complete this work.

I would like to thank all my beloved friends and students for their untiring help towards the successful completion of this research.

I wish to acknowledge my indebtness to *Mr. G. Manivannan* and a Special word of thanks to *Mr. G. Balaji,* Ganesh Computers, for their valuable help and the timely preparation of my work in an extraordinary way.

It is my heartfelt pleasure to thank *Mrs. D. Anita* and *Mrs. A.Vanitha,* Department of English (SF), *Ms. G.Mahoori Devi* and *Ms. G.K.Suganya,* Department of Commerce (CS), Vellalar College for Women, for their assistance in this study.

I express my profound gratitude to *Thiru. Ramakrishnan, Kavya Computers,* Coimbatore for his timely help in analysing the data.

A short acknowledgement seems to be very little to thank *My Parents, Sister* and *well-wishers* for their constant love and support and for the never-failing confidence they had in me.

In short, I would once again like to thank all those who assisted and contributed in one way or other towards this research.

—S. Kalaiselvi

CONTENTS

1

INTRODUCTION AND DESIGN OF THE STUDY

INTRODUCTION

The world has made rapid strides in recent years with economic progress linked to the explosion in Information Technology (IT), accompanied by globalisation-led shrinking of national boundaries. Physical borders no longer define markets. Companies have the freedom to source products from the lowest cost locations. The communication revolution has dramatically reduced response times. These sweeping changes resulting in global level of competitiveness are at the core of several challenges that confront Indian companies today. The biggest challenge to Indian companies lies in their ability to grow in the midst of competition.

The Indian IT industry has not only been among the fastest growing industries globally, it has played a key role in transforming India from a largely inward looking economy to an emerging knowledge power that is today perceived as being one of the most dynamic and entrepreneurial in the world. In 1991, the IT industry was modest sized, employing 12000 persons, and contributing an insignificant part of GDP. Between 2000 and 2004, it had emerged as the largest incremental contributor to GDP, with 6 per cent coming from this sector. Around 95 per cent of the absolute growth in foreign exchange inflows in the service sector during this period is estimated to have come from the IT and BPO industries alone.

In this decade, Information Technology has emerged as the leader for economic growth of India because each development in computer technology has presented new opportunities for business. With many Indian businesses having their competitive edge in the global market by using IT as a key enabler, a NASSCOM study has found that about 35 per cent of the organisations have moved to a level where almost all processes have been automated. The NASSCOM IT User Survey 2005, which covered 300 organisations has reported that 85 per cent of the organisations believe that they have been able to derive benefits out of the IT implementation. Assessing the impact of IT implementation on the company productivity, the survey said 80 per cent of the respondents felt that they have been able to trace productivity enhancements within their organisations. (*Source: The Hindu, Business Line, April 14, 2006, p. 4*)

Today, management has been placed under increasing pressure to implement financial strategies that create value for shareholders. Some of the methodologies used for traditional analysis of business performance have been ineffective in detecting the accounting manipulations that often take place. Profit is an opinion and cash flow is a fact. While reported profit can be manipulated or even distorted in so many ways, cash flow cannot be subjected to any form of creative accounting. Emphasis upon cash flow has set the format for the development of financial strategies linked to the creation of value.

In the past, management has formulated and introduced a strategy and then attempted to measure its impact. This approach has been largely influenced by the fact that a suitable strategy valuation technique has not been available in a simple and meaningful format. Fortunately a relatively simple approach does exist for estimating value created by business strategy. The challenge for the 2000's is to use performance measurements which can be integrated throughout the process of formulating strategy. It can help establish criteria for selecting the correct strategy using sensitivity analysis to maximise value creation. The shareholders/

owners are always the residual claimants who need to be satisfied with suitable returns. Without this, the business entity is no longer viable and is not likely to continue as a going concern.

The effective and healthy performance of any business is measured by its positive financial performance. Over the past few years, the global economic development has shifted the efficiency equation from measurement by accounting profits to the measurement by the economic profits. The financial function can play a lead role in emphasising things that are important to true economic performance. At the micro economic level, the goal of an enterprise is to create maximum shareholder value. With the globalisation of capital markets, intensification of competition and massive privatization initiatives, shareholders value creation is gaining the attention of executives all over the world including India. The growing predominance of the shareholders wealth culture is largely a consequence of several developments like:

- Globalisation and deregulation of the capital markets;
- Advances in Information Technology;
- More liquid securities markets;
- Improvements in capital market regulation;
- Generational changes in attitudes towards savings and investments;
- Expansion of institutional investment, etc.

In the new environment characterised by heightened sensitivity to return, investors invest their capital in the companies where management strategy is based on shareholder value maximisation. If the investors do not receive adequate compensation for the risk they are taking, they withdraw their funds and reallocate them to more attractive opportunities. With globalisation paving the way for greater mobility of capital, on the macro-economic level, investors move their capital across political borders in pursuit of relatively higher yields. This reveals that those countries whose economic systems are not based on the principle of maximisation of shareholder value will get starved of capital.

Role of EVA and MVA in Efficient Capital Allocation

Practitioner interest in shareholders value management has increased dramatically over the last decade. The increased interest stems largely from Stern Stewart's promotion of Economic Value Added (EVA), their trade marked measure of economic profit. EVA is purportedly a measure of the economic wealth creation that was devised in 1989. The measure has been used to evaluate companies or division of companies as complete entities; it may also be used to evaluate cash flows at the project level. A number of companies have employed EVA for analysing their performance, acquisitions, mergers, divestitures and investments. The actual calculation of EVA stems from the accounting value known as Residual Income (RI). RI is defined as the difference between all the net income before taxes and a capital cost that is determined by an explicit cost of the capital charged against the investment base.

Economic Value Added (EVA) is an encompassing measure that captures the true economic profit of an enterprise. A proprietary tool developed by Stern Stewart & Co, EVA is also a performance measure most directly linked to the creation of shareholder wealth over time. Besides guiding client companies, the implementation of a complete EVA-based financial management and incentive compensation system provides management with better information and motivation to make decisions that will enhance shareholders wealth. Several companies like Boeing, Coca-Cola, Monsanto, in the US and the Tata's and Godrej in India are using this system.

Indian companies are in expansion mode. Infusion of capital will skew profit and value addition in the short run. EVA does not discourage new investments. If a firm were to embark on an expansion or growth path, the total capital deployed would go up in the short run while the returns may not be immediate. This would result in lower EVA and expansion could be discouraged. Stern Stewart's uses a suspense account for new investments that do not payoff immediately. The amount in the suspense account is placed out the balance sheet and brought back as returns from the investments start accruing.

In India when Godrej implemented EVA, the shares were quoted at Rs.36; it was exactly 20 times greater as on June 2006. The adoption of the bonus scheme, way down deep amongst Godrej's employees led to an improvement in EVA. Similar was the case with TCS. Even when it was wholly owned, Tatas senior management decided to pilot EVA at TCS since the management was not given the shares or share options. Down to middle management, the improvement in EVA became the goal. TCS went public in August 2004 at about Rs. 800 plus. The shares were quoted at around Rs. 2000 as on June 2006. These are but two cases where management was deeply committed to EVA as a goal and implementation of the bonus scheme. Both are crucial; Success and EVA are linked by accountability.

EVA is considered important for companies as a performance measurement and controlling tool. EVA shows the financial performance with a new pair of glasses or offers new approach especially for the companies where equity is viewed as free source of funds and performance is measured by some earnings figure. At best EVA helps to create a mindset throughout the organisation that encourages managers and employees to think and behave like owners. At operational level this new approach leads to increased capital turnover. One of the EVA's more powerful features is, its suitability to management bonus systems. This has been empirically proved to be a way to increase shareholders value (*Wallace 1997, p. 116-www.eva.com*).

EVA is the measure of performance and can also serve as the centre piece of the strategy implementation process linked to various major functions like strategic planning, capital allocation, operating budgets performance measurement, management compensation, internal and external communication (with the capital markets). One of the EVA's great virtues is that targets can be devolved to operating divisions and departments. Firms create value for their shareholders when they invest in the projects, products, technologies or strategies that are expected to earn returns greater than the cost of capital.

One of the EVA's great strengths is that it provides a link between performance measurement and capital market valuation, helping to ensure that managerial performance is evaluated and rewarded in a manner that is consistent with sound corporate finance theory. EVA attempts to measure a corporation's actual rate of return as against the required rate of return.

EVA Basic Premise

The idea behind EVA is that shareholders must earn a return that compensates the risk taken. EVA is based on the common accounting based items like interest bearing debt, equity capital and net operating profit. The EVA concept is often called as Economic Profit (EP). The number of companies adopting EVA is increasing rapidly. EVA is a measure to assess the extent to which companies have succeeded in achieving the objective of enhancing shareholders wealth. It is a useful tool for performance appraisal of divisions and cost centers.

EVA is the only financial management system that provides a common language for employees across all operating and staff functions, allows all management decisions to be modelled, monitored, communicated and compensated in a single and consistent way in terms of value added to shareholder investment. EVA is aimed to be a measure that tells what has happened to the wealth of the shareholders. Earning a return greater than the cost of capital increases the value of the company and earning less return decreases the value of the company. For the listed companies Stewart defined another measure that assesses if the company has created shareholders value. If the total market value of a company is more than the amount of capital invested in it, the company has managed to create shareholders value. If the case is opposite, the company has destroyed shareholders value.

EVA has become a very popular performance measure because applying it has some powerful impacts on organisational behaviour. Unlike conventional profitability measures EVA helps the management and also other employees to understand the cost of equity capital. Application of EVA in small companies is useful because traditional performance measures used by the small companies are unable to describe the company's true business results and sometimes lead to the wrong business decisions. EVA reflects company's performance in money. Positive EVA indicates the value creation and the negative EVA indicates the value destruction. Series of negative EVA is a signal that restructuring in a company may be needed. In small companies managers can make the EVA concept transparent to all employees in a short time and a useful tool for allocation of small company's scarce capital resources.

The management in a small company can improve EVA by trying to improve return with no or with only minimal capital investment. EVA helps enormously the management and the employees to see what should be the real objective of the company, since it makes clear to all what profitability really is. EVA is an excellent bedrock on which an integrated financial management system can be constructed. It serves as an anchor for all internal system of corporate governance that motivates everyone to work co-operatively and enthusiastically to achieve the best attainable performance.

Market Value Added (MVA) is one of the external indicators which gives the utmost satisfaction to the investors. Investors always desire an increase in the share prices. The most reliable measure of management's long term success in adding value is known as "Market Value Added". MVA is the difference between company's current market value and the amount of capital that shareholders have committed to the firm throughout its existence, including earnings that have been retained in the business. MVA is the best external performance indicator as it indicates the market assessment of the effectiveness with which companies' managers have used the scarce resources under their control. Market value added refers to the value added to the shareholders wealth by the firm.

Shareholders Value Added (SVA)

SVA is a creation of Dr. Alfred Rappaport and LEK/Alcar Consulting Group. It origins from the Discounted cash flow model and has gained publicity and established position, although is far less used than EVA or Cash Flow Return On Investment (CFROI). The idea of SVA is probably to discount estimated future cash flows to present and hence continuously, to calculate the value of the firm. The popular method of calculating SVA is to add Equity Dividend to Market Value Added.

NEED FOR THE STUDY

The Information Technology (IT) sector is doing remarkably well and is registering high growth rates for the past few years. The software industry, which is a part of the IT industry has been the major driver of the IT industry and has been responsible for the phenomenal growth achieved by the IT industry. The exports are pioneering the software industry. Maximising shareholder value is becoming the new corporate standard in India. The corporates, which gave low preference to the shareholder inquisitiveness are now bestowing the utmost inclination to it. In order to help the corporates to generate value to the shareholders, value-based management systems have been developed. If a business enterprise is determined to maximise the economic value of the shareholders claim to the assets, then it is quite beyond price to all those who are patronised stakeholders.

Creating value is the core principle on which the economic system is based. No enterprise survives or glows if it fails to generate wealth for the stakeholders. EVA is basically a broader financial measure of judging the output of a corporate in particular and the industry in which such corporate works in general to the economic growth and the development of the nation. EVA is a blossoming model for the corporate financial disclosure in India. Economic valuation is based on the assumption that all companies are engaged in the business of allocation, managing and redeploying scarce resources. In the context of an impressive performance by the IT sector and realising the significance of EVA, the researcher has made an attempt to study the Economic Value Added performance in the Indian software industry.

STATEMENT OF THE PROBLEM

The Indian IT sector has proved to be the country's fastest growing segment, even in troubled times. The software and service industry, a major component of India's IT sector, showed significant momentum, higher than that of other industries in the country. India continued to be a compelling investment destination, as leading companies either set up shop here or enhanced their existing infrastructure. The IT services sector has witnessed tremendous growth in the last decade, fuelled by an increasing number of business expansions, acquisitions and green field projects funded both with domestic and foreign private investment. Some of the services typically rendered by the IT companies include Application Development (AD), Application Management (AM), consulting and testing services performed either off shore (in India) or onsite (at the client location outside India). India has become one of the most favoured destinations for outsourcing and IT-Enabled Services (ITES).

The shift in the role of IT from merely supporting business to transforming business, which is driving productivity gains and creating new business models, has increased the importance of IT to the success of companies worldwide. The ability to design, develop, implement and maintain advanced technology platforms and solutions to address business and customer needs has become a competitive advantage and a priority for corporations worldwide.

According to NASSCOM (National Association of Software and Services Companies) strategic Review Report 2005, the Indian IT industry employed nearly 700000 software professionals as of March 31, 2005, making it the second largest employer in the IT services industry after the United States. India accounts for almost 84 per cent of the outsourcing and faces competition from Canada, China and Vietnam. Canada seems to be the next best stop for outsourcing.

In the present economic scenario, the investor's perception of the world around is constantly undergoing a change. They need appreciation in the value of the investment made. As such maximisation of wealth has become the objective of many firms. In India, the goal of sustainable long term value creation for shareholders is well understood by all the business groups. The companies that have implemented EVA or another measure of value, credit it with dramatic improvement in operating and financial results. These in turn have been rewarded with the hefty appreciation in stock price.

The ultimate goal of EVA is to maximise shareholder value, but the best tool of EVA to do this is to convert employees into value change agents. This allows teams of employees to work to extract maximum performance with the theme, "Waste not, Want not". This controls discretionary costs and improves working capital management.

The ultimate success of a firm is not measured only by its capacity to grow its sales, produce profits or generate cash from its operations. The real fact is whether the firm's activities are creating value for its owners. Motivated employees, delighted customers and efficient suppliers are an integral part of a successful receipe for enhancing the firm's value. In this respect the researcher seeks answer to the following aspects:

- Whether the entrepreneurs are really increasing the Networth of the company or they reduce it gradually?
- Should entrepreneurs try to assess the real growth they add to shareholder's wealth?
- Whether or not funds are being efficiently utilised?
- Is there significant difference between the real rate of EVA and the rate the enterprise expects?
- To what extent MVA and SVA enhance shareholder's wealth?
- How sensitive is EVA towards its components?

RESEARCH OBJECTIVES

Value Added indicates the Net wealth created by the production of goods or services during a specified period in the corporate. An enterprise may exist without making profit but cannot survive without adding value. Indian markets are awakening to the reality that several companies are using capital incompetently and destroying value. Companies that add value to their enterprise often rank high when it comes to Market capitalisation. International markets also look at economic value when it comes to sizing up of a company. The main goal of the business enterprises is to protect and maximise the interest of shareholders by maximising the overall goal of the business units. For carrying out the study, the following specific objectives have been set:

- To analyse the trends and patterns of capital structure of the select Indian software companies;
- To analyse the cost of components of capital structure;
- To compute and analyse EVA and rank the sample companies on the basis of EVA, MVA, Return On Capital Employed (ROCE), Earnings Per Share (EPS), Net Operating Profit After Tax (NOPAT) and Weighted Average Cost of Capital (WACC) and examine the difference, if any, in the rankings;

— To observe the influence of EVA components on EVA, segment-wise and also for the industry;

— To study the relationship between EVA and Select financial variables;

— To compute MVA and SVA of the sample companies and to study EVA's impact on MVA and SVA;

— To assess the relationship between MVA and Select financial variables;

— To examine the extent of awareness and adaptability of EVA among the select Indian Software Companies;

— To make suggestions and recommendations for the use of EVA as a measure of financial performance to the Indian Corporate Managers.

HYPOTHESES OF THE STUDY

To fulfil the objectives of the study, the following hypotheses have been formulated and tested:

➢ There is no significant difference in the average amount of capital employed of the sub-groups;

➢ There is no significant difference in the average proportion of debt to total capitalisation of the sub-groups;

➢ There is no correlation between total capital employed and the proportion of debt to total capitalisation;

➢ There is no correlation between debt to capital employed and average capital employed;

➢ There is no correlation between Capital Employed and Debt Equity Ratio of above median capital employed and below median Capital Employed Companies;

➢ There is no significant variation in averages of cost of debt of different sub-groups;

➢ There is no perceptible and distinctive difference in cost of equity among sub-groups of sampled companies;

➢ There is no significant variation in WACC among the sub-groups of sampled companies;

- There exist no significant differences in the paired samples;
- There is no significant relationship between EVA and Selected financial variables;
- There is no significant relationship between EVA and MVA;
- There is no significant difference between actual EVA and expected EVA;
- There is no significant relationship between MVA and Select financial variables;
- The different variants of value added in the Indian Software Companies under study are uncorrelated.

RESEARCH METHODOLOGY

Sample Selection

The data used in this study relate to those software companies listed in the Bombay Stock Exchange (BSE) for which the data are available in the Capitaline database. The analysis is confined to the BSE listed Indian software companies only. This is due to the fact that BSE has the second largest number of domestic quoted companies on any stock exchange in the world after New York Stock Exchange (NYSE) and has more quoted companies than either the London or the Tokyo Stock Exchange.

Capitaline database contained data relating to 465 BSE listed software companies. Stratified sampling technique was used and hence the total population was sub-divided into three standard sub-groups namely Large (Turnover greater than Rs.900 Crores), Small-Medium (Turnover less than Rs.900 Crores) and Converts (diversified companies), in such a way that each strata was more homogeneous than the total population. Accordingly, it was found that there were 10 Large, 407 Small-Medium and 48 Converts. For selection of sample companies in each stratum, companies for which data were available for minimum of eight years were identified. The researcher selected all those companies from each stratum which fulfilled the above condition. Thus the final sample consisted of 102 software companies as detailed in the following table:

Composition of Sample Companies

No. of years for which data were available	Sub Groups			Total
	Large	Small-Medium	Converts	
8	2	14	7	23
9	-	23	3	26
10	5	42	6	53
Total No. of Sample Companies	**7**	**79**	**16**	**102**

Further it could be observed that the total sample of 102 software companies fall into following trading groups in BSE: 16 'A' group companies, 5 'Z' group companies, 8 'S' group companies, 28 'T' group companies, 17 'B1' group companies, 22 'B2' group companies and 6 'TS' group companies.

The list of sample companies selected for the study is furnished below:

Sl. No.	Company Name	Trade Name
1.	Digital Global Soft Ltd.	DIGITALEQP
2.	Hewlett Packard Global Soft Ltd.	HP
3.	Iflex Solutions Ltd.	I-FLEX
4.	Infosys Technologies Ltd.	INFOSYS
5.	Satyam Computer Service Ltd.	SATYAM
6.	Tech Mahindra Ltd.	TECHM
7.	Wipro Ltd.	WIPRO
8.	ABACUS Computers Ltd.	ABACUS
9.	ABM Knowledge Ware Ltd.	ABMANO
10.	ACE –Software Exports Ltd.	ACESOFT
11.	Advent Computer Services Ltd.	ADVENT
12.	Aftek Infosys Ltd.	AFTEK LTD

(Contd...)

Sl. No.	*Company Name*	*Trade Name*
13.	Asian CERC Information Technology Ltd.	ASIANCE
14.	Avantel Softech Ltd.	AVANTELQ
15.	Aztech Software and Technology Service Ltd.	AZTECH
16.	B2B Software Technologies Ltd.	B2BSOFT
17.	Bluestar Infotech Ltd.	BLUESTINFO
18.	Brels Infotech Ltd.	BRELS
19.	California Software Company Ltd.	CALIFSOF
20.	CG-VAK Software Enterprises Ltd.	CGVAK
21.	Contech Software Ltd.	CONTECH
22.	Cranes Software International Ltd.	CRANES
23.	Cressanda Solutions Ltd.	CRESSAN
24.	CS Software Enterprise Ltd.	CSSOFT
25.	Cybertech Systems & Software Ltd.	CYBERTE
26.	Datasoft Application Software (India) Ltd.	DATASOFT
27.	Dynacons Systems & Solutions Ltd.	DYNACON
28.	E-serve International Ltd.	ESERVE
29.	European Software Alliances Ltd.	EUROSOFT
30.	Ez-comm Trade Technologies Ltd.	EZCOM
31.	Financial Technologies (India) Ltd.	FINTECH
32.	Frontier Information Technologies Ltd.	FRONTINF
33.	Genesys International Corporation Ltd.	GENESYS
34.	Geometric Software Solutions Company Ltd.	GEOMETRIC
35.	Gold Stone Technologies Ltd.	GOLDTECH
36.	GTL Ltd.	GTL
37.	Hexaware Technologies Ltd.	HEXAWERE
38.	Hinduja TMT Ltd.	HINDTMT

(Contd...)

Sl. No.	*Company Name*	*Trade Name*
39.	Info-drive Software Ltd.	INFDS
40.	Infotech Enterprises Ltd.	INFOTECENT
41.	Innovation Software Exports Ltd.	INSOE
42.	Intellvisions Software Ltd.	INTELVIS
43.	Intra Infotech Ltd.	INTRAINF
44.	It Microsystems (India) Ltd.	ITMICRO
45.	Jetking Infotrain Ltd.	JETKINGQ
46.	Jindal Online.Com Ltd.	JINDONL
47.	Kashyap Tele Medium Ltd.	KASHYAP
48.	Kedia Infotech Ltd.	KEDIN
49.	KLG Systel Ltd.	KLG
50.	KPIT Cummins Infosystems Ltd.	KPITCUMM
51.	Lee & Nee Software Exports Ltd.	LEENEE
52.	Maars Software International Ltd.	MARRSOF
53.	Magnum Ltd.	MAGNUM
54.	Mangalya Soft-Tech Ltd.	MANGASOF
55.	Mastek Ltd.	MASTEK
56.	Melstar Information Technologies Ltd.	MELSTAR
57.	Micro Technologies (India) Ltd.	MICROTECH
58.	Mid Point Software & Electro Systems Ltd.	MIDPOINT
59.	Mindtech (India) Ltd.	MINDTEK
60.	Mphasis BFL Ltd.	MPHASIS
61.	NCC Finance Ltd.	NCCFIN
62.	Nucleus Software Exports Ltd.	NUCLEUSSOFT
63.	Odyssey Technologies Ltd.	ODYSSEY
64.	Onward Technologies Ltd.	ONWARD

(Contd...)

Sl. No.	*Company Name*	*Trade Name*
65.	Orient Information Technology Ltd.	ORIENTINFO
66.	OTCO International Ltd.	OTCO
67.	Pal Soft Info Systems Ltd.	PALSOFT
68.	Pentasoft Technologies Ltd.	PENTASOFTTE
69.	Pioneer Technoparks Ltd.	PIOTECH
70.	PSI Data Systems Ltd.	PSI
71.	Ram Informatics Ltd.	RAMINFO
72.	Ramco Systems Ltd.	RAMCOSYS
73.	Rolta India Ltd.	ROLTA
74.	Sanra Software Ltd.	SANRASOF
75.	Silverline Technologies Ltd.	SILVERLINE
76.	Sindu Valley Technologies Ltd.	SINDUVA
77.	Softsol India Ltd.	SOFTSOL
78.	Sonata Software Ltd.	SONATA
79.	Svam Software Ltd.	SVAMSOFT
80.	Teledata Informatics Ltd.	TELEDATA
81.	Tera Software Ltd.	TERASOFT
82.	Twinstar Software Exports Ltd.	TWINSOFT
83.	Virtual Soft Systems Ltd.	VIRTUALS
84.	Visual Soft Technologies Ltd.	VISUALSOFT
85.	VJIL Consulting Ltd.	VJIL
86.	Zensar Technologies Ltd.	ZENSAR
87.	Choksh Infotech Ltd.	CHOKSHIN
88.	Corcomp Info Systems Ltd.	CORCOMP
89.	Danlaw Technologies India Ltd.	DANLAW
90.	Encore Software Ltd.	ENCORE

(Contd...)

Sl. No.	Company Name	Trade Name
91	ICSA (India) Ltd.	ICSAIND
92.	IECs Software Ltd.	IECSOF
93.	Infotrek Syscom Ltd.	INFOTREK
94.	LCC Infotech Ltd.	LCCINFO
95.	Mascon Global Ltd.	MASCONGLO
96.	Millenium Cybertech Ltd.	MILLENCY
97.	Netvista Information Technology Ltd.	NETVISTA
98.	Omega Interactive Technologies Ltd.	OMEGAIN
99.	SRG Infotech (India) Ltd.	SRGINFO
100.	Synergy Log in System Ltd.	SYNLOG
101.	Trillenium Technologies Ltd.	TRILLENT
102.	Vakrangee Softwares Ltd.	VAKRANG

Period of the Study

The data collected for the study pertains to a period of ten years from 1996-97 to 2005-06.

Sources of Data

The study is based on the secondary data collected from the Capitaline and EBSCO databases. The data for the sample companies as obtained from Capitaline are supplemented with the information from various financial dailies, business magazines, reports, websites etc. Information regarding bank interest rates have been collected from 'The Indian Banker' (IBA Bulletin). In order to assess the awareness and applicability of EVA in Indian Corporates, a questionnaire has been prepared and responses collected.

SELECTION OF VARIABLES

In the present study, a number of key financial variables have been identified for the purpose of analysis and they are: EVA, MVA, Turnover, NOPAT, ROS, ROTA, ROCE, EPS, Market Price and SVA. Computation of these variables has been made for a period of ten years. An epigrammatic explanation of the selected variables is outlined below:

(a) *Economic Value Addition (EVA)*

EVA model is based on the hypothesis that rational investor takes into account just two things.

- The cash to be generated over the life of a business; and
- The risk of the cash receipts

EVA = NOPAT – Cost of Capital Employed.

Cost of capital or Weighted Average Cost of Capital (WACC) is the average cost of both equity capital and the interest bearing debt. Cost of equity capital is the opportunity return from an investment with same risk as the company has. Cost of equity (K_e) is generally defined in Capital Asset Pricing Model (CAPM). K_e is the shareholder's expected rate of return.

Average cost of time deposits of Scheduled Commercial Banks in India has been considered as a proxy for risk free rate of return. The market rate of return has been calculated by using index number of security prices (Sensex Index) from year to year basis.

The idea behind EVA is that shareholders must earn a return that compensates the risk taken. In other words, equity capital has to earn atleast same return as similarly risky investments at equity markets

(b) *Market Value Added (MVA)*

MVA describes the value added to a particular share over its book value. It enlightens how much value a shareholder has added to his wealth, which he has invested in the share. Accordingly, a company with an objective of enhancing the shareholders wealth should attempt to capitalize on its MVA. MVA is derived by deducting the book value of the firm from its market capitalisation. The book value of the firm is equity share capital plus reserves and surplus, minus any revaluation reserve and miscellaneous expenses. Market Value of the firm can be arrived at by dividing Earnings Before Interest and Taxes (EBIT) by overall cost of capital.

(c) *Earnings Per Share (EPS)*

This is calculated by dividing the net profit after tax and preference share dividend or net profit available to the equity shareholders divided by the number of ordinary shares. It indicates the net profit available to the ordinary shareholders on a per share basis. EPS has an effect on the share prices and consequently on MVA. Thus, the selection of EPS as an independent variable is quite understandable.

$$EPS = \frac{\text{Net Profit (After taxes and preference share dividend)}}{\text{Number of ordinary shares}}$$

or

$$EPS = \frac{(EBIT - I)\ (1 - t)\ Pd}{N}$$

Where EBIT = Earnings Before Interest and Taxes; I = Interest

t = Tax; P_d = Preference Share Dividend

N = Number of Common shares Outstanding

(d) *Return On Sales (ROS)*

Return on Sale in derived by dividing Profit Before Interest and Tax (PBIT) by sales.

$$ROS = \frac{PBIT}{Sales}$$

(e) *Return On Total Assets (ROTA)*

This gives productivity of all assets taken together. It can be calculated using the following formula:

$$\text{Return on Total Assets} = \frac{\text{PBIT} - \text{Tax Provision}}{\text{Total Assets}}$$

ROCE

ROCE establishes the relationship between profits and the capital employed. In conventional accounting, ROCE is measured as the most appropriate method of calculating profitability and efficiency of a business. This is put in plain words as profit after tax/networth x 100. For that reason, counting ROCE as an independent variable is quite coherent with the logic that the market appraises the firm on the basis of its long-term profitability.

NOPAT

NOPAT is the profit derived from the company's operations after taxes but before financing costs and non-cash book keeping entries. Depreciation is subtracted to arrive at NOPAT. In other words NOPAT is equivalent to income available to shareholders plus interest expenses.

Shareholder Value Analysis (SVA)

Share Holder Value Analysis (SVA) calculates the value of a company to its shareholders by looking at the returns it gives to shareholders and is based on the view that the objective of company directors is to maximise the wealth of the company's shareholders. Correctly performed SVA reveals that the more a business earns above its cost of capital, the higher its market value relative to invested capital.

Market Price

Market price is the price that a good or service is offered at or will fetch in the market place; it is of interest mainly in the study of micro economics. Market value is the total market price of a given quantity of a good. In the case of a company the total market values of the company's shares is its market capitalisation.

FRAMEWORK OF ANALYSIS

Economic Value Added (EVA) has been computed with the following steps:

Step 1:

Proportion of debt to capital employed =

$$\frac{\text{Total Debt}}{\text{Capital Employed}} \times 100$$

Step 2:

$$\text{Cost of Debt } K_d = \frac{\text{Interest \& Financial Charges}}{\text{Total Debt}} \times 100$$

Step 3:

$$\text{Weighted Cost of Debt (WCD)} = \frac{\text{Proportion of debt to capital employed} \times K_d}{100}$$

Step 4:

Risk free rate of return, R_f = Average Cost of time deposits of Scheduled Commercial Banks in India.

Step 5:

$$\text{Expected market return } (R_m) = \frac{\text{Current Year Index- Previous Year Index}}{\text{Previous Year Index}} \times 100$$

(Sensex Index)

Step 6:

Expected Risk Premium = $R_m - R_f$

Step 7:

Beta Variant (β) obtained from the Capitaline Database

Step 8:

Cost of equity (k_e) $= R_f + b_i (R_m - R_f)$

Step 9:

$$\text{Proportion of equity to capital employed} = \frac{\text{Total shareholders Equity}}{\text{Capital Employed}} \times 100$$

Step 10:

Weighted cost of Equity (WCE) =

$$\frac{K_e \times \text{Proportion of Equity to Total Capital Employed}}{100}$$

Step 11:

Weighted Average Cost of Capital (WACC) = WCD + WCE

Step 12:

Cost Of Capital Employed (COCE) = Capital Employed x WACC

Step 13:

Net Operating Profit After Tax (NOPAT) = PAT + Interest expenses after Tax

Step 14:

EVA = NOPAT – COCE

Market Value Added (MVA)

MVA has been computed with the following formula:

MVA = Market Value of the firm – Book Value of the firm

$$\text{Market Value of the firm} = \frac{\text{EBIT}}{K_o}$$

Where EBIT = Earnings Before Interest and Taxes

K_o = Weighted Average Cost of Capital (WACC)

Book Value of the firm=Equity Share Capital + Revaluation reserves + Miscellaneous Expenses.

Shareholders Value Added (SVA)

SVA = MVA + Equity Dividend.

STATISTICAL TOOLS USED FOR ANALYSIS

The role of statistical tools is important in analysing the data and drawing inferences there from. Various statistical tools like Mean, Standard Deviation, Variance, Kurtosis, Skewness, Correlation, Regression, ANOVA, Factor Analysis, Kendall's tau-b, Logit Analysis have been accomplished through Excel and SPSS softwares. Some of these statistical techniques particularly Correlation co-efficients, the Paired-Samples, Durbin Watson Test, t-Test, Kendall's test and the Chi-Square test have been used to interpret the sense of mathematical relationship amongst values of different variables so computed in the study.

The following statistical tools are used for the analysis and interpretation of data. This section briefly explains the context in which the tools are applied.

Summary Statistics such as Mean, Standard Deviation, Range and Variance have been used to study the mean differences. Both skewness and kurtosis has been used to estimate the distribution (symmetric/asymmetric).

Skewness characterises the degree of asymmetry of a distribution around its mean. Positive Skewness indicates a distribution with an asymmetric tail extending toward more positive values. Negative Skewness indicates a distribution with an asymmetric tail extending toward more negative values.

Ranking based on ten year average of select financial variables has been done to examine the difference, if any, in the rankings.

Kurtosis: A measure of the extent to which observations cluster around a central point. For a normal distribution, the value of the kurtosis statistic is 0. Positive kurtosis indicates that the observation cluster more and have longer tails than those in the normal distribution and negative kurtosis indicates the observations cluster less and have shorter tails.

The Paired Samples: T-test procedure compares the means of two variables for a single group. It computes the differences between values of the two variables for each case and tests whether the average differs from zero. It is used in this study to analyse the differences of EVA, WACC and NOPAT between the years.

Analysis of Variance (One Way) based on F-statistics has been applied to ensure whether there is any significant variation in the average amount of capitalisation and debt to total capitalisation of the sub groups as compared to the overall amounts of the entire group.

Average Growth Rate and Annual Compound Growth Rate have been computed to analyse the growth pattern of the sample companies on various parameters.

Correlation Analysis, Correlations (alias PEARSON CORR) produces Pearson product-moment correlations with significance levels and, optionally, univariate statistics, covariances, and cross-product deviations. It has been done in order to test whether there exist any significant relationship between EVA and MVA with regard to the whole sample as well as for the sub-groups for the ten year period from 1996-97 to 2005-06.

Kendall's tau-b, a non-parametric measure of association for ordinal or ranked variables that take ties into account is used in this study to test the association between EVA and each of the select financial variables.

Regression, Multiple Linear Regression estimates the coefficients of the linear equation, involving one or more independent variables, that best predict the value of the dependent variable. In the present study it is used to select the best predictor among the select financial variables on EVA and also on MVA.

The Logit Loglinear Analysis procedure is used to model the values of one or more categorical variables given one or more categorical predictors. This is accomplished through analysis of the cell counts of the cross tabulation table formed by the cross-classification of the response and predictor variables. Logit loglinear models are "ANOVA-like" models for the Logit-expected cell counts of cross tabulation tables. Logits are formed by the log-ratios of cell counts, where the cells in a given logit are correspond to pairs of values of the dependent variable, for a given cross-classification of factors. It is used to study the influence of EVA components on EVA, segment wise and also for the industry.

Discriminant analysis is useful for building a predictive model of group membership based on observed characteristics of each case. The procedure generates a discriminant function (or, for more than two groups, a set of discriminant functions) based on linear combinations of the predictor variables that provide the best discrimination between the groups. The functions are generated from a sample of cases for which group membership is known; the functions can then be applied to new cases that have measurements for the predictor variables but have unknown group membership. It is used to study the effect of positive EVA (Wealth Creators) and negative EVA (Wealth Destroyers) on the select financial variables.

The Chi-Square Test is used to test the goodness-of-fit. It compares the observed and expected frequencies in each category to test either that all categories contain the same proportion of values or that each category contains a user-specified proportion of values. In the present study it is used to compare observed EVA and the expected EVA.

Factor Analysis attempts to identify underlying variables, or factors, that explain the pattern of correlations within a set of observed variables. Factor analysis is often used in data reduction to identify a small number of factors that explain most of the variance that is observed in a much larger number of manifest variables. Factor analysis can also be used to generate hypotheses regarding causal mechanisms or to screen variables for subsequent analysis. In this study it is used to identify which variable contribute more towards the wealth creation.

't'-test has been applied to examine whether the variants: Economic Value Added (EVA), Market Value Added (MVA) and Shareholders Value Added (SVA) are correlated or not.

LIMITATIONS OF THE STUDY

The generality of this research is restricted due to certain limitations. Most of these limitations are offshoots of the self imposed restrictions during the process of research, for keeping research within manageable limits.

- The present study is mainly confined to one hundred and two software companies only, which are listed in Bombay Stock Exchange;
- For the purpose of computing EVA, Beta value from Capitaline database has been considered;
- Risk free rate of return can be taken either as Interest Rate of Government Bonds or Average Cost of time deposits of Scheduled Commercial Banks in India. In this study, average cost of time deposits of Scheduled Commercial Banks in India is taken as risk free rate of return and it has been collected from 'The Indian Banker';
- Only 11 responses had been obtained towards awareness and applicability of EVA and hence, further analysis is not carried over;
- Negative Capital Employed is found due to differences in the method of computation. The data obtained from Capitaline Database has been used.

CHAPTERISATION SCHEME

The present study has been organised into seven chapters. The layout of these chapters is delineated below:

Chapter I

Encompasses the research methodology of the study. This chapter contains eights parts, which include Introduction, Need for the Study, Research Problem, Objectives of the Study, Hypotheses, Research Methodology, Limitations of the Study and Chapterisation Scheme.

Chapter II

Presents a brief review of related literature.

Chapter III

Outlines the profile of Indian software industry.

Chapter IV

Analyses the overall trends and patterns of the capitalisation and capital structure of the sample companies as a whole and segment-wise.

Chapter V

Assesses the Economic Value Added performance of select Indian software companies.

Chapter VI

Depicts the impact of Economic Value Added on MVA and SVA of the select Indian software companies.

Chapter VII

Embodies the summary of research findings and some workable recommendations for the maximisation of shareholders wealth.

Towards the end of this research work, comprehensive bibliography on the subject have been added.

2

INFERENCES ON EVA
A REVIEW OF PREVIOUS RESEARCHES

INTRODUCTION

EVA application crosses all industrial and commercial boundaries and allows meaningful understanding among different corporates that are working towards the economic upliftment of their nation. No corporate may persist to exist if it fails to create adequate wealth. The corporates not making value addition in their wealth may become sick and vanish over a period of time. Hence, EVA may be a broader gauge of judging the contribution of an organisation towards the national economic development and growth.

EXCERPT FROM EARLIER STUDIES

The present section briefly thrashes out the researches carried out so far by the scholars actively engaged in the field. The studies have been classified as concept oriented and research related and are put under précis appraisal in the order of their occurrence.

CONCEPT RELATED LITERATURE

Stern Stewart (1990)[1] observed that EVA as a performance measure captures the true economic profit of an organisation.

EVA-based financial management and incentive compensation scheme gives manager better quality information and superior motivation to make decisions that will create the maximum shareholders wealth in an organisation.

Accordingly, EVA should be made the focal point for financial reporting, planning and decision-making. The executives of an organisation need to look out for appropriate techniques that will protect them against any future attacks by corporate marauders. The best way of maximising shareholders return is to offer incentives to managers for making decisions that boost long-term value. A major step is to provide cash bonus or stock option arrangements with incentives that create built-in share value. The main objective is to motivate the mangers to look beyond short-term measures of economic performance by essentially turning managers into owners.

The managers may be guided by EVA and pursue such objectives that improve operating profits investing more capital. Managers can be remunerated a proportion of both the total EVA and the positive change in EVA.

Tully (1993)[2] Tully has confirmed that there is no tricky situation about the technique through which the EVA can be augmented. It is a basic measure of return on capital and there are three ways to increase it:

- Earn more profit without using more capital;
- Use less capital; and
- Invest capital in high return projects.

Jain (1994)[3] has argued that the value added statements have certain advantages like comparison of performance, productivity measurement, resource allocation and incentive schemes for employees. The value added approach shows how the corporate quiche has been alienated among various contributors of value.

Mc Conville (1994)[4] concluded that EVA is an accountant's pleasure. But it is not the exclusive territory of finance department of an organisation. To determine the profits from operations of the corporate as a whole, a division or any activity within a division – simply subtract from the net operating profit after taxes, the value of the capital employed to produce that profit value. It is increased by earning returns greater than shareowners or lenders require; EVA is diminished when the return is less. It is being used increasingly to equate manager's salaries and bonuses with EVA replacing ROI (Return On Investment), sales goals or budget-based percentage.

Stewart (1994)[5] has expanded that EVA is a powerful new management tool that has gained worldwide recognition as the standard tool of corporate performance. EVA presents an integrated framework of financial management and incentive compensation. The adoption of EVA system by more and more companies throughout the world clearly states that it provides an integrated decision-making framework, can reform energies and redirect resources to create sustainable value for companies, customers, employees, shareholders and management.

Ochsner (1995)[6] brought into being that EVA is a performance measure that examines the company's financial results in economic language. It also quantifies the annual constituent of free cash inflows minus total capital expenses. EVA technique is popular because the managers can gauge whether a firm is generating economic returns. This capability satisfies investors who want companies to record such returns. In addition, EVA can be used as a tool for assessing financial performance. This measure also has downside that makes it unacceptable to some managers, who include, the fact that EVA uses software in computing financial results, so that managers cannot actually know, how performance numbers are derived.

Carr (1996)[7] considers that there are still generous problems with measuring the value created by companies. In recent times, even the stockbrokers have been giving the issue great attention. The traditional measures of earnings per share, dividend yield, and dividend per share remain popular, but growing emphasis is also being given to financial performance ratios based on cash flow and capital efficiency. Among valuation methods of operating performance, EVA, which measures the return on capital and its cost, has become predominantly well-liked.

Luber (1996)[8] confirmed that MVA is in compliance with the direction of the market. Studies have shown that a company which shows a positive EVA over a period of time will also have an increasing MVA while negative EVA will bring down MVA as the market looses confidence in the competence of a company to ensure a handsome return on the invested capital. The five top most companies as the wealth creators-Coke, GE, Micro Soft, Merck and Philip Morris-have strong EVAs and are expected to remain in the top niche in the upcoming years.

O'Hanlon and Peasrell (1996)[9] observed that the ability to create wealth of the shareholders is crucial to the survival of the companies in today's business environment. This gives rise to the question of which tools best measure the extent to which shareholder's value is being enhanced or destroyed. Traditionally, the corporate performance has been measured in terms of Earnings Per Share (EPS). However this methodology is believed to encourage myopic behaviour and to propagate that shareholders are a free source of funds. The 'economic profit' (EP) and EVA have been proposed as more sensible alternatives. The EP/EVA approach is very similar to 'residual income' concept.

Bacidore, et.al (1997)[10] Observed that the operating performance measures are evaluated in the context of shareholder value creation. EVA performs well in correlation with shareholder value creation. A refinement of Economic Value Added called Refined Economic Value Added is proposed. This measure is theoretically and empirically superior in measuring a firm's financial performance.

It has been observed that change in shareholder value can be fittingly depicted by applying market derived cost of capital to market value of company assets / organisation value. They have described the phenomenon with the help of an improved concept termed as Refined Economic Value Added (REVA). This new concept has been defined as:

REVA t = NOPATt - Kw (MVt-1) where,

MVt -1 = Total market value of the company's assets at the end of the period t-1. Kw = weighted average cost of capital.

As per these philanthropists REVA provides an analytical framework to evaluate operating performance in the context of shareholders value creation. EVA is an adequate measure of shareholder's value creation but REVA is considered a theoretically superior measure to assess whether a firm's operating performance is adequate from the viewpoint of compensating the firm's financers for the risk to their capital. In a wide-ranging statistical study of both EVA and REVA, it has been demonstrated that REVA statistically out-performs EVA in its ability to predict shareholder value creation.

Blair (1997)[11] observed that EVA has generated much interest in the business community. This financial tool advocates debt finance, as evidenced by its basic formula, which uses the weighted cost as the cost of capital, thus becomes cheaper than equity, partly due to the tax deductible interest.

Booth, Rupert (1997)[12] has observed that economic profit should be a part of company's performance measurement framework. Value based management and shareholder value analysis have been well known concepts in 1980s. Recently, there is a transformed interest in them and also the newer related concept of EVA. Previously many corporate strategies were utilised for destroying rather than creating shareholder value. A device, which can be used to reduce this risk, is to build an analysis of shareholder value into selection of corporate strategy.

Burkette and Hedley (1997)[13] explained that the EVA concept can be used to assess organisational performance known as economic profit. It can be applied for profit companies, public sector organisation and the non-profit organisations. EVA is being used by these entities in a number of ways, i.e., as a management communication base, as a measure of corporate and divisional performance, to tighten management, stock holder interests and to emphasise the long-term benefits of industrial research and employee training. Profit can be ascertained by determining the company's cost of equity capital, weighted average cost of the firm, adjusted operating income, operating income plus back expenses providing a future benefit, assets employed on a book basis, capital investment and the difference between the readjusted operation and the capital change.

Chen and Dodd (1997)[14] concluded that EVA measures provide relatively more information than the traditional measures of accounting in terms of the stock return association, but that EVA should not entirely replace the traditional measures since measures such as E/P, ROA and RONW have incremental value in monitoring firm performance. It was also observed that there was no significant difference between EVA and the traditional RI in terms of the association with stock returns.

Coggan (1997)[15] held that EVA has been applied to individual companies and has also been used for stock markets. It was high when stock price were high at the end of 1980s and latter fell to become suppressed during 1991 and 1992. EVA has again risen according to Goldman sachs, with better inventory and labour management seen as two factors behind the rise. High EVA levels do not mean that stock price will rise, but buy-backs may occur because returns cannot be sustained.

Elliott (1997)[16] established that a number of consulting firms and financial officers are searching for the ways to apply EVA to the oil and gas industry. EVA is a performance measure which determines whether a particular company creates value for the shareholders. However, queries have been raised to the researcher on the application of EVA to the industry and the significance of discounted cash flow in measuring value.

Kroll (1997)[17] explained with the help of paradigms that business with the intention of making use of an EVA system or a system oriented to the cost of capital find that it improves both financial and operating results. Those that achieve the best results usually run the system with their organisational and business strategy.

Mayfield (1997)[18] has statistically established that the shareholder value can be increased by investing in all those projects, which give a positive NPV, and by discontinuing all those products and projects whose return on capital is less that the cost of capital. The major task is to encourage the managers to create long-term value. The traditional accounting techniques are familiar with concept of residual value. When this concept is used in economic value measurement as a means of evaluating business performance it involves some important modifications in traditional accounting concepts. EVA as a measure of financial performance provides an excellent tool for strategy planning, investment appraisal pricing decisions and a basis for incentive compensation.

Myers (1997)[19] put forward that the companies should consider first the nature of their business or their objective before they decide, what value-based performance metrics to use. Those firms that aim to achieve balance sheet efficiency, control over capital and increase in asset turnover, can utilise free cash flow methods or EVA, method. However, the firms that have undertaken cost cutting and re-engineering should avoid using cash flow return on investment and return on net assets.

Putnam (1997)[20] pointed out that the investors were bullish on US equities in 1995 and 1996 whereas, 1997 was a much more volatile year. To understand this phenomenon a framework of analysis such as EVA is extremely useful. EVA highlights five important factors to analyse the creation of shareholders value:

— Net operating profit after tax and before interest;

— Weighted average cost of capital;

— Investment in the business;

— Rate of return in investments;

— The competitive advantage period.

Rajeshwar (1997)[21] stated in his study that EVA can also be used as a device for shareholder's communication and manager incentive systems, apart from measuring the financial performance of an organisation. Demand for EVA among the corporate world has spurred competition among financial consultants, who help in computing EVAs in business organisations.

Smith (1997)[22] Pioneered that many insurance companies are embracing the concept of econometrics measurements through mathematical and statistical criteria to help assess the financial performance. The insurance industry is using these as a supplemental evaluative measure, primarily because insurers still have success with existing systems of measurements such as Total Business Return and EVA find significant application in the insurance industry.

Smith and Marinak's (1997)[23] held that Human Resources departments are increasingly compelled to justify their costs and value added to their organisations. One way of achieving this is through business intelligence. Generating timely information about the organisations human resources, enhances the HR functions strategic valuc, enabling to contribute to the company's bottom line and transforms it into a true business partner. Specifically, the HR function can increase its EVA to the rest of the company by using business intelligence in evaluating and assessing its own value and in helping other departments improve their workforce related processes.

Teitelbaum (1997)[24] the concept of EVA is becoming more and more popular as a measure of financial performance, as an analytical tool and as a management device. The author has shown that EVA is used extensively by various organisations like community hospitals, US postal, etc in order to run their operations. Many investors use EVA for evaluating scripts while investing in shares. He stated that MVA provides a large picture on company's economic well – being than its better-known substitute EVA. MVA subtracts all money ever invested in a company from its current market value.

Tully (1997)[25] brought to book EVA as a method for understanding as to what is happening to the financial performance of an organisation. The paper presents the method for calculating EVA and also shows some pictorial presentations of EVAs of several companies like Bajaj Auto, Asian paints, Procter and Gamble (India) Ltd, Siemens India. It has been concluded that EVA can be a better financial performance evaluation measure than other traditional measures.

Chhabria (1998)[26] Confirmed that many companies are taken as wealth destroyers due to the reason that they are in commodity business. Their fortunes are closely linked to the cyclical swings of these industries. 'Intelligent Investor' took 1638 companies for the period 1993 to 1998 and analysed, which companies were creating or destroying wealth. A number of measures like Total shareholder's return, EVA and MVA have been evolved to find out the wealth creating companies. Of these EVA is quite popular. It is not without limitations and cannot be used in isolation. The author is of the view that while seeking for the stocks to invest in, keep away from capital-intensive commodity businesses. Finally, a wealth creator is that which can expand and strengthen its existing business.

Ethiraj (1998)[27] derived that in the Indian market many companies are using capital inefficiently and thus destroying value. The tool to measure capital efficacy and economic value is Economic Value Added. Taking EVA as a tool of financial performance, HLL and ITC stand at the top of the list. The relation between EVA and total operating capital employed is also important. This would show how much value the company has generated in relation to the assets it has deployed. It is argued that the stock prices move up as a company adopts EVA as an internal performance criterion.

Lahiri (1998)[28] affirmed that Reliance Industries approach of measuring long – term success in adding value is slightly different. It is called Market Value Added. MVA is obtained when all EVA figures are discounted to present value. Still EVA is the most hotly debated concept in the Indian corporate sector. However, the disputes regarding its computation are rampant.

Pattanayak and *Mukherjee* (1998)[29] discussed that there are traditional methods to measure the corporate income called accounting concept and there are also a modern method known as economic concept. EVA, which is based on economic concept, is professed to be a superior technique to identify whether, the organisations NOPAT during a particular period is covering its WACC, thus generating value for its owners. Companies trying to implement EVA are asked to incorporate 164 amendments to their financial accounts.

Riley (1998)[30] stated that United Kingdom stock prices are rising although earning growth has not been especially increasing. EVA is seen as a more precise way of representing corporate performance than market value. EVA measures net profit in relation to capital costs and can help explain a word – wide boom in stocks. Corporate Governance council of western economics have focussed more attention on stockholder's interests. This has helped to prevent over capitalisation.

Saxena (1998)[31] elucidated that there is no one method to measure financial performance that is totally perfect. A measure should be such that it satisfies shareholder's expectations and is also being committed by top management. EVA is a measure that should be used by top management to evaluate investment centre managers, because it considers goal congruence between shareholders and managers.

Anand, et.al (1999)[32] stated that EVA, REVA (Refined Economic Value Added) and MVA are the better measures of business performance than NOPAT and EPS in terms of shareholders value creation and competitive advantage of a firm. Since conventional management compensation systems emphasize sales / asset growth at expense of profitability and shareholder's value. Thus, EVA is a measure that shifts focus on an organisational culture of concern for value.

Harihar (1999)[33] highlighted some myths as regard EVA. According to the author, Stern and Stewart were not the founders of EVA concept; rather it was first propounded by General Motors in early 1920's. Further, EVA calculations are not simple and need a lot of adjustments in the financial books. The author is also of the view that EVA cannot be used for comparison among companies. The next myth is that EVA figures can be manipulated to suit the needs of management. The last and most dangerous myth discussed is that the high EVA companies are cash rich. For looking at cash adequacy another measure called CVA (Cash Value Added) can be used.

Ken C. Yook (1999)[34] in his paper "Estimating EVA using compustat pc plus" states that EVA is gaining popularity in leading corporations and the investment community. Unlike traditional accounting measures of performance, EVA attempts to measure the value that firms create or destroy by subtracting a capital charge from the returns generated on invested capital. In this paper EVA is measured using compustat pc plus based on the methodology that Stewart defines. The author concludes that there exists high correlation between the estimates. A caveat is the accuracy with which cost of capital can be estimated. Although same theoretical framework followed to estimate WACC, diverse approaches to estimate each component lead to very different capital costs for the same company.

Ravishankar (1999)[35] elucidated that whatever be the chosen value goal, value reporting is vital. As a corollary, no longer is the CEO concerned with raising and allocating money, but has emerged as the custodian of value. According to the author, much of what has been published as EVA could well be incorrect. The author further states that EVA may treat an item as capital item, what would be a revenue item under Generally Accepted Accounting Principles (GAAP). Other issues regarding EVA include:

- A big lot of non–critical accounting adjustments;
- Determination of level of capital used in an operating unit;
- Determination of cost of capital;
- Irrationality of using EVA as a project evaluation technique.

Singh A.K (1999)[36] tried to present a new framework of decision-making based on EVA and BPR. Both have gained more attention of corporate managers in the Fortune 500 companies but still a lot to be done. Many finance managers in India are not able to appreciate the potential of EVA and BPR. Although Indian corporate sector has slowly started giving recognition to these critical concepts of success in the light of competitive global village it seems that it may take a few more years for the corporate executives to realise the potential of the buzzwords of 21st century. It can be concluded that maximising the value of shareholders is the prime concern of any business organisation and it should be kept in mind that change is the only thing, which is permanent in nature.

Thenmozhie (1999)[37] discussed the concept of EVA and compared it with some other traditional measure of corporate performance viz., ROI, EPS, RONW, ROE, ROCE, etc. She used the co-efficient of determination to demonstrate that traditional measures do not reflect the real value of shareholders and hence EVA has to be taken into account to measure the value of shareholder's wealth. She has also described the concept of EVA in the Indian scenario with specific reference to companies like NIIT, Hindustan Lever and ITC. The author has referred to some of the shortcomings of the concept of EVA but maintains that EVA is a better measure of corporate performance as compared to the traditional measures.

Kumar S (2000)[38] concluded that using EVA as the best financial indicator blindly may not be correct, since it is not without pitfalls. The pitfalls in EVA calculation and manipulation have been discussed. According to the author positive EVA figures do not ensure high financial performance. He suggests that EVA should be used for making comparison between companies in the same industry group. He observes that computing COC at flat rates is meaningless. To make EVA relatively comparable, EVA should be expressed in terms of EVA (in Rs.) per unit of capital employed.

William G. Sullivan and ***Kimlascola Needy (2000)***[39] in a study "Determining EVA for a proposed investment in new manufacturing" has said that one of the most highly touted financial metrics of the 1990s is Economic Value Added (EVA). For the past 10 years, EVA has been adopted by many large manufacturing companies such as AT & T, Eastman Chemical, Coca-cola and Eli lilly, as a means of retrospectively aligning executive compensation plans with corporate shareholder returns. This matching of management salaries and bonuses is possible because of the strong statistical correlation that EVA has with wealth creation in some companies. EVA is equivalent to the Annual Worth measure of after-tax profitability. The study concludes that even though EVA has been applied predominantly to retroactive equity valuation of entire manufacturing companies, EVA can also be utilised to evaluate proposed capital investments because it is equivalent to the Annual Worth (AW) of a project's after-tax cash flows. Since EVA is done on an after-tax basis, it eliminates possible distortions that may result when engineers in industry perform before-tax engineering economy studies on proposed capital investments. After-tax studies are important because income taxes are an integral part of any cash flow analysis.

Chen Shimin and ***James L Dodd (2001)***[40] in a study presented evidence on the value relevance of several profitability measures, like operating income, residual income and EVA. Based on a formal valuation model, the authors found the three profitability measures have information content in terms of value-relevance. However contrary to the claim of EVA advocates, the data do not support the assertion that EVA is the best measure for valuation purposes. The market may see through various accounting conventions differently than Stern Stewart does when it calculates EVA. It also suggests that the market may place higher reliance on audited accounting earnings than the unaudited EVA metric. The study further states that Residual Income measures contain significant incremental information that is not available in operating income measures.

Janardhan N. Rao (2001)[41] in "*ESOPs* Vs *EVA*: Alignment of interests"; Employee Stock Options (ESOPs) have been widespread in US since 1990s. Its objective is to motivate employees to perform better and improve shareholder's value. They create a sense of belonging and ownership among employees. Employees are typically awarded stock options entitling them to purchase a certain number of shares in one or two years' time at the prevailing market price. The reward to the employee directly vests with any increase in share price over the intervening period. Studies in US suggest that ESOPs increase shareholder wealth when used purely as employment benefit vehicle.

EVA is also considered to be an instrument that can be used for compensation for executives to align their interests with those of shareholders. The relative attractiveness of EVA is gaining momentum in the light of stock market turmoil. ESOPs provide employees with a long-term incentive and EVA short-term. ESOPs are a claim on shares while EVA is an annual accounting measure.

Madhav V. Rajan (2001)[42] in a discussion of EVA Versus Earnings; The paper begins with a consideration of practitioner claims regarding the superiority of various metrics and of whether the R^2 metric for each measure relative to price is a sensible criterion for judging superiority. The paper concludes with the message that a researcher who is unaware of the parameters governing the metrics for a firm can make use of a complex nonlinear function of the metric's correlation with price to compute the value of adopting EVA.

A firm that is considering adoption of EVA as a metric in addition to earnings and the share price knows the signal properties of its metrics. It seems reasonable that a consultant implementing EVA in a firm would have access to sufficient data about the metrics to obviate the need for R^2 information.

Garvey (2001)[43] revealed that dissatisfaction with traditional accounting-based performance measures has spawned a number of alternatives of which EVA is clearly the most prominent. There is currently a heated debate among practitioners as to whether the performance measures have a higher correlation with stock values and returns than do traditional accounting earnings. Academic researchers have instead relied on the variance of performance measures to gauge their relative accuracy. The analysis pits EVA against earnings as two candidates performance measures. A relatively standard principal agent model was used and recognised that while the variability of each measure is observable, their exact information contents is not. The model provides a formal method for ascertaining the relative value of such measures based on two distinct uses of a stock price. First, prices provide a noisy measure of managerial value-added. The novel insight is that the stock prices can also reveal the signal content of alternative accounting-based performance measures. Then how to combine stock prices, earnings and EVA is shown to produce an optimally weighted compensation scheme.

It is found that simple correlation between EVA or earnings and stock returns is a reliable guide to their value as an incentive contracting too. This is not because stock returns are themselves an ideal performance measure; rather it is because correlation places appropriate weights in both the signal and noise components of alternative measures.

Russ Ray (2001)[44] in "Economic Value Added: Theory, Evidence, A Missing Link", suggested that the missing link in the EVA process is productivity, a factor, which has so far been ignored by both the proponents and the critics of EVA. It is further argued that EVA is simply a measuring tool, which points out where value is being created by the firm, and where it is not. EVA does not create value – it simply measures it. The real reason why a firm's financials might improve after EVA adoption is two fold:

- The measurement effect; and
- Productivity increases—the real missing link between EVA and better financials.

EVA allows a firm to identify where the return on its capital is out stripping the cost of that capital. For those areas of the firm where the former is indeed greater than the latter, EVA analysis allows the firm to concentrate on the firm's productivity in order to maximise the value created by the firm.

Salmi, Timo and ***Ilkka Virtanen (2001)***[45] in "Economic value added: A simulation analysis of the trendy, owner-oriented management tool; the value-based management performance measure", EVA is an incarnation of the underlying Residual Income (RI) concept. The concept evaluated and compared with the traditional profitability measures within a controlled simulation framework. It was observed that EVA is very sensitive to its cost of equity component, but insensitive to its cost of debt component under regular conditions. EVA and its variability were observed to be strongly affected by the firm's growth policies because of coverage effects. EVA was observed to be much more unstable than the traditional return on investment and directly related to the return on equity measures.

Weaver (2001)[46] observed that over the past decade, a number of companies, consultants, and a few investment analysts have heralded Economic Value Added. In theory, it is NOPAT (Net Operating Profit After Tax) less a capital charge for the Invested Capital (IC) employed in the business. This survey bridges the gap between "theory" and "practice" by detailing how EVA proponents measure EVA. This survey is important because its fieldwork identifies significant inconsistencies in the measurement of EVA and its major components.

Bardia S.C (2002)[47] revealed that EVA concept has caught on the fancy of investment analysis recently to measure corporate performance. In the dynamic corporate environment, a common investor finds difficult to monitor his investments. The method of EVA guides the investors in evaluating the performance of the company and monitoring their investments. It is claimed that EVA is the single method of accounting properly for various dimensions by which a company's value may be added or lost. The method emphasises the quality of earning and not just the quantity. The number of companies adopting EVA as a tool of performance measurement is increasing sharply in India. No system or technique will bear fruits until it is well implemented, and has the support of all the concerned parties. EVA is no exception to this rule. If the concept of EVA is implemented well taking the limitations into account, it will produce better results in analysing the performance of a corporate entity.

Mangala and Simpy (2002)[48] discussed that maximising shareholders value had become the new corporate paradigm. Although shareholders wealth maximisation has been recognised by the managers and researchers, the maxim has gained a new dimension only in the recent years due to the introduction of the concept of EVA. Shareholder's wealth is equal to the market price of shares multiplied by the number of equity shares outstanding.

Stern who coined the term EVA believed that EVA is the most important driver influencing the market value of a share. So, if the company improves EVA by increasing its return on capital employed and lowering its cost of capital, its market value will increase. This paper attempts to study the relationship between EVA and market value among various companies in India. The EVA of 15 companies among five industries (Fast Moving Consumer Goods, Information Technology, Pharma, Automobile, Textile) has been computed. The results of the analysis confirm stern's hypothesis and conclude that the company's Current Operational Value (COV) is more significant in contributing to a change in the market value of shares in the Indian context.

Shrieves (2002)[49] concluded that the researcher should help the user of DCF methods by clearly setting for the relationship of Free-Cash Flow (FCF) and Economic Value Added (EVA) concepts to each other and to the more traditional applications of DCF thinking. The research team follows others in demonstrating the equivalence between EVA and NPV, but their approach is more general. It links the problem of security valuation, organisation valuation and investment project selection. In addition it relates more directly to the use of standard financial accounting information. The FCF approach focuses on the periodic total cash flows obtained by deducting total net investment and adding net debt issuance to net operating cash flow, whereas the EVA approach requires defending the periodic total investment in the firm. In a project valuation context, both FCF and EVA are conceptually equivalent to NPV. Each approach necessitates a myriad of adjustments to the accounting information available for most corporations.

Adsera, Xavier; Vinolas, Pere, (2003)[50] in their paper "FEVA: A Financial and Economic Approach to Valuation", present a financial and economic approach to valuation. In addition to traditional discounted cash flow methods, one family of valuation models, Economic Value Added (EVA) and other franchise factor approaches, has become a favorite methodology for corporate valuation. In EVA approaches, the key value driver is the spread between the return on the existing investments and their average cost of capital. Therefore, this approach focuses on the left-hand side of the balance sheet. The important aspect of this issue is not its technical interest or which of the different values of a company is correct, but what the value drivers are that each method identifies.

Ferguson, Robert ; Rentzler, Joel; Yu, Susana, (2005)[51] in their article "Does Economic Value Added (EVA) Improve Stock Performance Profitability?" used event study methodology to investigate whether firms adopt Stern Stewart's EVA system due to poor stock performance (i.e.. poor profitability) and whether adopting EVA leads to better stock performance (i.e.. greater profitability). There is insufficient evidence to conclude that poor stock performance leads firms to adopt EVA or that adopting EVA improves stock performance. Firms that adopt EVA appear to have above average profitability relative to their peers both before and after the adoption of EVA; further, there is some evidence that EVA adopters experience increased profitability relative to their peers following adoption.

De Wet, J. H. V. H., Du Toit, E., (2007)[52] in their article "Return on Equity: A popular, but flawed measure of corporate financial performance" aimed at analysing the impact of popular financial performance measures on shareholders' wealth. It tests the strength of the linear relationships between these performance measures and shareholders' returns, which consist of dividends and changes in the share price. The Return on Equity (ROE) is weighed up against the present favourite, Economic Value Added (EVA) and the merits and flaws of each approach were discussed. Other approaches, such as a combination of performance measures and the expectations theory were also discussed briefly. The statistical tests performed found Spreads (a standardised EVA) to be slightly superior to ROE in explaining changes in shareholders' returns. However, the use of same year data resulted in very weak linear relationships between all the performance measures tested, relative to shareholders' returns. When 5-year medians were used in the analysis, significant correlations were obtained between current shareholders' returns and the future results for the internal performance measures. This engenders some support for the expectations theory with its contention that the most effective positive impact on shareholders' returns can be accomplished by managing expectations about future financial results, rather than maximising these results now. It is clear that the debate about the effectiveness of traditional accounting performance measures, as well as the search for the real drivers of shareholder value, will continue and increase in intensity.

EMPIRICAL LITERATURE

The first empirical study regarding the association between EVA and MVA was conducted by ***Stewart (1991)***[53]. Based on a sample of 613 US companies and regarding the period from 1984 to 1985 relatively to the period from 1987 to 1988, the author states that there is a strong relation between the average standardised values of EVA and MVA, only the relation between negative EVA and negative MVA does not correspond very well. According to the author, this is due to the potential of liquidation, recovery, recapitalisation sets a floor on a company's market value.

Kusum L. Ailawadi, Norm Borin and ***Paul W. Farris (1995)***[54] in "Market Power and Performance: A Cross-industry analysis of manufacturers and retailers", MVA serves as an indicator of market power, which is being accumulated for future earnings. If retailers have indeed been increasing their market power and therefore their ability to increase EVA in future, then efficient capital markets will recognise this potential for future earnings and the market participants will incorporate this knowledge in their valuation of the retailers. For this empirical analysis, financial data for the period 1982-1992 was collected from the COMPUSTAT and university of Chicago CRSP database. The standard industry classification–coding manual was used to categorise the companies with specific SIC codes into various industries. The sample contains 909 manufacturers and 274 retailers.

Trends in the mean values of certain variables have been examined for retailers and manufacturers in each industry. Means of all the ratio variables are weighted by their denominator. This paper has examined the purported shift in power from manufacturers to retailers using more complete measures of market power and broader sample of industries and retail classes. Out of 14 consumer goods industries analysed only a few of them exhibit a shift in market power towards retailers. This apparent shift is highly influenced by a small number of retailers within a single retail class. It was suggested that retailers are not significantly better off compared to manufacturers on any of the performance measures. Retailer EVA and MVA have increased at a significantly slower rate than manufacturers. The results do not support the contention that retailers have increased their power relative to manufacturers.

Dodd and ***Chen (1996)***[55] studied the correlation between stock returns and EVA, Residual Income (RI), ROA, ROE and EPS. The data is from the ten-year period 1983 through 1992 and the sample consists of 566 US companies. In their study ROA explained R^2 best with an R^2 of 24.5 per cent; R^2 for other performance measures; EVA 20.2 per cent, RI 19.4 per cent and between 5 per cent to 7 per cent for ROE and EPS. The authors conclude that adjusted EVA offers few advantages over unadjusted EVA or residual income.

Grant (1996)[56] found that the EVA concept may have everlastingly changed the way real profitability is measured. Pioneered by Stern Stewart Management Services in the 1980s, EVA is a financial tool that focuses on the difference between company's after tax operating profit and its total cost of capital. A survey was conducted to examine the empirical relations between EVA and corporate valuation. Results suggest that EVA significantly bangs the Market Value Added of a firm and that this wealth effect stems from the company's residual return on capital.

Lehn and *Makhija (1996)*[57] affirm that EVA and market value Added (MVA) are increasingly being eyed as alternative measures of business performance and strategic development. Despite the attention, however, the empirical research has been devoted to these two metrics. A study, which examines the effectiveness of EVA and MVA as measures of performance, was conducted. It used data from 241 firms for the time slab 1987-96, showed that EVA and MVA effectively measured the quality of strategic decisions and served as signals of strategic change. They were found to be significantly correlated with stock price performance and inversely related to turnover. Firms having greater focus in their business activities had higher MVA than less focused counter parts.

Lehn and *Makhija (1996)*[58] studied EVA and MVA as performance measures and signals for strategic change. Their data consists of 241 US companies and cover years 1987, 1988, 1992 and 1993. The researchers first found that both measures positively correlate with stock returns and that the correlation is slightly better than with traditional performance measures like Return on Assets (ROA). Return on Equity (ROE) and Return on Sales (ROS). In addition they studied how companies perform as measured in terms of EVA.

O' Byrne (1996)[59] compared the information content by regressing firm value of EVA and earnings measured as NOPAT. The sample consists of 6551 firm year observations, for the period between 1985 and 1993. The author reports all adjusted R^2 of 31 per cent for the EVA regression and 33 per cent for the NOPAT regression. The author concludes that EVA outperforms earnings in explaining firm values.

O'Byrne (1996)[60] analysed the relationship between operating performance and market value for the years 1985-93 for the companies in the 1993 Stern Stewart performance 1000 data base and compared the explanatory power of Free Cash Flow (FCF), Net Operating Profit After Tax (NOPAT) and EVA. The study shows that a simple EVA – regression model explains less variance than a standard NOPAT – regression model with a non-zero constant term, but that EVA explains more than twice as much of the variation in market/capital ratios as NOPAT when the EVA model has positive and negative EVA coefficients and an in (Capital) term and the NOPAT model is truly a "NOPAT only" model with a zero intercept.

Padgett (1996)[61] recognised that the ranking of top 100 banks in terms of MVA and EVA by the financial consulting company Stern Stewart and company reveals that the 100 banks had an average return of 12.37 per cent. The figure was only 97 basic points higher than their average weighted cost of capital of 0.11, which indicates that the value of bank's capital to their shareholders has stagnated. The bank that had the best position for creating MVA in 1995 was Citicorp, which created $ 13.5 billion.

Telaranta (1997a)[62] studied how residual income variables explain movements in market valuation of Finnish Companies. The data consisted of 42 Finnish industrial companies during 1988-1995. Only 26 of the companies were listed for the whole period and 16 were listed for shorter period. During the research period both the aggregate MVA and the non-weighted average return as stock among the sample companies were negative, since the whole Finnish economy and the stock markets experienced a severe recession in the middle of research period around the turn of the decade (1990). The researcher used different methods in assessing the ability of different measures to explain market movements.

As dependant variables the researcher used MVA, market-to-book ratio and excess return on stock and as independent variables two versions of economic profit (residual income) and three versions of Eduard – Bell – Ohlson – figure (near residual income) as well as traditional accounting based performance measures like operating profit, Net earnings and cash flow were used.

The results indicated the level of Economic profit to explain 30.7 per cent of the level of Market value added as the next best measure NOPAT explain 30.16 per cent. The author concluded that residual income variables are found to explain the movements in market capitalization with statistical significance. The author also presents that residual income variables are not better than accounting based measures. Finally it stated that Economic profit is the best variable in the study explaining market movements but that the difference compared to other measures is insignificant.

Banerjee (1997)[63] has conducted an empirical research to find the superiority of EVA over other traditional financial performance measures. Ten industries have been chosen and each industry is represented by four/five companies. ROI and EVA have been calculated for the sample companies and a comparison of both has been undertaken, showing the superiority of EVA over ROI. Indian companies are gradually recognising the importance of EVA. Some such companies are Ranbaxy Laboratories, Samtel India Ltd. and Infosys Technologies ltd.

Kramer and *Pushner (1997)*[64] compared EVA's effectiveness as a proxy for MVA and changes in MVA to the traditional accounting measure Net Operating Profit After Taxes (NOPAT) over 8855 firm years. They find no clear evidence that EVA is the best proxy for MVA and that the market seems to be more focussed on earnings than EVA.

Wallace (1997)[65] studied the effects of adopting management bonus plans based on residual income measures. The sample in the study consists of forty firms that have some residual income measure, mainly EVA, as bonus base. This sample was compared to the sample of same size consisting of similar companies where the bonus is tied to accounting based measures. The researcher tested with various methods, the management actions in these sample groups and concluded and interpreted that the results were consistent with a residual income-based performance measure providing incentives for managers to act more like owners, thus mitigating the inherent conflict between managers and the shareholders. The firms that adopted residual income based compensation outperformed the market over the twenty-four month period by over 4 per cent points in cumulative terms.

KPMG – BS study (1998)[66] assessed top 100 companies on EVA, sales, PAT, and MVA criteria. The survey has used BS-1000 list of companies using a composite index comprising sales, profitability and compounded annual growth rate of those companies covering the period 1996-97. Sixty companies have been found able to create positive shareholder value whereas 38 companies have been found to destroy it, 24 companies have destroyed shareholder value by reporting negative MVA.

Banerjee and ***Jain (1999)***[67] made a research based on empirical data. Among the selected independent variables (EPS, EVA, Kp,Lp and ARONW) EVA has proved to be the most explanatory variable when MVA was taken as the dependent variable. Backward Elimination method was applied to find the most explanatory independent variable. For this purpose the time frame was of eight years and all the variables were calculated over this period for the sample companies.

Bao and Bao (1999)[68] revealed the association between EVA and the value of the Indian firms, which are included in the COMPUSTAT – Global vantage database. The results of the study show that EVA is positively and significantly correlated with the firm value. The results are consistent with the theory in that firms with EVA created value and firms with higher created value have higher stock prices. The study also reveals that explanatory power of EVA is lower than that of earnings and book value of firms under consideration.

Evans, John (1999)[69] argued that despite a growing literature, the relationship between the structure of executive compensation and firm performance is not fully understood. Furthermore, little work has been done on the link between EVA as a measure of firm performance and the form of executive compensation. An examination of the compensation structure and EVA of 209 companies in 1995-98 provides evidence supporting incentive compensation. EVA is found to be positively and significantly related to incentive-based compensation. Cash-based remuneration was found to be unrelated to EVA performance.

Banarjee (2000)[70] had made an attempt to find out whether Stewart's claim that market value of a company is equal to the discounted value of all future EVAs, holds good in the Indian context or not. For this purpose the researcher selected a sample of 200 companies over a period of four years (1994-95 to 1997-98). According to him, market value of the firm is the function of two components i.e., Current Operational Value (COV) and Future Growth Value (FGV).

COV is equal to book value of beginning invested capital plus the capitalised value of current years EVA, whereas FGV represents the present value of all future expected future improvements. Based on the analysis he comes to the conclusion that in many cases there is a considerable divergence between MVA and sum total of COV and FGV. He points out that this divergence may be due to the short time span of the study, thus leading to the inability of FGV to capital the growth potential factored in the market value of company's shares.

Oral Erdogan, Niyazi Berk and ***Erol Katircloglu (2000)***[71] in a study on the "Economic profit approach in firm performance measurements-Evidence from the Turkish Stock Market" covered the non-bank firms for which detailed financial data are available for the 1993-98 period and whose equity shares were traded on the Istanbul Stock Exchange during the period 1991-98. The aggregate market values of 123 companies in the study are examined on a yearly basis. It is observed that the market capitalization share of the sample companies in the stock market has never dropped below 50 per cent. To calculate the 6 coefficients, the rate of returns for 48 months preceding the end of each accounting period are used.

Economic profit approach is mathematically equivalent to discounted cash flows. The market inefficiencies and the uncertainly related to the future estimations restrict the practical use of EVA as one of the economic profit measurements. In evaluating company performance, cost of capital and wealth maximization become the most important issues. In the calculation of economic profit in the study, EVA, MVA and SVA measures are considered. Required descriptions in connection with the efficiency of use have been given after suggesting static CAPM in the measurement. Almost all of the EVAs for the period 1994-98 resulted in negative values. It is concluded that the sample companies have not created any economic value added in terms of macro economic significance.

Parasuram (2000)[72] discussed the EVA position of 14 major public sector banks, 7 new private sector banks, 5 old private sector banks and 2 Foreign banks. Among the strength indicators, deposit, return on assets, interest income as a percentage of total assets, interest yield spread as a percentage of total assets and EVA were considered. The study concluded that EVA is an important measure to judge a bank's performance in view of the current scenario of banks. EVA has been found to have a high degree of correlation with ROA and not with any of the other measures. It stages a fact that banks realise the importance of measuring EVA separately even if they do well on other filed. Some of the banks, which have higher net profit and otherwise ranked high, have been found to have a negative EVA. This study expects that EVA will soon displace other measures of bank performance.

Parasuraman.N.R., (2000)[73] in "Economic Value Added – its computation and impact on select Banking Companies" concluded that EVA is an important measure to judge a bank's performance in view of the current scenario of banks having to satisfy a large body of shareholders. The position of 14 major public sector banks, 7 new private sector banks, 5 old private sector banks and 2 foreign banks were studied. Ranking has been done on the basis of certain parameters like Deposits, Return on Assets, Interest income as a percentage of total assets, interest yield spread as a percentage of total assets and EVA. It was found that in certain observed cases, ranking under EVA is high not so high under the criterion of ROA. It is explained that the banks concerned have a more than average working funds and when return is computed as a percentage thereof, the rank is pretty low, whereas in terms of EVA, which just takes the return as a percentage of Networth the Banks are doing pretty well. It is concluded that in the light of intense competition in the forthcoming years, it is likely that EVA will soon displace other measures of bank performance and ultimately a bank will get to be judged by the extent of shareholder value creation.

Jonathan K.Kramer and ***Jonathan R.Peters (2001)***[74] made an inter Industry analysis of Economic Value Added as a proxy for Market Value Added across 53 industries. The objective of the study is to determine whether the level of capital intensity affects the ability of EVA to serve as an effective proxy for MVA. Compustat pc plus was used to find the Fixed Asset Turnover ratio (FAT) of each firm in the SS1000, and FAT ratio was used as an indicator of capital intensity. The results indicate that using EVA as a proxy for MVA is not FAT dependent. EVA outperformed NOPAT as a proxy for MVA in only ten of the 53 industries studied. In 11 cases for EVA and 6 for NOPAT, the sign of the coefficient was negative and statistically significant, indicating an inverse relation between EVA and changes in MVA. The relationship between MVA and changes in EVA and NOPAT was also examined. It showed that a high correlation exist among them.

Kalaiselvi. S., (2001)[75] in her study entitled "Economic value added performance and financial efficiency of Hindustan lever limited" examined the impact of merger of Broker bond with HLL on HLL's financial efficiency and assessed the shareholders wealth maximisation strategies of HLL. The study covered a period of ten years from 1991 to 2000. The financial health of HLL on the scores of liquidity, stability, profitability, efficiency and solvency during the study period as analysed through the application of ratios has been quite satisfactory. HLL has enhanced shareholders take by its excellent EVA performance through a spurt in EVA from Rs.46 crores to Rs.848 crores during the selected decade.

All the nine growth indicators and 14 of the 17 financial ratios computed in the study had maintained an upbeat trend in the post-merger period. This proves that the merger of brooke bond had favourable impact on the HLL. The findings of the study prove that Hindustan Lever Ltd is committed to the strategy of growth with efficiency and has succeeded in it.

Thampy and ***Beheli (2001)***[76] studied the economic profits to commercial banks in the public and private sectors during 1990s. It also moves the benchmark of performance of banks from accounting profits of the economic profits and shareholder wealth creation. The study has been restricted to 12 commercial banks consisting of 4 public and 8 private sector banks. The period covered is three years starting from 1995-96 to 1997-98. Beta has been calculated on the basis of daily stock price data with Bombay Stock Exchanges BSE 200 index returns during January 1, 1997 to march 31, 1998 as the proxy for the market returns. The study reveals that the performance of Indian banks as measured by EVA is not very satisfactory. The results of the study reveal that the commercial banks under consideration have not created any positive EVA. It also suggests that banks should improve and strengthen their credit assessment technique and monitoring mechanism to bring down the NPAs so as to improve the earning capacity.

Adnan M. Abdeen and ***G. Timothy Haight*** **(2002)**[77] in an Empirical Study of the fortune Five Hundred Companies compared the performance of EVA user companies with non-user Fortune 500 corporations, the largest corporations in the United States, as published in the April 26, 1999 issue. Fortune rates the 500 companies not just on revenues, but on 12 other performance criteria by showing the highest 50 performing companies in each of the criteria. This research examined how many EVA users made the highest fifty companies lists in order to support or deny any conclusion may be reached about the EVA users. It also ranks the EVA users within the same industries in order to see which industry uses this evaluation measure the most.

It was found that only 47 companies specifically stated that they use EVA as a performance measure. Most of the 500 companies referred to shareholders value enhancement through profitable growth and the introduction of value added products, services, customers, advice, solutions, operations, internet services and others. The performance of the Fortune 500 companies using EVA as revealed in this research was better than the performance of the non-EVA users for the categories of profits as percentage of revenues, assets and shareholders equity. It was concluded that EVA will become less popular in its use as an instrument to measure value creation to shareholders and that EVA will join the other traditional metrics used by business firms.

Eduardo Sandoval **(2002)**[78] in an empirical study for Chilean companies examined a sample of 62 Chilean companies over the period 1994-1999 using quarterly data. This sample comprises the most traded and representative industrial companies on the Chilean stock market. The study shows evidence about whether EVA dominates REVA. The results indicated that REVA outperforms competing alternatives in associations between their current and lagged realisations and value creation. When past realisations for EVA and REVA are taken into account and once controlled for other accounting measures, REVA outperforms EVA for the whole sample.

At the Chilean industry level, REVA explains by itself value creation for construction and investment industries. For the remaining industries, the findings indicate that in addition to the high explanatory power associated to REVA, the net income and operating cash flows explain only a low portion of value creation volatility.

Costigan and ***Linda (2002)***[79] observed that EVA is a new measure of performance that is purported to better align manager's incentives to that of the shareholders. Firms that experience higher agency conflicts should be more inclined to use this performance evaluation system. The organisational strategy of the firm must influence the likelihood of employing EVA. Prospector firms are firms that apply a differentiation strategy while the defender firms focus on being cost-leaders. Those firms identified as the prospectors should be less likely to use EVA. 115 firms were identified as being adopters of EVA.

Logistic regression was performed to contrast these firms to a control group of 1271 non-adopters. The results show that firms using EVA exhibit percentage of institutional ownerships and a lower percentage of insider ownership than the non-adopters. The prospector firms as defined by a high ratio of research and development to sales tend to use EVA less than defender firms. Accounting adjustments are a focal point of the EVA formulation and the results presented in this study suggest that providing appropriate incentives may be more complex than the developers of EVA.

Cyrus A. Ramezant, Luc. Soenen and ***Alan Jung (2002)***[80] in a study relating to "Growth, Corporate profitability and value creation", used the data from the annual compustat files on US companies for the period 1990 through 2000. The sample consisted of approximately 2156 companies. Two broad measures of growth were considered. Sales growth was measured as the average of quarterly sales growth rates over the past 20 quarters. Earnings growth was measured as the average of earnings growth rates over the past 20 quarters. This study was based on two objectives:

- To investigate the link between measures of growth and corporate profitability; and
- To judge whether maximizing corporate profitability enhance shareholder value.

Univariate and multivariate analysis was made. The univariate results point to a complex and U – Shaped relationship between performance and growth. Multivariate analysis showed that although corporate profitability measures generally rise with earnings and sales growth, an optimal point exists beyond which further growth destroys shareholders value and adversely affects profitability.

Further an inverted U- Shaped relationship between EVA and measures of sales and earning growth was found. It was concluded that maximising growth is not necessarily consistent with maximising shareholder wealth. Shareholder value is a concave function of growth.

Dr. Niranjan Swain, Dr. Chandra Sekhar Mishra, Dr. Mukesh Kumar and ***Dr. S.Vijayalakshmi (2002)***[81] in "EVA and MVA; A study of Indian Pharmaceutical Industry", examined how MVA-a measure of external performance which is considered to be the best indicator of shareholder value creation is correlated with the firm's performance in terms of financial measures of the company such as EVA, Net Operating Profit After Tax (NOPAT), Return On Capital Employed (ROCE), Return On Networth (RONW), Earnings Per Share (EPS) on the one hand and the purely economic factors of the company such as Labour Productivity, Capital Productivity, Total Factor Productivity, Sales and R&D expenditure on the other hand. A sample of 28 companies has been taken from Pharmaceutical industry. The study concludes that EVA, NOPAT and sales outperform other financial and economic measures in predicting MVA in most of the companies in Indian Pharmaceutical Industry.

Eugene W. Anderson, Clacs Fornell and ***Sanal K. Mazvanchery (2004)***[82] in a study, "Customer satisfaction and shareholder value", develops a new conceptual framework that links customer satisfaction to shareholder value and that brings the role of market structure into the nomological network that links the two key constructs. The study builds on research that relates customer satisfaction to accounting-based measures of financial performance and to the one previous study that examines the association between customer satisfaction and shareholder value. To test the hypotheses, the American Customer Satisfaction Index (ACSI) database of nearly 200 publicly trade fortune 500 firms from 1994 to 1997 were employed. Tobin's Q, a measure that is forward looking, risk adjusted, comparable across firms, and well-grounded in economic theory was selected. The findings indicate that the association between ACSI to Tobin's q is positive and significant. It was also found that ASCI is positively associated with two measures:

- ➢ Equity prices; and
- ➢ Ratios of price to book value.

Finally a significant systematic variation in the association between ACSI and Tobin's q across industries was found. A test for underlying industry characteristics that moderate the association indicates that it is weaker in more fragmented industries that are characterised by a high degree of rivalry.

Karampal (2005)[83] in his study "Awareness and applicability of EVA among Indian corporate's: A survey-based analysis" approached the select Indian companies from BSE 200 through a well structured questionnaire to evaluate the realistic face of EVA in India. The questionnaire was mailed to all 50 selected Indian companies listed at the Mumbai Stock Exchange (BSE) at the end of 2000 and constituting the BSE-200 index. The final results of the survey are drawn on the basis of 39 companies of the BSE-200 or BSE-Dollar Index at Mumbai Stock Exchange (BSE).

Majority of the respondents who filled up the questionnaire were either corporate managers (46.2%) or owner-manager (28.2%). The preponderance percentage of the companies selected for the purpose of the survey is more than fifteen years old established business organisations and all companies are willing to maximise their shareholders wealth, 90 per cent of the companies are operating in the global market, 48.7 per cent have been using basic costing techniques or Traditional cost accounting and only about 30 per cent of the companies have put in practice either cost centres of Activity Based Costing (ABC).

All respondents consider only 4 variables as significant and all these variables demand better performance on the part of the corporate organisations. It sounds that the efficiency and effectiveness if go up may be observed as significant variable in the growth of the organisation and same is expected from a corporate generating positive EVA.

23.08 per cent respondents assigned 1st rank to EVA as the best indicator of performance evaluation of all organisation followed by rate of return, return on capital employed and profit margin. About 85 per cent of the respondents are either familiar or very familiar with the concept of EVA. Nearly 23 per cent of the respondent companies have already implemented EVA, 48.6 per cent are planning to implement in the near future and about 9 per cent are collecting information for winning in-house support for its implementation. Only about 18 per cent of the companies disclose their EVA in the annual report. More than 3/5th of the respondents consider EVA as most important factor in decision-making.

89.7 per cent of the respondents make a clean breast about the future of EVA in Indian corporates. It holds up the researcher's view that the concept of EVA has been emerging in the brains of the top brass of the corporate world in India and has nurtured a remarkably excellent time ahead.

Prakash Singh (2005)[84] in a study, "EVA in Indian Banking: Better information content, more shareholders value" examined an appropriate way of evaluating bank's performance with the help of EVA and MVA which tell what the institution is doing with the investors hard earned money. The study is based on 28 Indian private and public sector banks between 1998-1999 and 2002-03. The banks that are listed on the Bombay stock Exchange were selected and data are collected from a financial database of Centre for Monitoring Indian Economy (CMIE) called "Prowess".

While conducting the EVA analysis for banks, all banks were ranked on the basis of EVA, percentage change in EVA over last year, market capitalisation, enterprise value, percentage change in enterprise value over last year, market value added and percentage change in MVA over last year. The study shows that over 80 per cent of the banks were unable to earn a return sufficient to meet their cost of capital. Further the study suggests that the relationship between EVA and MVA statistically significant, some finer models, such as industry - specific models may provide additional insights.

RESEARCH GAP AND NEED FOR THE PRESENT STUDY

In India, for a particular business or company there is no one particular set of shareholders. The firm has a number of stakeholders with differing and sometimes conflicting goals. The stake holders include the owners, lenders, management, personnel, customers, suppliers and creditors. Situations may arise when the company ends up satisfying one set of stakeholders at the cost of another set. We have large business houses in India which started off with one business but diversified during the course of time. In the entire process, they ended up creating many sets of shareholders, thus making the spread of value creation all the more complicated task.

EVA, as an emerging tool of financial management has strong standards and regulations. It appears that the entire business world is moving towards greater transparency, supporting financial disclosures and superior corporate governance. In such an environment, the investor friendly financial performance measure is the need of the hour, for the globally competing companies. These companies opt for lower cost of capital to enhance risk-adjusted returns.

From the synoptic review, it is apparent that the concept has limited applicability in the Indian scenario. Many researchers have applied sophisticated econometric tools to assess the impact of EVA concept on corporate financial performance. In the initial years of EVA application conceptual aspects alone were highlighted, but later some empirical studies have also been accomplished. The present study has been made with regard to more than 100 Indian software companies for a period of ten years thereby establishing the cross-relationship of MVA concept with EVA, EPS, ROCE, NOPAT, Turnover, ROS, ROTA, Market price and SVA. Further a comprehensive survey of these companies through a well-structured questionnaire regarding their awareness and adoptability of EVA has been attempted and its introduction with component analysis would perhaps plug the research gaps in the field. This work is an attempt to offer a detailed examination of EVA with special reference to the research objectives.

REFERENCES

1. **Stern, Joel,** "One Way to Build Value in Your Firm, Executive Compensation", *Financial Executive*, Nov-Dec. 1990, pp. 51-54.

2. **Tully, Shawn.,** "The Real Key to Creating Wealth", *Fortune*, Sept. 20, 1993, p. 563.

3. **Jain. S.K.,** "How much Value are you Adding". *The Management Accountant*, August 1994, pp. 610-11.

4. **McConville. D.,** "All About EVA". *Industry Week*, April 18, 1994, Vol. 243, No. 8, p. 55(3).

5. **Stewart, G. Bennet,** "EVA™ Fact and Fantasy", *Journal of Applied Corporate Finance*, June 1994, pp. 71-84.

6. **Ochsner,** "Welcome to the New World of Economic Value Added", *Compensation and Benefits*, March-April, 1995, Vol. 27, No. 2, p. 30(3).

7. **Carr. R.,** "Towards a Truer Measure of Value", *The Financial Times*, Dec. 11, 1996, p. 19.

8. **Luber, R.B.,** "Who are the Real Wealth Creators", *Fortune*, Dec. 9, 1996, pp. 2-3.

9. **O'Hanlon, J. and Peasvell, K.,** "Measure for Measure", *Accountancy-International Edition*, Feb. 1996, pp. 44-46.

10. **Bacidore, J.M.; Boquist, J.A., Milbourn, T.T.; Thakor, A.V,** "The Search for the Best Financial Performance Measure", *Financial Analysts Journal*, May-June 1997, pp. 11-20.

11. **Blair, A.,** "EVA fevers", *Management Today*, Jan. 1997, p. 42(4).

12. **Booth, Rupert,** "EVA as a Management Incentive", *Management Accounting*, April 1997, pp. 48-50.

13. **Burkette, G., Hedley, T.,** "The Truth About Economic Value Added", *The CPA Journal*, June 1997. No. 7, p. 46(4).

14. **Salmi, Timo and Ilkka Virtanen,** "Economic Value Added: A Simulation Analysis of the Trendy", Owner-oriented Management Tool, *Acta Wasaensia* No. XX, 2001, p. 2.

15. **Coggan, P.,** "Evaluating EVA for Markets", *The Financial Times*, Sept. 29, 1997, p. 26(1).

16. **Elliot.L.,** "Is EVA for everyone?" *Oil and Gas Investor*, Feb. 1997, Vol. 17, No. 2, p. 46.

17. **Kroll. K.,** "EVA and Creating Value: Almost Everybody Agrees on the Goal-covering Capital and Economic Value Added the Way to Reach it?" *Industry Week*. April 7, 1997, Vol. 246, No. 7. p. 102(4).

18. **Mayfield, John,** "Economic Value Management", *Management Accounting*, Sept. 1997, pp. 32-33.

19. **Myers, Randy,** "Measure for Measure", CFO: *The Magazine for Senior Financial Executives*, 1997, No. 11, p. 44(7).

20. **Putnam, Bulford,** "EVA Analysis Predicts Tough Time in US Markets", *Global Investor*, April 1997, pp. 42-44.

21. **Rajeshwar, C.,** "Economic Value Added: Rediscovery Value" *Financial Analyst,* Dec. 1997, pp. 39-44.

22. **Smith, L.,** "Beyond Profit and Loss", *Best's Review-Property-Causality Insurance Edition,* 1997. Vol. 97. No. 12. p. 40(4).

23. **Smith, M., Marinakis, S.,** "Measuring HR Value Added from the Outside in", *Employment Today,* Autumn 1997. Vol. 24, No. 3, p. 59(15).

24. **Teitelbaum. R.,** "America's Greatest Wealth Creators", *Fortune,* Nov. 10, 1997, Vol. 136, No. 9, p. 265(5).

25. **Tully, Shawn,** "Adding Value". *Business Today,* Sept. 22, Oct. 6, 1997, pp. 68-73.

26. **Chhabria, Vishal,** "The Untouchable", *Intelligent Investor.* August 26, 1998, pp. 46-49.

27. **Ethiraj, Govindraj,** "The EVA Feather in the Market Cap", *The Economic Times,* 21 Sept. 1998, p. 1.

28. **Lahiri, Arjun,** "All About EVA", *Business India,* Sept 21-Oct 4, pp. 32-33.

29. **Pattanayak, J.K., Mukherjee, K.,** "Adding Value to Money", *The Chartered Accountant,* Feb. 1998, pp.8-12.

30. **Riley. B.,** "Conjuring up New Value", *The Financial Times,* Feb. 28, 1998, p. 11.

31. **Saxena, Pankaj,** "Economic Value-added and Performance Evaluation", *The Management Accountant,* May 1998, pp. 341-42.

32. **Anand, Manoj, Garg, Ajay; and Arora, Asha,** "Economic Value Added: Business Performance Measure of Shareholder Value", *The Management Accountant,* May 1999, pp. 351-56.

33. **Harihar, T.S.,** "EVA Prorating Myths", *Chartered Finance Analyst,* Nov. 1999, pp. 8-9.

34. **Ken C. Yook,** "Estimating EVA Using Compustat PC Plus", *Financial Practice and Education–Fall/Winter,* 1999, pp. 33-37.

35. **Ravishankar. T.J.,** "Value for Money Sir". *The Economic Times* (Corporate Possier), 26 April, 1999. p. 1.

36. **Singh. A.K.,** "Maximising Wealth of Shareholders Through EVA and BPR", *Pranjana,* Vol. 2, No. 1, Jan-June, 1999. pp. 65-75.

37. **Thenmozhie. M.,** "Economic Value Added as a Measure of Corporate Performance", *The Indian Journal of Commerce,* Vol. 52. No. 4, October-December 1999, pp. 72-85.

38. **Kumar, Satheesh,** "Economic Value Added—A Critique", *Indian Management,* March 2000, pp: 57-62.

39. **William G. Sullivan, Kimla Scola Needy,** "Technical Note–Determination of Economic Value Added for a Proposed Investment in New Manufacturing", *The Engineering Economist*, 2000, Vol. 45, No. 2, pp. 166-179.

40. **Dr. Niranjan Swain, Dr. Chandra Sekhar Mishra,** "Economic Value Added-Concepts and Cases", *ICFAI PRESS*, 52 Nagarjuna Hills, Hyderabad, India–500082, pp. 109-113.

41. **Janardhan Rao. N.,** "*ESOPs* Vs. *EVA*: Alignment of Interests?", *Chartered Financial Analyst*, September 2001, pp. 140-151.

42. **Madhav Rajan. V.,** "Discussion of EVA Versus Earnings: Does It Matter Which is More Highly Correlated with Stock Returns?", *Journal of Accounting Research*, Vol. 38, Supplement 2000, pp. 247-254.

43. **Garvey, T. Herald,** "EVA Versus Earnings: Does It Matter Which is More Highly Correlated with Stock Returns", No. 52, 2001 at http://econ. claremontmckenna.edu/papers/.

44. **Russ Ray,** "Economic Value Added: Theory, Evidence, A Missing Link," *Review of Business, Summer 2001*, pp. 65-69.

45. **Salmi, Timo and Ilkka Virtanen,** *Op.cit*., p. 33.

46. **Weaver, Samuel,** "Measuring EVA: A Survey of the Practices of EVA Proponents", *Journal of Applied Finance*, Vol. 2. Nov. 2001, pp. 141-53.

47. **Bardia, S.C.,** "Economic Value Added: Overall Consideration", *Economic Challenger*, April-June 2002, pp. 1-7.

48. **Mangala, Deepa and Joura Simpy,** "Linkage Between Economic Value Added and Market Value: An Analysis in Indian Context", *Indian Management Studies Journal*, June 2002, pp. 55-65.

49. **Shrieves, E. Ronald,** "Free Cash Flow (FCF), Economic Value Added (EVA), and Net Present Value (NPV): A Reconciliation of Variations of Discounted Cash Flow (DCF) Valuation", *European Management Journal*, Vol. 21, No. 2, June 2002, pp. 386-93.

50. **Adsera, Xavier; Vinolas, Pere.** "FEVA: A Financial and Economic Approach to Valuation", *Financial Analysts Journal*, March-April 2003, Vol. 59, Issue 2, p. 16.

51. **Ferguson, Robert ; Rentzler, Joel; Yu, Susana,** "Does Economic Value Added (EVA) Improve Stock Performance Profitability?", *Journal of Applied Finance*, Fall/Winter 2005, Vol. 15, Issue 2, pp. 101-113.

52. **De Wet, J.H.V.H.; Du Toit, E.,** "Return on Equity: A Popular But Flawed Measure of Corporate Financial Performance", *South African Journal of Business Management*, March 2007, Vol. 38, Issue 1, pp. 59-69.

53. **Dr. Prakash Singh,** Asst. Prof. Management Groups, BITS, Pilani, "EVA in Indian Banking: Better Information Content, More Shareholder Value", 2005, pp. 40-49.

54. **Kusum L. Ailawadi, Norm Borin, Paul W. Farris,** "Market Power and Performance: A Cross-Industry Analysis of Manufacturers and Retailers", *Journal of Retailing,* Vol. 71, No. 3, 1995, pp. 211-245.

55. **Dodd, James L and Chen, Shimin,** "EVA: A New Panacea?" *Business and Economic Review,* Vol. 42, July- Sep 1996, pp. 26-28.

56. **Grant, J.,** "Foundation of EVA for Investment Managers; Just in Time, EVA", *Journal of Financial Management,* Fall 1996, Vol. 23, No. 1, p. 41(8).

57. **Lehn,K., Makhija, A.K.,** "EVA and MVA as Performance Measures and Signals for Strategic Change", *Strategy and Leadership,* Vol. 24, May/June, 1996, p. 35.

58. Ibid, pp. 36-38.

59. **O' Byrne S,** "EVA and Market Value", *Journal of Applied Corporate Finance,* 1996, Vol. 9, No. 1, pp. 116-125.

60. **Stephen F.O' Byrne,** "EVA and Shareholder Return", *Financial Practice and Education*—Spring/Summer 1997, pp. 50-54.

61. **Padgett, T.,** "Cold Water on Idea of Banks as Not Performers", *American Banker,* July 24, 1996, p. 1(2).

62. Department of Accounting and Finance, *"Economic Value Added as a Management Tool"*, p. 12.

63. **Banerjee, Ashok,** "Economic Value Added (EVA): A Better Performance Measure", *The Management Accountant,* December 1997, pp. 886-88.

64. **Kramer J.K. and G.Pushner,** "An Empirical Analysis of Economic Value Added as a Proxy for Market Value Added", *Financial Practice and Education,* Spring/Summer 1997, pp. 41-48.

65. Department of Accounting and Finance, *Op.cit.,* p. 13.

66. **KPMG-BS,** "Corporate India: An Economic Value Scoreboard", *The Strategy,* Jan-March, 1998, pp. 22-25.

67. **Banerjee, Ashok and Jain,** "Economic Value Added and Shareholder Wealth: An Empirical Study of Relationship", *Paradigm,* Vol. 3. No. 1, January-June. 1999, pp. 99-135.

68. **Bao. B.H. and Bao, D.H.,** "The Association Between Firm Value and Economic Value Added". *Indian Accounting Review,* Vol. 3, No. 2, Dec. 1999, pp. 161-64.

69. **Evans. John,** "An Examination of Economic Value Added and Executive Compensation". Sept. 1999 at htlp://www.40wdubai.ac.in.

70. **Banerjee, Ashok,** "Linkage Between Economic Value Added and Market Value: An Analysis", *Vikalpa,* Vol. 25, No. 3, July-September, 2000, pp. 23-36.

71. **Oral Erdogan, Niyazi Berk and Krol Katir Cioglu,** "The Economic Profit Approach in Firm Performance Measurement—Evidence from the Turkish Stock Market", *Russian and East European Finance and Trade,* Vol. 36, No. 5, Sep-Oct 2000, pp. 54-75.

72. **Parasuraman. N.R.,** "Economic Value Added—Its Computation and Impact on Select Banking Companies", *The ICFAI Journal of Applied Finance,* Vol. 6, No. 4, Oct. 2000, pp. 14-23.

73. *Ibid,* pp. 171-78.

74. **Jonathan K.Kramer and Jonathan R.Peters,** "An Inter Industry Analysis of Economic Value Added as a Proxy for Market Value Added", *Journal of Applied Finance,* 2001, pp. 41-48.

75. **Kalaiselvi.S.,** "Economic Value Added Performance and Financial Efficiency of Hindustan Lever Limited", 2001.

76. **Thampy, A. and Beheli, R.,** "Economic Value Added in Banks", *The ICFAI Journal of Applied Finance,* Vol. 7, No. 1, October 2001, pp. 180-89.

77. **Adnan M.Abdeen, G.T. Haight,** "A Fresh Look at Economic Value Added: Empirical Study of the Fortune Five-Hundred Companies", *The Journal of Applied Business Research,* Vol. 18, No. 2.

78. **Eduardo Sandoval,** "Financial Performance Measures and Shareholders Value Creation: An Empirical Study for Chilean Companies", *The Journal of Applied Business Research,* Vol. 17, No. 3.

79. **Costigan, M.H. and Lovata Linda,** "Empirical Analysis—Adopters of Economic Value Added", *Management Accounting Research,* Vol. 13, No. 2, June 2002, pp. 40-46.

80. **Cyrus A. Ramezani, Luc Soenen and Alan Jung,** "Growth, Corporate Profitability, and Value Creation", *Financial Analyst Journal,* 2002, pp. 56-65.

81. **Dr.Niranjan Swain, Dr. Chandra Sekhar Mishra,** *Op.cit.*, pp. 152-159.

82. **Eugene W. Anderson, Claes Fornell and Sanal K. Mazvancheryl,** "Customer Satisfaction and Shareholder Value", *Journal of Marketing*, Vol. 68, Oct 2004, pp. 172-185.

83. **Singh. K.P. and M.C. Garg,** "Economic Value Added in Indian Corporates", Deep and Deep Publications Pvt. Ltd, F- 159, Rajouri Garden, New Delhi-110027.

84. **Dr.Prakash Singh,** *Op.cit.*, p. 42.

3

INDIAN SOFTWARE INDUSTRY

A PROFILE

INTRODUCTION

The modern business and marketing have a major role to play in the new liberalised and globalised business era. In India, the trend of developing business has been positive until now. For this progress the Information Technology field has played an important role. There was a time probably till a decade ago, when no Indian company would dream of becoming a global player. Then the software industry showed what was possible with a combination of enterprise, quick thinking and luck. Now the entire world thinks of India as one of the places from where to execute its Information Technology strategy. The IT Industry is India's first truly global industry.

The Indian IT industry has been steering the growth of the Indian economy like no other industry in the past decade by generating jobs, pushing exports, enticing FDI, creating wealth, bolstering forex exchange reserves and in umpteen other visible and invisible ways. It has grown at an incredible rate of 50 per cent per annum over the past few years and has the potential to grow even further and faster. It is highly export oriented and extremely knowledge intensive. The nation is pinning high hopes on this industry in its developmental agenda.

The year 2005 witnessed the coming of age of the Indian IT multinationals, with the traditionally India – Centric indigenous players beginning to build noticeable presence in other locations – through crossborder acquisitions, onshore contract wins and organic growth in other low-cost locations. This was complemented by global majors continuing to significantly ramp-up their offshore delivery capabilities – predominantly in India, vindicating the success of the global delivery model and highlighting India's increasingly important role in the new world IT order.

The size of the software business in the domestic market in the 1970's was not big enough for these companies to generate revenues year after year. As a result they had to look towards foreign shores to generate revenues. In the 1980's, technological changes in the IT sector offered new opportunities for the Indian software firms. The big opportunity and potential to earn huge revenues attracted firms like Wipro, HCL, Infosys, Satyam and others to enter the software business. These firms acquired considerable expertise in various types of IT related work. The excellent skill sets possessed by Indian engineers and the 12 hour time difference between India and the US attracted a few foreign companies to locate their software development centers in India. These foreign companies also realised the cost advantage of using the services of Indian engineers.

In the early 1990's India adopted globalisation and competition through its New Economic Policy dispensation. By this time the reputation of Indian Engineers as excellent software programmers has spread and a number of Multinational Companies (MNCs) like British Telecom, Digital Equipment, AT&T and Northern Telecom, have established software development centers hiring Indian professionals. These centers acted as low cost outsourcing locations where Indian engineers developed software. This type of business model gave rise to a new type of software services model, known as 'offshore model'. The Indian software companies also started setting up offshore development centers right in India dedicated to specific US clients to take advantage of higher margins on projects, as the billing rates in USA were higher. To win more projects from the US and to compete with the big US IT Vendors, the Indian software firms realised the need to move away from being bracketed as low-price and low-quality producers to competitively priced and high – quality producers. The large Indian

IT companies such as TCS, Wipro and Infosys adopted the ISO 9000 international standard for quality management and assurance.

By 2000, the top Indian software firms gained expertise in onsite model. In order to meet the increasing competition from the established players and emerging companies, both foreign and local, in outsourcing business, various steps were taken. They got actively involved in the setting of certification norms for service production like the Capability Maturity Model (CMM) of Carnegie Mellon University's Software Engineering Institute. TCS, Wipro, Infosys, and Satyam opened representative offices in the US. Seeing the growth and success of Indian Software Industry, global IT vendors such as Accenture, EDS and IBM Global Services have rushed to set up their software development in India. NASSCOM (National Association of Software and Services Companies) has reported that the growth rate of these global companies was almost twice that of the Indian IT companies.

The world software market is growing rapidly due to fast technological change, freer trade and strong competitive pressures. Two of the developments which provided avenues for the growth of software firm's world wide were Millennium bug and Internet.

The last decade has seen the Indian software industry make impressive strides and carve out an identity for itself in the international technology services market. This industry has successfully withstood many business challenges in the past. The emergence of IT enabled business process outsourcing, the sustained interest of global majors in sourcing software and related services from India and the proliferation of captive development arms of multinational companies are indications of the continued importance of the Indian IT industry.

The internal structure of the Indian IT industry has exhibited some peculiar developments. The larger players have managed to sustain their high growth rates and have grown from strength to strength. An analysis of NASSCOM membership shows that between 1994-95 and 2001-02, there was a four-fold increase growing from 262 to 854. These 854 members together account for about 95 per cent of the revenues of the software industry in India, virtually the entire industry.

Development of Information Technology Field in India

In Information Technology field, India is super power nation. Indian IT professionals and companies are considered top-notch. After many years of phenomenal growth, the first year of the new millennium saw enormous challenges confronting the Indian IT software and service industry. In the year 2006, the software and service industry accounted for 16 per cent of the country's over all exports, for 5 lakh jobs and over $ 1.5 billion in investments.

Information Technology has developed Indian corporate sector and business field. "The Information Technology plus Indian Talent is equal to Indian Tomorrow (IT + IT + = IT)" said Mr. Narendra Modi, Hon. Chief Minister, Gujarat. With the help of Information Technology the market in India has also been moving inexorably towards the path of increased sophistication on the whole. In India the IT industry is in a strong position to take on the global software opportunity and establish India as the IT destination.

History highlights that industrial revolution took centuries to spread to different areas of the world but Information Technology has created a super imposed impact on human society in a much shorter time than anything ever. IT's power to promote innovations has brought a revolution in BPO industry. From the early 1990s, revolution in Information Technology has changed the whole life style of entrepreneur of large and small organisations by its new technologies in terms of speed of processing, data transportation and communication, database maintenance and electronic resources. Since the last decade IT has brought a tremendous change in the methods of doing business. The role of Information Technology is to boost up the business operation of an organisation. The emergence of the Indian software industry offers a unique setting to ask whether globalisation can promote convergence in corporate governance. India is home to a globally competitive set of software powerhouses, the success and generally positive reputation of India's software firms – in contrast to most of India's other firms – provides at least surface firms credence to the idea that the global markets to which these firms are exposed has affected their governance systems.

Software has played an unforgettable part where database management system, data warehouse, management information system, decision support systems, ERP (Enterprise Resource Planning), CRM (Customer Relationship Management) and many other softwares are used to carry out the operation of BPO industry.

As per a NASSCOM study for the year 1996-97, over 127 new software products were launched by domestic software companies and over 156 new software products were launched by overseas companies in the Indian domestic market. There was also 48 per cent increase in the CAD / CAM software market; an increase of 46 per cent in ERP solution market; 23 per cent increase in sale of RDBMS packages; 25 per cent increase in sale of financial accounting packages and 65 per cent increase in sale of networking products.

TCS has emerged as the top software and service exporter in the country during 2004-05 followed by Infosys and Wipro. As per the 'Top 20 IT software and service exporters in India (excluding ITES – BPO revenues)' ranking by National Association of software and services companies (NASSCOM), TCS topped the list with export revenues of Rs. 7449 crore followed by Infosys (Rs. 6806 crore) and Wipro (Rs.5426 crore). Software exports, the mainstay of the industry, grossed $ billion in 2004-05, up from $ 9.2 billion in 2003-04, indicating a growth of 30.4 per cent for the year. With offshore adoption amongst the Fortune 500 companies increasing rapidly from 300 in 2003 to 400 companies in 2004, NASSCOM expressed optimism about the long-term potential of this industry.

Structural Determinants of the Industry

Buyers

The customers of the Indian software Industry can be broadly classified into two categories 'domestic buyers' and 'overseas clients'.

Suppliers

There are three kinds of suppliers to this industry:

- Hardware and peripheral suppliers;
- System software suppliers;

- Human resources—This resource constitutes a very crucial element in the success of any software firm.

New Entrants

There are a large number of small firms setting up operations in India to exploit the software boom. A number of these firms are trying to use existing Indian software majors as their customer base. Apart from a few small firms who are in the areas of new technology or new product development, most of the startups typically perform low-end jobs like data entry and maintenance of existing software.

India is increasingly being used as a support base by many MNCs who set up 100 per cent subsidiaries in STPs and export-zones.

Substitutes

The Indian computer industry does not face any substitution threats from other products.

Role of Government

GOI (Government of India) views the rise of Information Technology favourably and it is viewed as a tool to become a strong, prosperous and self – confident nation. The government has taken a host of steps for providing a thrust to this sector. One of these initiatives is the development of Export Processing Zones (EPZ), where export production is organised on an internationally competitive basis with requisite infrastructure and duty-free imports. Another initiative is in the area of Software Technology Parks (STPs). An autonomous organisation called Software Technology parks of India (STP1) has been set up by GOI through the Department of Electronics to promote these parks. The objectives for setting up these STPs were:

- To establish and manage infrastructural resources;
- To provide services like import certification, software valuation, project approvals etc.;
- To provide technology assessments, market analysis, Marketing support etc.

There are a set of crucial parameters which have significant impact on the success of a software company. They are product mix, project quality, employee productivity, customer base, processes, investment in infrastructure, foreign Tie-ups and marketing network and internal reward systems.

SOFTWARE EXPORTS FROM INDIA

The software development activities of Indian companies for the global market can be broadly classified under 3 major heads:

- *Body Shopping:* Where the brokers send professionals abroad, who develop programmes after taking the specifications from the customer;
- *On Shore Development:* Where an Indian software company undertakes to execute all or some of the phases of software development for a project at the clients site;
- *Off Shore Development:* Where generalised solutions for specific computing needs like accounting and word processing are developed.

The Electronics and Computer Software Export Promotion Council (EPC) plays a crucial role in promoting exports of electronic hardware, computer software and services. It has over 2000 exporting companies as members. From the time of its formation (1988), the EPC has succeeded in raising exports of electronic hardware, software and services. Out of the total IT exports of India, the share of software and services has been predominant. The bulk of exports in the past came from supply of on-site services. Till 1990-91, such services constituted 80 per cent of the total exports of software. Since then, the share of on-site services has been declining gradually and being replaced by off-shore services, the share of which is rising. Internationally, half to two-thirds of the market is dominated by software packages and 15 per cent by professional services.

Indian companies are increasingly adapting to international quality standards. Today, the world looks forward towards the Indian software industry for its cost and quality advantage. A world Bank-funded study on the demand for Indian software found that more and more vendors in the USA preferred to get their software developed in India for its quality and cost advantage. A comparison of the Indian software industry with those of many other countries has proved that India is in the best position to supply high quality software at relatively low cost.

Marketing Channel Used by Software Companies

Marketing is the most critical issue for the development of the Indian software industry. The size of the Indian software export industry is very small compared to what exists in the world. To emerge as a major player in the world software market, there has to be significant expenditure of marketing. In India, the software vendors operating in the export market have traditionally depended upon direct marketing to end-users. However, lately many software companies have set up their own offices in various countries. In an effort to expand their software operations, many global and system hardware companies are sub-contracting software development to a consortium of software companies.

India is increasingly emerging as a software development centre, with more overseas companies setting up operations in India. They are operating in the Indian market either through:

- 100 per cent Equity holding;
- Joint ventures with Indian companies;
- Marketing or Technical collaborations.

IT–enabled services offer scope for employment of more than a million professionals throughout the country. These services cover:

- Preparation of financial accounts;
- Back–office work of Banks and insurance companies;
- Publishing ;
- Medical Transcription.

The IT software and services industry has emerged as the biggest contributor towards Indian exports with a share of 16.5 per cent in 2001-02. The impressive growth rates of software sector as a whole as well as its increasing share in the various national parameters have been kept up by the export segment. Software is widely held as the country's engine of growth and earner of essential foreign exchange.

As per NASSCOM report, India's market share in global packaged software during 1998-99 was less than one per cent, whereas in 'customised' software, it was a high as 18.5 per cent. This indicates that a major portion of the global software comprises of products and packages.

Export Structure

India's software export is dominated by software services which have always remained above 94 per cent. In 1989-90 it was 99.32 per cent and finally remained as 97.9 per cent in 2000-01. As regards packages, from a mere 0.68 per cent in 1989-90 it went upto 4.33 per cent in 1990-91 and 4.47 per cent in 1991-92. It stood at 2.10 per cent in 2000-01. Export earnings accounted for 64 per cent of the total IT-ITES aggregate in FY 2004-05. Strong fundamentals including a large base of skilled talent, demonstrated quality and service delivery expertise at a significant cost advantage and an enabling environment have ensured that India attracts a disproportionately larger share of the global IT-ITES demand for offshored services and continues to drive India's export-led growth. India's Stock of foreign exchange earnings is amongst the highest in the world, with reserves having risen from USD 5.8 billion in FY 1990-91 to USD 139 billion in January 2006.

Within software services, the three main components are custom software development, turnkey projects/services and consultancy services. The major share goes to custom software development. Its share has never been less than 75 per cent of production and reached 90 per cent in 1999-00 and 90.65 per cent in 2000-01. For turnkey projects/services, the export share is in the range of 45 to 76 per cent. The share of consultancy services has been highly significant, being in the range of 78 to 90 per cent. Within packages, the representation of both system software as well as applications software has never been significant. A few software products have been launched by Indian companies, as instanced by I–flex which is under use by over 240 financial institutions in about 70 countries. The banking solutions developed by Infosys, viz., Financle, Bankaway and payaway have found adoption and application in several countries. Wipro has successfully launched products like Instaplan, Teleprodigy and websecure. Similar attempts are from smaller software companies.

America and Europe remain the key markets, accounting for over 90 per cent of IT-ITES exports. However, export earnings from markets other than the US and the UK are also witnessing significant double-digit year-on-year growth. While Indian service providers have built delivery centers in key source markets, they are expanding their foot prints in specialist locations like China for engineering and design, South Africa for insurance and near-shore locations like Eastern, Europe and Mexico. Apart from companies in the US, organisations from Europe, South East Asia, Australia, Japan, Hong-Kong, New Zealand, etc, are also reaching out for Indian software expertise, supported by the conductive policy environment and incentives for software exports offered by India.

EVOLUTION OF INDIAN SOFTWARE INDUSTRY

Though the Indian software industry has risen to prominence in the last decade, it has a history of well over thirty years. The process of evolution has been chronicled from multiple perspectives. The common factors that are widely perceived to have been positive influences on the evolution and growth of this industry are availability of skilled, English speaking manpower, export orientation, policy initiatives of the government and the wide network of expatriate Indians in the global customer organisations.

Rapid advances in Information Technology and its convergence with communication technologies gave rise to a few growth accelerators. Some of the accelerators were in the form of new opportunities (Y2K and the internet) and some were in the form of new business models (offshore development and remote services).

The growth in the number of firms in any industry is a direct consequence of the perceived attractiveness of the industry. Low entry barriers, high profitability, a favourable regulatory regime and a buoyant high growth market encouraged entry of new players to the software industry at a rapid pace. The market for software services comprises three distinct segments. First, and by far the largest in terms of potential is the enterprise segment, whose core business is not IT. The second segment is the Independent Software Vendors (ISVs), whose core business is the development and sale of packaged software products and tools, along with a certain level of implementation and customisation. The third segment consists of the intermediaries who service the requirements of enterprise customers.

Rapid advances in information and communication technologies and their convergence have significantly altered the role of IT in all organisations. This changing role of IT has in turn altered their outsourcing strategy and buying behaviour. The IT spend of any organisation can be seen to provide a hierarchy of benefits. At the higher end of the hierarchy are the ideas and solutions that generate the competitive advantage for the organisation. At the lower end of the hierarchy is the operation and maintenance of the IT infrastructure, covering all aspects of the organisations operations. Large enterprises are likely to have a greater proportion of their IT spend occurring at the lower end of the hierarchy. The ISVs are likely to spend a greater proportion of their IT budgets at the higher end of the hierarchy since IT products are their core business. Incase of intermediaries, their IT spend is directed towards building their core competence and hence will tend to get bunched at the higher end of the hierarchy.

The history of the Indian software industry may be reckoned from 1974, when Tata Consultancy Services (TCS) started off its operations. TCS with its joint ventures became one of the largest software exporters in the early days. However, exports became the core focus of companies sometime around the late 1980s and early 1990s. A major event in the industry was when Texas Instruments proposed to start a 100 per cent export-oriented, foreign owned and operated subsidiary. This caught on rapidly, with large software companies like Siemens, Motorola and many more setting up shop in India as subsidiaries. Software companies became R&D partners for big multinational firms, helping them to reach market faster.

Much of the growth that the Indian software industry saw came from the outsourcing wave. Increasing cost pressures on global corporations, a growing focus and core operations by customers and technological advances made offshoring to India the most viable option and the Indian software and service industry turned the slowdown into an opportunity.

Small and Medium IT Companies (SMITs) constitute over 60 per cent of the software industry and their contribution to the total software exports increased from 25 per cent in 2000-01 to 35 per cent in 2001-02. SMITs with a sound business model and focussed activity grew despite a challenging market environment. The successful technologies that SMITs focused on were:

❖ Manufacturing of chips and software that dramatically cut the cost of internet access devices needed for sending voice, video and data on the net;

❖ Specification in telecom software solutions embedded on the chip used in wide band CDMA phones;

❖ E – security solutions to customers.

Fragmentation

- The Indian IT industry, software in particular, is highly polarised. At one end of the spectrum, large companies with global operations and infrastructure have emerged, while on the other, many small techno-entrepreneur-driven companies functioning in niche segments have started playing an important role in the evolution of the software industry. However, a significant number of companies which were earlier involved primarily with low-end services, have disappeared because of the challenging market conditions made worse by the lack of any core-competence.

There are two major delivery models in use for software and services exports, namely on site services and offshore services. Onsite services involve project implementation at the client facility overseas. Offshore services involve the use of high-speed data communication links, which allow computers situated anywhere in the world to be used by programmers in India on a real-time and on-line basis. The off shore model allows a client located anywhere in the world to monitor the software development on a minute –by-minute basis, ensuring quality checks, easy communication with remote programmers, and efficient software development translating into significant time and cost savings. The gross margins in the offshore business are typically higher than the margins in onshore business.

Revenue from software services is derived from technology and software services provided on either variable–price, variable-time frame basis or fixed price, fixed-time frame basis. Revenue from services provided on variable time-and-materials basis is recognised in the period in which the services are provided and costs incurred. Revenue from fixed price, fixed-time frame projects is recognised only on a percentage of completion basis.

Government Policies—Impact on Software Sector

- **Zero Duty Regime**

India joined the Information Technology Agreement (ITA) on 25.3.1997 which is a multilateral agreement within the WTO which aims to expand world trade in Information Technology products. According to the agreement, customers tariff on IT items were to be brought down in stages to zero by 2005.

- **Excise Duty at 8 per cent**

Reduction of excise duty from 16 per cent to 8 per cent on IT and IT related products in January 2004 will help in combating grey market, reducing price and give boost to demand.

- **STPs**

Software Technology Park (STP) is an autonomous body and comes under the department of electronics of Government of India. The STP scheme allows 100 per cent export oriented firms a tax-free status for five years from the first eight years of operation. The scheme provides them project approvals, market analysis, marketing support and training. The GOI has promoted several STPs in several locations across India. Units located in STP enjoy the benefits of single-window clearance for all regulatory compliance issues. The units enjoy duty free imports of professional equipment and duty free purchases.

➢ **100 per cent FDI**

The GOI allows for 100 per cent FDI equity in ITES companies.

➢ **Liberalising of the Telecom Sector**

Liberalization of the telecom sector allowing private players in International Long Distance (ILD), National Long Distance (NLD) and Leased line services.

➢ **State Governments**

Various state governments have introduced initiatives to encourage investments in the ITES sector.

The demand for software services over the short to medium term is likely to be export-led. However, India has a significant presence in only 2 of the 10 major IT services worldwide. ie, custom Application development and Application outsourcing.

Impact of IT

The rapid growth of ITES – BPO (Information Technology–Enabled Services–Business Process Outsourcing) and the IT industry as a whole is having a deep impact on the socio-economic dynamics of India. The sector has become the biggest employment generator with the number of jobs added almost doubling every year. India has become one of the most favoured destinations for outsourcing and ITES and is estimated to have achieved an export value of $ 12.8 billion in 2003-04. India ranks high in several, critical parameters including level of government support, quality of the human resource pool, English language skills, cost advantages, project management skills and overall quality control.

Communication has paved the way for business opportunities, such as BPO and network management services as well as new technologies and applications such as mobile phones and the internet. The IT industry grew 24 per cent (Rs. 92924 crore) in 2003-04 and the domestic market (Rs. 33374 crore) and exports (Rs. 59550 crore) shared the same growth of 24 per cent.

The Buoyancy in Export Market

India has become one of the most preferred destinations for sourcing software and IT enabled services. India in comparison to other low cost locations ranks high in several critical parameters including level of government support, quality of the labour pool, cost advantage, entrepreneurial culture, strong customer relationships and exposure to new technologies. As per the 'Top 20 IT software and service Exporters in India' ranking by NASSCOM, TCS topped the list followed by Infosys, Wipro, Satyam Computers and HCL. These five companies have been consistently maintaining their ranks in the same order since 2002-2003.

At a time when Indian software product companies are marking significant headway in overseas markets such as West Asia and Africa, the $ 4.8 billion domestic IT market, with a healthy forecast of a 25 per cent growth continues to prove elusive for most players. These home-bred companies feel that despite the advantages attached to choosing Indian vendors, including their deep understanding of the local markets, and assurance of strong onsite support, a slow decision-making process, temptation of the Indian buyer to opt for products offered by global companies and sometimes huge product discounts offered by MNC players to grab significant chunks of market share, are factors that are cited as severe constraints when it comes to doing IT business in their own market.

It is not unusual to find foreign players offering huge discounts to gain market share. Indian companies find it difficult to compete on this front, given the financial prowess of the MNC firms. The players feel this is because the global companies, while making inroads into a new market, may not be looking for 'profitability on every sale'. In many cases where foreign joint venture partners are involved, particularly in the insurance business, the overseas firm may prefer to go with a more visible standard product from the international market rather than choosing a local one. Indian companies are, in fact, in a better position to serve clients in the local markets, but given the hurdles, product become a tough business in the Indian market.

Average annual growth rate of exports for ten years from 1995-96 to 2005-06 is 39 per cent.

The most high profile and commonly understood services in the ITES area are the call centers and the medical transcription services. ITES also includes several other services viz, Customer

Top 20 IT Software and Service Exporters (India based companies)

Rank	*F.Y. 2005-06*	*F.Y. 2004-05*	*F.Y. 2003-04*
1.	TCS	TCS	TCS
2.	Infosys Technologies	Infosys Technologies	Infosys Technologies
3.	Wipro Tech	Wipro Tech	Wipro Tech
4.	Satyam Computer Services	Satyam Computer Services	Satyam Computer Services
5.	HCL Tech	HCL Tech	HCL Tech
6.	Patni Computer Systems	IBM Global Services India	Patni Computer Systems
7.	I Flex Solutions	Patni Computer Systems	I Flex Solutions
8.	Tech Mahindra Ltd.	I Flex Solutions	Mahindra British Telecom
9.	Perot Systems TSI (I) Ltd.	Mahindra British Telecom	Polaris Software
10.	L & T Infotech Ltd.	Polaris Software Lab	Digital Global Soft
11.	Polaris Software Lab Ltd.	Perot Systems TSI (India)	NIIT
12.	Hexaware Technologies Ltd.	Hexaware Technologies Ltd	Perot Systems TSI
13.	Mastek Ltd.	L&T Infotech	i-GATE Global Solutions
14.	Mphasis BFL Ltd.	Mastek	Birla Soft
15.	Siemens Info Systems	i-GATE Global Solutions	MPhasis BFL
16.	Genpact	Siemens Info Systems	Mastek
17.	i-Gate Global Solutions Ltd	MPhasis BFL	Hexaware Technologies Ltd.
18.	Flextronics Software	Tata Info Tech	L&T Info Tech
19.	NIIT Technologies Ltd.	NIIT Tech	Tata Info Tech
20.	Covansys India Ltd.	Flextronics Software	Hughes Software

Table 3.1

A decade of Indian IT industry Exports

Year	*Software Export (US$m)*	*Export Growth(%)*	*Year*	*Software Export (US$m)*	*Export Growth (%)*
1980	4.00		1993-94	314.00	43
1981	6.80	70	1994-95	480.00	53
1982	13.50	99	1995-96	668.00	39
1983	18.20	35	1996-97	997.00	49
1984	25.30	39	1997-98	1650.00	65
1985	27.70	9	1998-99	2180.00	32
1986	38.90	40	1999-2000	3600.00	65
1987	54.10	38	2000-2001	5300.00	47
1988-89	69.70	29	2001-2002	6200.00	17
1989-90	105.40	51	2002-2003	7550.00	22
1990-91	131.20	24	2003-2004	8800.00	17
1991-92	173.90	33	2004-2005	12400.00	41
1992-93	219.80	26	2005-2006	17500.00	41

Source: Indian Department of Electronics Annual Reports, Dataquest (India) Surveys.

interaction services, Business process outsourcing, Back office operations, Transcription and translation services, Legal Databases, Digital content/Animation, Website services, Remote Education, Data Digitization, Global information systems and Market Research.

IT industry has over the past decade emerged as a key growth engine of the economy. The IT industry continues its winning streak, registering a 34 per cent increase in exports in 2005-06, the highest in over a decade, while retaining its leadership position in the global off-shoring market with 64 per cent and 46 per cent market share in IT and Business Process Outsourcing respectively. As the Nasscom Mckinsey Annual survey released in December 2005 highlights, the industry has demonstrated that it has truly come of age, not merely as a niche player in software services, but has also acquired the capability to become one of the leading export sectors by 2010. The report further states that in the next five years, India's offshore industries could generate $ 60 billion in export revenues, accounting for 17 per cent of incremental GDP growth, and sustain 9 million jobs, thus making it one of the largest export sectors in the world.

Exhibit 3.1

Indian IT Exports

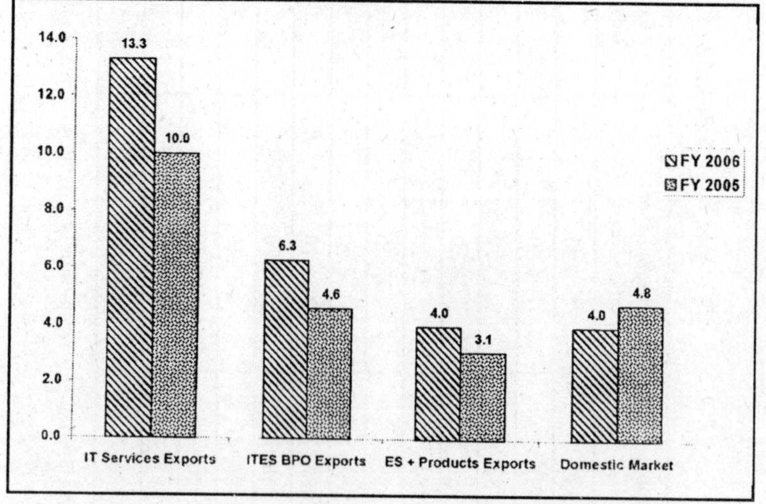

Source: The Economic Challenger, No. 9 Issue 34, Jan-March, 2007.

Table 3.2

Revenues from Global IT Services and Products

Year	*1994-95*	*2002-03*	*2003-04*	*2004-05*
Revenue ($mn)	28	625	943	1353

10 year CAGR 57%

Source: Wipro Annual Report 2004-05.

Table 3.3

Operating Income and Product Sales

Year	*Operating Income (Rs. mn)*		*Product Sales (Rs. mn)*	
	Global IT Services and Products	*India and Asia Pac IT Services and Products*	*Global IT Services and Products*	*India and Asia Pac IT Services and Products*
2002-03	8451	557	8395	30487
2003-04	9539	792	9762	43575
2004-05	16041	1042	13964	60753

Source: Wipro Annual Report 2004-05.

The NASSCOM Mckinsey report identifies the following key challenges that could slow down growth:

- The lower global demand for off-shoring in the face of increasing political opposition and costs;
- Potential shortage of skilled workers;
- Competition from new countries; and
- Inadequate urban infrastructure.

IT—The Road Ahead

The future of Indian IT is important not merely from a sector-wise perspective, but from a larger economic stand point as well. There is more at stake here than just the future of one million persons that the IT industry currently employs, which is only a minuscule proportion of the country's total work force of 300 million, as is apparent when one looks at the evolution of this industry; and the remarkable role it has played in the transformation of the Indian economy and its image in the world.

IT in many parts of world, has been acknowledged as a new tool of cyberspace in which a 'seamless information society' is taking place. In such society a digitalisation process occurs where information of numerous fields are converted into the computer language and the sound, text, files, data, music, voice, image etc., fly back and forth computer to computer and user to user. This information process hinges on cyberspace infrastructure consisting of millions of servers, routers, switches, optical fiber, satellites, mobile phones, cables, information super images and personal computers.

This tremendous revolution in IT has fundamentally transformed the quality of life of citizens, political process, governmental operations, commercial and economic transactions, power of NGO's and civil society activists and cultural ethos of the society as a whole.The shift in the role of IT from merely supporting business to transforming business, which is driving productivity gains and creating new business models, has increased the importance of IT to the success of companies worldwide. The ability to design, develop, implement, and maintain advanced technology platforms and solutions to address business and customer needs has become a competitive advantage and a priority for corporations world wide.

According to the worldwide services spending forecast, a report published by International Data Corporation in May 2005, the global IT services market is estimated to grow from approximately $383 billion in 2003 to approximately $512 billion by 2008. Companies are increasingly using external professional services as an effective tool to meet their IT requirements. Outsourcing IT requirements enable companies to acquire high quality and cost competitive services.

Challenges and Opportunities Before the IT Industry

Despite a very impressive growth profile, the Indian IT industry is facing a number of challenges.

❖ **Scarcity of Trained Manpower**

Indians comparative advantage in software industry development is primarily based on the availability of trained manpower of good quality. Several countries including United Kingdom, Germany, Japan, South Korea, Switzerland and France have announced their intention to import IT trained manpower from India. A major challenge before the industry is to retain experienced software professionals from migrating to abroad due to wide differences in their pays and perks in India and abroad.

❖ **Competition from MNCs**

Global software giants such as Microsoft, and Oracle stepped up their Indian presence considerably in the year 2003. Global IT vendors such as the IBM, Accenture and EDS have set up their software development centers in India. Competition in future will be at two levels, domestic and global.

❖ **Protectionist Policies of U.S. Government**

On 23rd January 2006, U.S Senate passed a law restricting contractors from sub-contracting Government projects to firms in other countries. According to experts, this step has the potential to harm the Indian software industry, which is excessively dependent on US in the long run.

❖ **Emerging Competition from other Countries**

A survey conducted by the Carnegie Mellers University found that 82 per cent of the competitors of the Indian software firms were located within India. The second largest source of competition was US based firms that extensively recruit Indian software professionals (Arora et al 2000). In future, Indian software companies may face more competition in high-end jobs from firms based in Israel, Ireland, Singapore, East Europe, among others; Philippines, China, Malaysia and other South Asian countries are fast emerging as strong competitors for low-end routine jobs.

❖ **Infrastructural Bottle Necks**

The rapid growth of the IT industry can be sustained only by ensuring that the infrastructural development keeps pace with the growth trajectory. More important of the infrastructural improvements that are urgently called for are adequate bandwidth for data transfer, built-up space for software development and other facilities. According to the industry association, available band width is not adequate and is becoming a bottle neck.

❖ **Low R&D Thrust**

The Indian software industry has not given adequate importance to R&D to commensurate with its knowledge intensity and international orientation. A NASSCOM study (2000) found that R&D spending in the industry has increased from 2.5 per cent of total spending on R&D in 1997-98 to about 4 per cent during 2000-01. A bigger R&D thrust will be necessary for Indian software enterprises to upgrade their export profile to higher value adding services and products and technologies rather than just providers of coding and programming services.

Opportunities

IT is today the foremost productivity tool of our times. Information and communication technologies play an important part. The use of IT tools and e-learning present an unprecedented opportunity for enhancing the capabilities of knowledge of the poor for creating, sharing and exchanging knowledge and knowledge products and for accessing new and profitable markets.

In recent years, there is increased awareness among global corporations about the potential of off shoring. Today over 70 per cent of the fortune 500 firms off shore some of their internal business processes. Indian firms started offering customer services, accounting services and CAD services. Talk about the Indian IT industry almost invariably boils down to a highly adrenalised discussion on our success in the software exports arena. Software and services exports from the country have been growing at an enviable pace.

India has emerged as a global player in Information Technology with software exports of US Dollars 12 billion in 2003-04 and $17.2 billion in 2004-05. The revenue from exports of IT and related services is expected to reach US $ 57 billion by 2008, according to a Mckinsey report. Of the fortune 500 companies 220 outsource their software from India. 80 out of world's 117 SEI CMM level – 5 companies are from India. Indias IT and ITES exports go to 133 countries. Indian IT companies train people in 55 countries; NIIT and APTECH have 200 training centres in China.

Software exports, the mainstay of the industry grossed $ 12 billion in 2004- 2005, up from $ 9.2 billion in 2003-04, indicating a growth of 30.4 per cent for the year. In an economically challenging environment that characterised global markets, the export- oriented software and services sector logged in 26 per cent growth during 2002-03. It was a creditable performance marked by a hike in software and services exports and a major jump in ITES.

CONCLUSION

The Indian IT industry has not only been among the fastest growing industries globally, it has played a key role in transforming India from a largely inward looking economy to an emerging knowledge power that is today perceived as being one of the more dynamic and entrepreneurial in the world. The NASSCOM report states that India's economic growth will be greatly accelerated if India based IT and BPO industries sustain their global leadership and are also to generate $60 billion in export revenues by 2010.

A dynamic and entrepreneurial leadership, a large talent pool, global delivery capabilities and operational excellence are areas where India has demonstrated its leadership. IT may well be the key to harness the energies and unlock the enormous potential of millions of ordinary Indians for transforming India into a truly developed country.

4

CAPITALISATION AND CAPITAL STRUCTURE

TRENDS AND PATTERNS

INTRODUCTION

Capital structure plays a vital role in attracting investment in the corporate field. Apart from attracting different types of investor, it also affects the value of the firm by affecting its expected earnings and cost of capital. It helps in maintaining suitable debt management policy, investment—worthiness and growth of an organisation.

Capital structure refers to the relative composition of long-term different source of funds such as debenture, long-term debts, preference and ordinary share capital and retained earnings. Capital structure can be built up in different ways such as:

- Exclusive use of equity capital;
- Combination of equity and preference share capital;
- Combination of equity, preference and long-term debt capital.
- Equity and long-term debt.

The cost of a particular source of finance is the minimum return expected by its suppliers. The expected return depends on the degree of risk assumed by the suppliers. A high degree of risk is assumed by shareholders than debt holders. Debt is a cheaper source of fund than equity capital and preference capital because the interest payment on debt is fixed. A company borrows capital in order to maximise the profits for its shareholders and it would continue to use this source of finance until the incremental return on it is higher than its incremental cost. So, there must be a combination of debt and equity capital that minimises a firm's average cost of capital and maximises the market value per share.

In designing the capital structure, the existing management may desire to continue control over the company and also to manage the company without any outside interference. If the company issues new shares, there is a risk of loss of control, particularly in the case of closely held company. To avoid this risk, the company can use debt capital to maintain control. Every company has its own level of debt capital, beyond which management cannot use or else it has to face a high degree of financial risk. The financial plan of a company should be flexible enough to change the composition of capital structure. It must keep itself in a position to substitute one form of financing for another to customise the use of funds.

The capital structures of firms are different at various stages of their development. As a firm grows in size, the rate of its internal expansion declines and the retained earnings replace the sources of bonded debts. In each field of economic activity, the capital structure and the nature of debt are influenced by the size of a company and equity ratios tend to be varying directly with this size. Informational and operating efficiency, and liquidity, are institutional features of financial markets that may play a role in determining firm's financing mix.

Significance of Capital Structure

Capital structure decision is very important for a firm, because the nature and quality of capital structure directly affects the cost of capital as well as the market value of a firm. Every source of capital has its own cost. Though debt creates a fixed financial charge, it is the cheapest source of funds, due to the tax treatment of interest. Retained capital also has a less cost than the equity cost. Dividend is to be paid after paying tax in case of preference capital. Hence, before tax, cost of preference capital is high. The cost of equity capital is the highest as equity shareholders are the last claimants of earnings of a firm. Considering the different nature of cost of capital of each source, it is essential to frame the capital structure that minimizes the overall cost of capital and gives the maximum benefits to the owners of a business. The impact of leverages and trading on equity need to be considered by the management in framing the capital structure.

CAPITAL STRUCTURE ANALYSIS

Trends and Patterns

In recent years, there has been increasing recognition that small enterprises are different from larger ones and that these differences affect numerous aspects of small firms including their capital structure. In this respect the average capital employed and debt-equity have been analysed both with regard to large concerns and small concerns using ANOVA.

Small enterprises rely more heavily on their savings than large enterprises; the very largest and the very smallest enterprises finance a larger part of capital expenditure from their own savings. Cost is the crucial factor, which have the direct impact on wealth creation. Hence cost analysis has been made taking the three components namely cost of debt, cost of equity and weighted average cost of capital.

In theory though debt-equity, weighted average cost of capital and market share price are interrelated and interdependent on each other, in practice, they may not be so, as market share prices are still more being influenced by some other exogenous variables. Certain variables like debt-equity, ROCE, Turnover, EBIT, Total Debt and EBIT to capital employed were analysed for the period of ten years and the trends identified to assess the profitability and risk position of the sampled companies.

The present chapter has been devoted to analyse the overall trends and patterns of the capitalization and capital structures of the sampled companies.

Trends and Patterns of Capitalisation of the Sampled Group as a whole

Capital Employed of all the sample companies for the Study Period (1996-97 to 2005-06) is shown in Table 4.1. The total capital employed, its growth and the average capital employed are given in Table 4.1.

Table 4.1

Capital Employed

Year	*Total (Rs. in Crores)*	*Growth Index*	*Average (Rs. in Crores)*
1996-97	2851.13	100.00	33.82
1997-98	3341.21	117.19	37.63
1998-99	5144.58	180.44	51.78
1999-00	8831.04	309.74	90.21
2000-01	13215.75	463.53	140.64
2001-02	16594.35	582.03	168.22
2002-03	18647.42	654.04	189.72
2003-04	20403.55	715.63	205.01
2004-05	22963.96	805.43	249.61
2005-06	29388.87	1030.78	372.01
		Average	**153.87**
		ACGR (%)	**30.53**

It is delineated from the Table 4.1 that the overall average amount of capital employed of the sampled companies during the period was Rs.153.87 crores and with the passage of time, the amount of capitalisation continued to increase every year. The average compound growth rate of 30.53 per cent is a sign of buoyancy in the software industry.

Trends and patterns of capitalisation among sub-groups of the sampled companies.

As such, an attempt has been made to examine the patterns and trends of capitalisation among various sub-groups of the

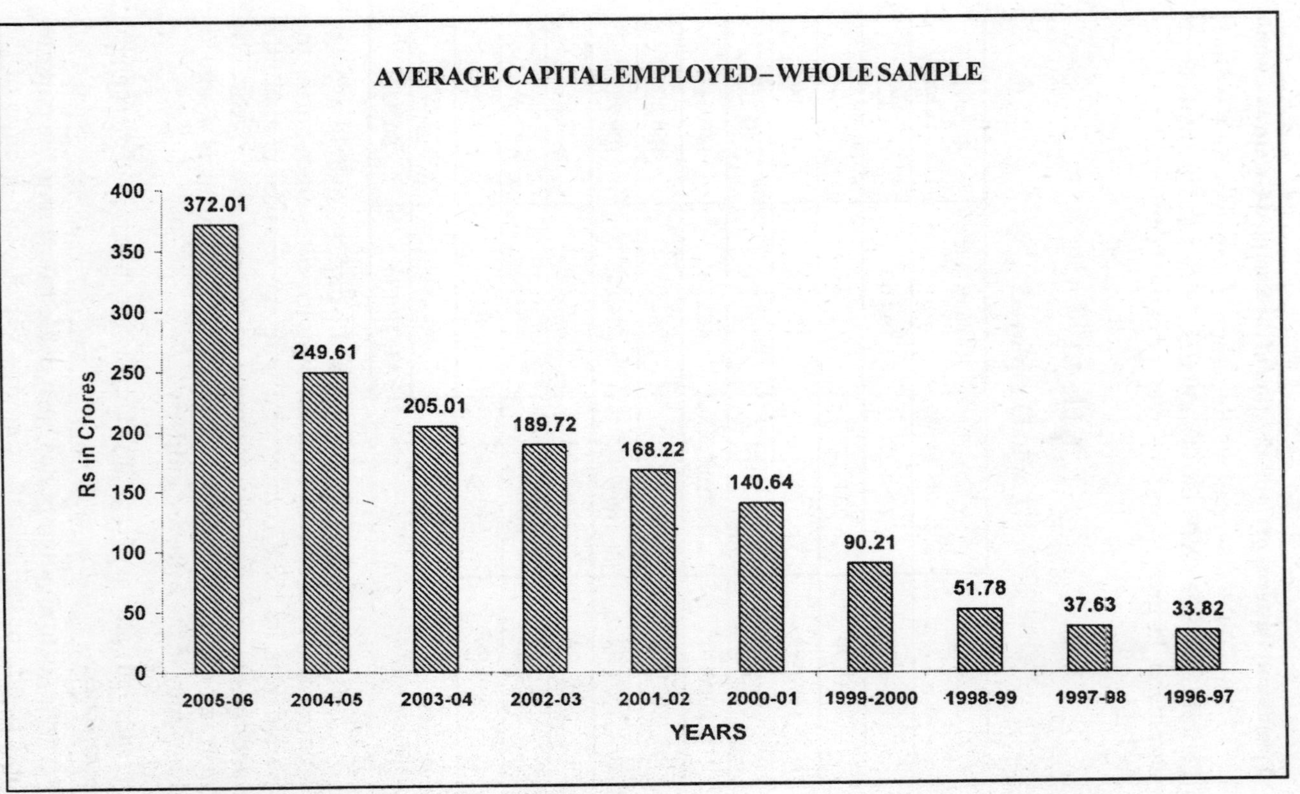
AVERAGE CAPITAL EMPLOYED – WHOLE SAMPLE
Rs in Crores
400
350
300
250
200
150
100
50
0
372.01
249.61
205.01
189.72
168.22
140.64
90.21
51.78
37.63
33.82
2005-06
2004-05
2003-04
2002-03
2001-02
2000-01
1999-2000
1998-99
1997-98
1996-97
YEARS

sampled companies, by computing average capital employed of each sub group as shown in Table 4.2.

Table 4.2

Average Capital Employed in different Sub-Groups

Years	*Large*	*Small-Medium*	*Converts*
1996-97	185.06	24.52	11.67
1997-98	238.42	26.13	10.70
1998-99	315.95	33.20	26.81
1999-00	408.72	69.78	46.48
2000-01	746.57	104.84	20.95
2001-02	1120.47	105.44	53.73
2002-03	1465.65	103.73	45.36
2003-04	1695.21	104.52	49.22
2004-05	2608.43	91.86	49.97
2005-06	3398.07	130.55	77.60
Average	**1218.26**	**79.46**	**39.25**
ACGR	**38.18**	**20.42**	**23.43**

According to Table 4.2, the overall average amount of capitalisation for different sub-groups, namely Large, Small-Medium and Converts for the entire study period were Rs. 1218.26 crores, Rs. 79.46 crores and Rs. 39.25 crores respectively. The annual compound growth rate for the same stood at 38.18 per cent, 20.42 per cent and 23.43 per cent respectively. A spurt in the capital employed is found among the biggies which rose from Rs. 185.06 crores to Rs. 3398.07 crores during the study period.

Like the increasing overall trend in the total capitalisation of the sample as a whole, every sub-group also showed an annual increasing trend, as it is obvious in Table 4.3.

Table 4.3

Summary table for Capitalisation, Trends and Growth

Details	*Large*	*Small-Medium*	*Converts*	*Whole Sample*
Average amount of capitalisation Rs. Crores	1218.26	79.46	39.25	445.66
Annual Amount of change in capitalisation Rs. Crores	321.30	10.60	6.59	112.83
Rate of Growth percentages	40.05	20.51	21.22	27.26

By comparing the annual amount of changes, it is found that large group of companies recorded higher annual amount of change than that of the amount of change in the whole sample. In a way, the average amount of change in capitalisation showed similar trends in the cases of the various sub-groups as compared to the overall average.

An attempt has also been made to find out the annual compound rates of growth in the total capitalisation. It could be seen from the Table 4.3 that the highest Compound Rate of Growth was found in the case of large as 40.05 per cent while the lowest compound rate of growth was found in the case of Small-medium as 20.51 per cent. It can be concluded that large companies had the higher compound rate of growth as compared to overall compound rate of growth of the sampled companies as a whole, while small-medium and converts had lower compound rate of growth.

In the Large category, HP recorded the minimum ACGR of 25.65 per cent and INFOSYS recorded a maximum of 57.93 per cent. A minimum of -176.11 per cent (PALSOFT) and the maximum of 275.50 per cent (RAMINFO) was found among Small-Medium group of companies. Among Converts, TRILLENT recorded the lowest ACGR of -11.99 per cent and MASCONGLO, the highest ACGR of 99.87 per cent. Fifteen negative ACGRs in case of Small-Medium and three negatives in Converts were observed.

Table 4.4 (1)

Capital Employed – Frequency Distribution of Sample Companies (1996-97 to 2000-01)

Capital Employed	*No. of Companies*									
	2000-01	%	*1999-00*	%	*1998-99*	%	*1997-98*	%	*1996-97*	%
Negative	0	0.00	0	0.00	0	0.00	0	0.00	0	0.00
Upto Rs. 1000 Cr	97	95.10	102	100.00	102	100.00	102	100.00	102	100.00
Rs. 1000 to Rs. 2000 Cr	4	3.92	0	0.00	0	0.00	0	0.00	0	0.00
Rs. 2000 to Rs.5000 Cr	1	0.98	0	0.00	0	0.00	0	0.00	0	0.00
Above Rs. 5000 Cr	0	0.00	0	0.00	0	0.00	0	0.00	0	0.00
	102	**100.00**	**102**	**100.00**	**102**	**100.00**	**102**	**100.00**	**102**	**100.00**

Table 4.4 (2)

Capital Employed – Frequency Distribution of Sample Companies (2001-02 to 2005-06)

Capital Employed	*No. of Companies*									
	2005-06	%	*2004-05*	%	*2003-04*	%	*2002-03*	%	*2001-02*	%
Negative	0	0.00	2	1.96	2	1.96	2	1.96	1	0.98
Upto Rs. 1000 Cr.	97	95.10	96	94.12	95	93.14	95	93.14	95	93.14
Rs. 1000 to Rs. 2000 Cr	2	1.96	1	0.98	2	1.96	2	1.96	4	3.92
Rs. 2000 to Rs. 5000 Cr	1	0.98	2	1.96	3	2.94	3	2.94	2	1.96
Above Rs. 5000 Cr	2	1.96	1	0.98	0	0.00	0	0.00	0	0.00
	102	**100.00**	**102**	**100.00**	**102**	**100.00**	**102**	**100.00**	**102**	**100.00**

Table 4.4 (3)

Average Amount of Capital Employed - Large group

Name of the Company (Rs. in Crores)	*Average (in percentage)*	*ACGR*
DIGITALEQP	200.29	27.73
HP	293.55	25.65
I-FLEX	677.09	39.93
INFOSYS	2341.66	57.93
SATYAM	1664.34	47.94
TECHM	276.39	44.23
WIPRO	2606.96	28.78
Average	**1151.47**	

Table 4.4 (4)

Average Amount of Capital Employed – Small-Medium Group

Name of the Company	*Average (Rs. in Crores)*	*ACGR (in percentage)*	*Name of the Company*	*Average (Rs. in Crores)*	*ACGR (in percentage)*
ABACUS	2.62	-3.44	KEDIN	5.83	9.95
ABMANO	9.27	4.43	KLG	35.68	25.02
ACESOFT	8.96	10.02	KPITCUMM	61.38	45.20
ADVENT	23.24	48.43	LEENEE	17.15	20.68
AFTEK LTD	186.72	55.88	MARRSOF	90.42	36.27
ASIANCE	3.23	6.52	MAGNUM	6.70	-1.33
AVANTELQ	14.41	13.15	MANGASOF	6.46	4.14
AZTECH	74.76	75.52	MASTEK	101.63	18.84
B2BSOFT	9.64	-5.05	MELSTAR	37.65	2.84
BLUESTINFO	35.01	151.33	MICROTECH	39.53	65.41
BRELS	29.97	7.34	MIDPOINT	1.46	-16.44
CALIFSOF	22.89	13.73	MINDTEK	19.77	11.53
CGVAK	9.69	8.38	MPHASIS	427.76	38.66

(Contd...)

Name of the Company	Average (Rs. in Crores)	ACGR (in percentage)	Name of the Company	Average (Rs. in Crores)	ACGR (in percentage)
CONTECH	8.74	-16.07	NCCFIN	5.35	-40.26
CRANES	121.62	125.59	NUCLEUSSOFT	44.16	24.82
CRESSAN	6.28	56.47	ODYSSEY	2.87	-1.49
CSSOFT	8.07	25.11	ONWARD	49.27	13.52
CYBERTE	49.18	15.34	ORIENTINFO	68.54	30.06
DATASOFT	3.31	-15.33	OTCO	1.65	18.92
DYNACON	20.48	58.36	PALSOFT	1.93	-176.11
ESERVE	42.49	15.88	PENTASOFTTE	670.92	50.40
EUROSOFT	36.94	12.69	PIOTECH	12.01	6.52
EZCOM	5.42	2.73	PSI	26.43	15.75
FINTECH	47.13	42.64	RAMINFO	274.42	275.50
FRONTINF	30.55	16.05	RAMCOSYS	34.36	30.88
GENESYS	37.99	79.00	ROLTA	539.14	22.45
GEOMETRIC	58.14	41.85	SANRASOF	5.86	2.30
GOLDTECH	29.89	3.93	SILVERLINE	388.13	2.03

(Contd...)

Name of the Company	*Average (Rs. in Crores)*	*ACGR (in percentage)*	*Name of the Company*	*Average (Rs. in Crores)*	*ACGR (in percentage)*
GTL	1001.12	19.99	SINDUVA	0.19	-24.40
HEXAWERE	271.83	17.22	SOFTSOL	73.60	59.66
HINDTMT	355.48	13.29	SONATA	101.44	24.90
INFDS	1.53	0.16	SVAMSOFT	19.26	-2.49
INFOTECENT	98.85	48.86	TELEDATA	139.33	93.24
INSOE	2.19	-7.93	TERASOFT	10.23	83.60
INTELVIS	6.27	19.20	TWINSOFT	21.35	2.39
INTRAINF	4.17	2.22	VIRTUALS	5.52	-10.81
ITMICRO	9.74	32.45	VISUALSOFT	138.95	52.49
JETKINGQ	3.48	23.40	VJIL	21.82	16.20
JINDONL	5.10	-3.06	ZENSAR	76.80	11.36
KASHYAP	4.48	-11.11	**Average**	**79.57**	

Table 4.4 (5)

Average Amount of Capital Employed – Converts

Name of the Company	*Average (Rs. in Crores)*	*ACGR (in percentage)*
CHOKSHIN	2.07	-7.65
CORCOMP	1.22	20.40
DANLAW	26.01	39.60
ENCORE	9.63	7.11
ICSAIND	9.04	24.03
IECSOF	20.80	13.69
INFOTREK	4.86	8.67
LCCINFO	62.94	26.08
MASCONGLO	218.84	99.87
MILLENCY	3.26	7.54
NETVISTA	20.58	-0.12
OMEGAIN	8.53	4.75
SRGINFO	203.26	8.72
SYNLOG	23.91	0.09
TRILLENT	6.79	-11.99
VAKRANG	42.32	18.76
Average	**41.50**	

Wide variations have been found in the average amount of capitalisation of the sub-groups as compared to the average of the entire sample. ANOVA technique has been used to test the significance of the differences in capital employed and hence the following hypothesis has been formulated:

H_0: There is no significant difference in the average amount of capital employed of the sub-groups.

Table 4.5

ANOVA for Averages of Capital Employed in Sub-Groups

Source of Variance	*df*	*Sum of Square*	*Mean Score*	*'F' ratio*	*Sig. level at 5%*
Between Groups	2	15417843.43	7708922.00	89.49	S
Within groups	99	8528164.12	86143.07		
Total	**101**	**23946007.55**			

Table 4.5 indicates that the calculated value of *F* was 89.49 as against the table value of 3.0 at 5 per cent level of significance. Thus the calculated value of *F* is greater than the table value of *F*; the null hypothesis is rejected at 5 per cent level of significance and hence it is concluded that there is significant difference in the averages of the sub-groups.

Pattern of Total Debt to Total Capital Employed

The general pattern of Total Debt to Total Capital Employed is analysed after preparing Table 4.1.2.

Table 4.6

Average Debt Equity (D/E)

(Ratio)

Years	*2005-06*	*2004-05*	*2003-04*	*2002-03*	*2001-02*	*2000-01*	*1999-00*	*1998-99*	*1997-98*	*1996-97*
(D/E)	0.131	0.156	0.123	0.110	0.095	0.084	0.083	0.171	0.216	0.217

Table 4.6 shows the general pattern of total debt to total capital employed of the sampled companies during the period of study (1996-97 to 2005-06). The highest debt proportion of 0.217 was found in the year 1996-97 and the lowest debt proportion of 0.083 in the year 1999-2000. A fluctuating trend has been found in the average debt to capitalisation over the study period. The average decreased from 0.217 to 0.131 during the study period. The overall average debt to total capitalisation of the sampled companies for the study period was found to be 0.139.

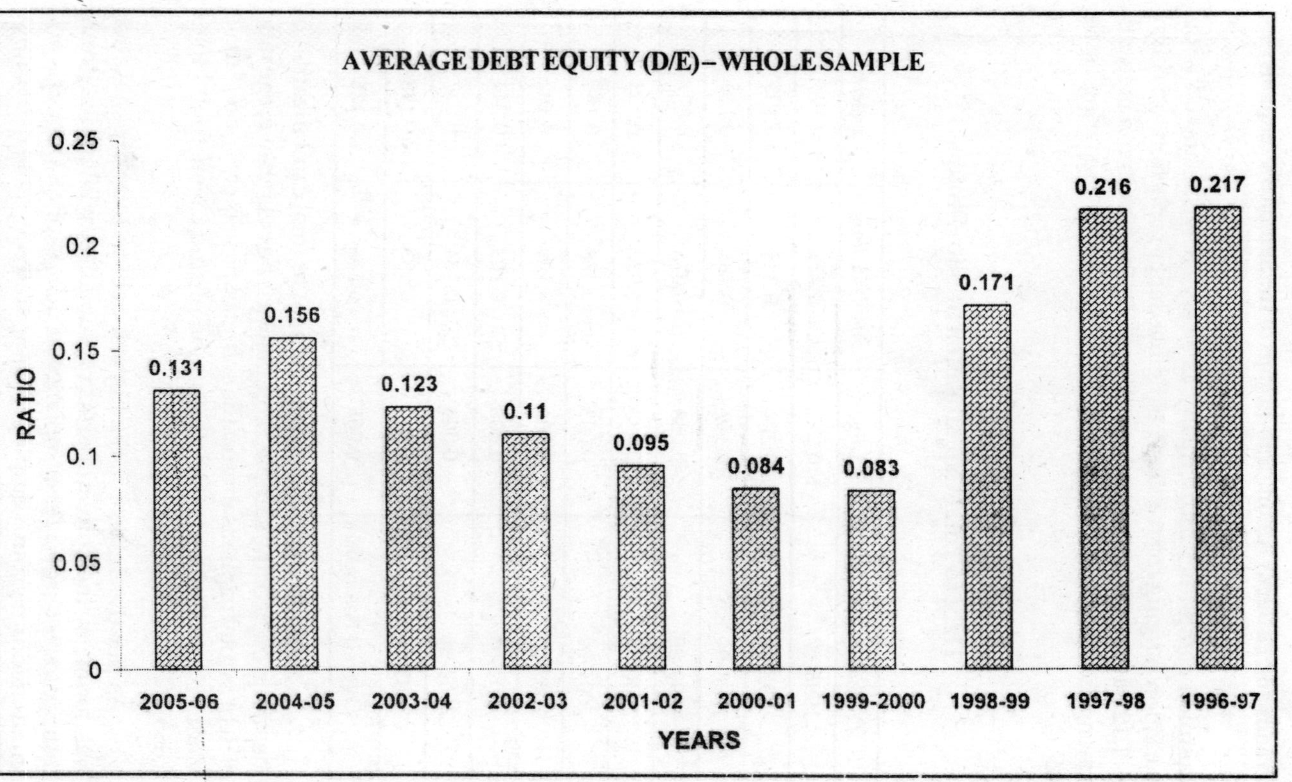
AVERAGE DEBT EQUITY (D/E)–WHOLE SAMPLE
RATIO
0.25
0.2
0.15
0.1
0.05
0
0.131
0.156
0.123
0.11
0.095
0.084
0.083
0.171
0.216
0.217
2005-06
2004-05
2003-04
2002-03
2001-02
2000-01
1999-2000
1998-99
1997-98
1996-97
YEARS

Trends and Patterns Among Sub-groups of the Sampled Companies

The figures of debt to total capitalisation of the sub-groups of sampled companies individually as also year wise showed wide variation ranging from a very negligible debt proportion to as high as 1.192. Hence, an attempt is made to study the trends and patterns among the sub groups of the sampled companies by preparing Table 4.7.

Table 4.7

Debt to Total Capitalisation of Sub-Groups

(Ratio)

Years	*Large*	*Small-Medium*	*Converts*
1996-97	0.151	0.229	0.193
1997-98	0.204	0.235	0.135
1998-99	0.157	0.186	0.111
1999-00	0.088	0.078	0.077
2000-01	0.033	0.092	0.153
2001-02	0.003	0.078	0.154
2002-03	0.006	0.109	0.162
2003-04	0.006	0.108	0.244
2004-05	0.004	0.134	0.337
2005-06	0.002	0.133	0.198
Overall Average	**0.065**	**0.138**	**0.176**

Table 4.7 evinces the pattern of debt to total capitalization of the sub-groups of the sampled companies. The overall average ratio of debt to total capitalisation of the sub-groups namely Large, Small-Medium and Converts over the period of study were found to be 0.065, 0.138 and 0.176 respectively.

As per the Table 4.7, the highest debt to total capitalisation was found in the converts group companies, while large group companies recorded lesser reliance of debt capital. Converts and small-medium groups employed comparatively more debt capital in their capitalisation than the overall average of 0.127 for the whole sample, while the large group of companies had this proportion much below the overall average. Unlike the general declining trend found throughout the large group, the Small-Medium group and converts recorded an upward swing since 2001-02.

In order to ensure whether there was any significant variation in the debt to total capitalization among the various sub-groups of sampled companies, the analysis of variance technique (ANOVA) was applied. In this connection the following hypothesis has been framed:

H_0: There is no significant difference in the average proportion of debt to total capitalisation of the sub-groups.

Table 4.8

Debt to Total Capitalisation in Different Sub-Groups – ANOVA

Source of Variance	*df*	*Sum of Square*	*Mean Score*	*'F' ratio*	*Sig. level at 5%*
Between Groups	2	5282.37	2641.18	20.79	S
Within groups	99	12579.21	127.06		
Total	**101**	**17861.59**			

As per Table 4.8, the calculated *'F'* value is 20.79, as against the table value of 3.0 at 5 per cent level of significance. Since the calculated value of *F* being much higher than the table value of *F*, the null hypothesis stands rejected and as such it is concluded that the differences among the average proportions of debt to total capitalisation of the sampled companies during the study period is significant.

Considering the entire sample it can be concluded that there is a general trend of lesser reliance on debt finance with the passage of time; however converts and small-medium sub-groups are found to be employing more debt finance than large companies.

Total Capitalization vis-à-vis Debt to Total Capitalisation (Trends and Patterns)

The trends and patterns with regard to total capital employed and the proportion of debt to total capitalisation of the 102 sampled companies and also in the sub-groups have been analysed to know whether or not there exists significant correlation between these two variables. The details of the correlation analysis are depicted in Table 4.9.

H_0: There is no correlation between total capital employed and the proportion of debt to total capitalization. (Whole Sample)

H_0: There is no correlation between debt to capital employed and average capital employed. (Sub-Groups)

Table 4.9

Analysis of Coefficient of Correlation and t-test of the 102 Sampled Companies and sub-groups

Details	*Coefficient of Correlation*	*df*	*t Test*		*Result*	*Remarks*
			Calculated Value	*Table Value*		
Whole Sample						
All sample companies as a gross	0.0667	101	0.0004	3.00	Insignificant	Hypothesis Rejected
Sub-Groups						
Large	0.6115	6	0.0123	2.45	Insignificant	Hypothesis Rejected
Small Medium	0.0834	78	0.0002	1.96	Insignificant	Hypothesis Rejected
Converts	-0.1484	15	0.2230	2.13	Insignificant	Hypothesis Rejected

As per Table 4.9, the values of the coefficient of correlation between the average capital employed and the ratios of debt to capital employed in the case of 102 companies as a group was found to be very insignificant as the calculated value of t was 0.0004 at 5 per cent level of significance. From this, it can be concluded that the reliance on leverage was found independent of the size of the sampled companies. It could be further observed that there is no significant relationship between the proportion of debt to total capital employed and average capital employed in each sub group.

Further, all the sample companies were classified into two categories on the basis of median value of their average total capital employed. Thus, the first group of companies comprised of those companies whose average total capital employed was above the median value and the second group comprised of those companies whose average capital employed was less than the median value and the results of analysis have been detailed out in Table 4.10.

H_0: There is no correlation between Capital Employed and Debt Equity Ratio of above median capital employed and below median Capital Employed Companies.

Median = Rs.23.57 Crores

Table 4.10

Results of Coefficient of Correlation and t-test of above Median and below Median Capital Employed

Details	*Coefficient of Correlation*	*df*	*t Test*		*Results*	*Remarks*
			Calculated Value	*Table Value*		
Companies CE Below Median	-0.1013	50	0.0002	1.96	Insignificant	Hypothesis Rejected
Companies CE Above Median	-0.0729	50	0.0001	1.96	Insignificant	Hypothesis Rejected

The Table 4.10 shows that there is no significant relationship between the debt and the total capital employed in the case of below median and also above median companies. Thus, the proportion of debt to capital employed and average capital employed above and below the median value did not show any significant correlation.

Overall Analysis of Capital Structure

Capital structure, the mix of debt and equity have been analysed sub-group wise in Table 4.11.

Table 4.11

Capital Structure of different sub groups

Sub Groups	*Capital Employed*		*Total Debt*		*Debt to Total Capital Employed*	
	Avg (Rs. in crores)	*ACGR (%)*	*Avg (Rs. in crores)*	*ACGR (%)*	*Avg (Ratio)*	*ACGR (%)*
Large	1151.47	38.88	32.44	-0.31	0.06	-15.19
Small-Medium	79.57	23.38	10.42	-11.95	0.14	-24.54
Converts	41.50	16.22	5.05	9.00	0.18	-3.02

Table 4.11 articulates the capital structure of different sub-groups. The average capital employed of large group companies was Rs. 1151.47 crores, It was Rs. 79.57 crores and Rs. 41.50 crores in the case of small-medium and converts companies respectively. The annual compound growth rates of the sub groups stood at 38.88 per cent, 23.38 per cent and 16.22 per cent respectively.

The average of total debt of large group of companies was Rs. 32.44 crores, for small-medium Rs. 10.42 crores and for converts Rs. 5.05 crores. Annual Compound Growth Rates for the same were -0.31 per cent, -11.95 per cent and 9.00 per cent respectively indicating the fact that contrary to the inclination of converts towards increased debt equity ratio, large and small-medium groups tend to borrow less.

Large group of companies registered an average debt-equity of 0.06, small-medium group of companies 0.14 and converts 0.18. The Annual Compound Growth Rates of all the sub-groups were negative and stood at -15.19 per cent, -24.54 per cent and -3.02 per cent in large, small-medium and converts group of companies respectively.

COST OF COMPONENT ANALYSIS

The cost of capital constitutes an integral part of investment decisions. A company uses more than one type of capital. The composite capital lies between the least and the most expensive funds. Table 4.12 puts forward the synoptic description of Cost of Equity, Cost of Debt and WACC.

Table 4.12

Yearly Average of Cost of Equity, Cost of Debt and WACC

(in percentage)

Years	*2005-06*	*2004-05*	*2003-04*	*2002-03*	*2001-02*	*2000-01*	*1999-00*	*1998-99*	*1997-98*	*1996-97*
Cost of Debt	0.18	0.09	0.11	0.23	0.21	0.23	0.33	0.74	0.34	0.83
Cost of Equity	37.82	32.83	11.06	52.74	4.99	-10.13	-9.42	46.64	-8.61	15.89
WACC	34.87	27.95	10.75	50.25	5.44	-8.68	-7.31	42.78	-3.75	16.33

It is obvious from Table 4.12 that, the cost of debt has declined over the years while the cost of equity has exhibited wide variations. An attempt has been made to study the average cost of debt for the different sub- groups of the companies.

The averages of cost of debt capital of the sample companies varied from year to year. In order to verify whether there is any significant variation in the averages of cost of debt of different sub – groups, the following hypothesis has been framed and tested.

H_0: There is no significant variation in averages of cost of debt of different sub-groups.

Table 4.13

Cost of Debt of sub-groups – ANOVA

Source of variance	*d.f*	*SS*	*MS*	*'F' ratio*	*Sig. level at 5%*
Between Groups	2	1.085	0.542557	0.884	NS
within groups	99	60.790	0.614042		
Total	**101**	**61.875**			

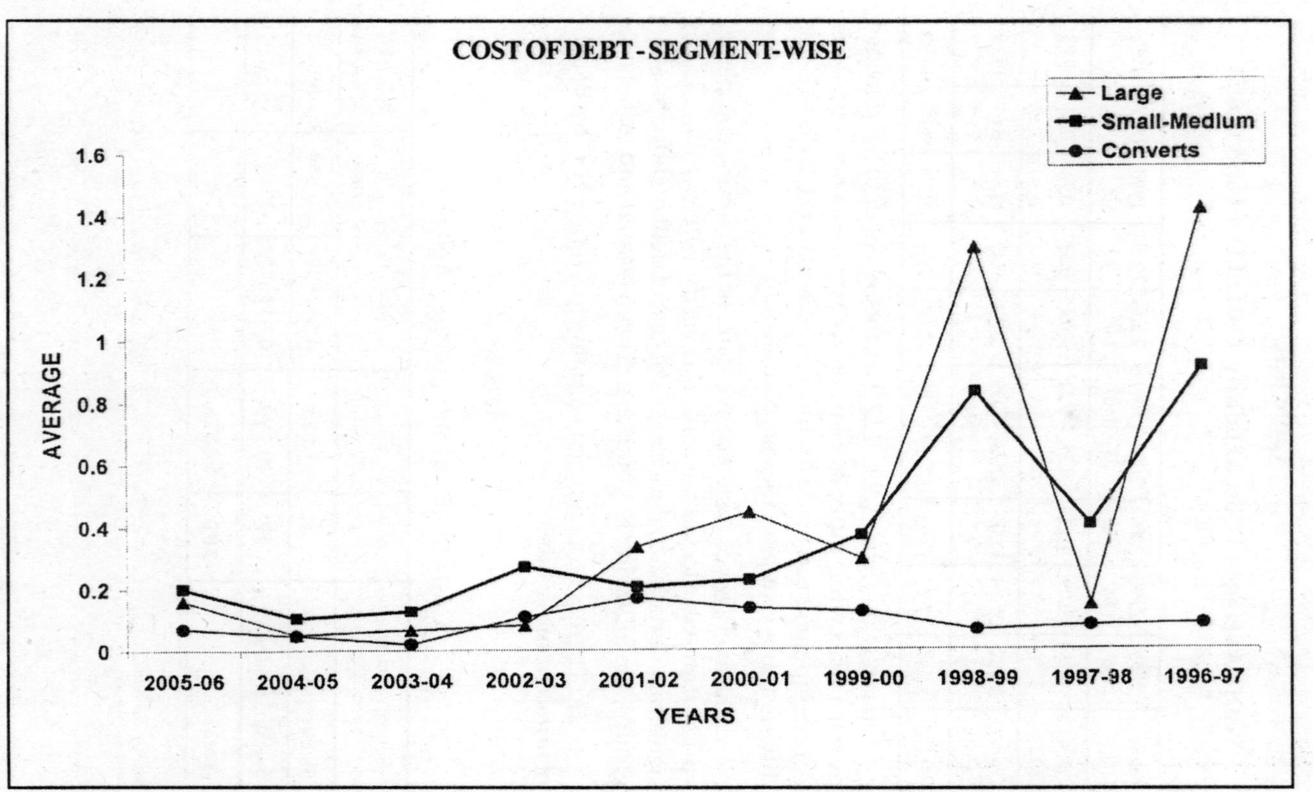
COST OF DEBT - SEGMENT-WISE
Large
Small-Medium
Converts
AVERAGE
1.6
1.4
1.2
1
0.8
0.6
0.4
0.2
0
2005-06
2004-05
2003-04
2002-03
2001-02
2000-01
1999-00
1998-99
1997-98
1996-97
YEARS

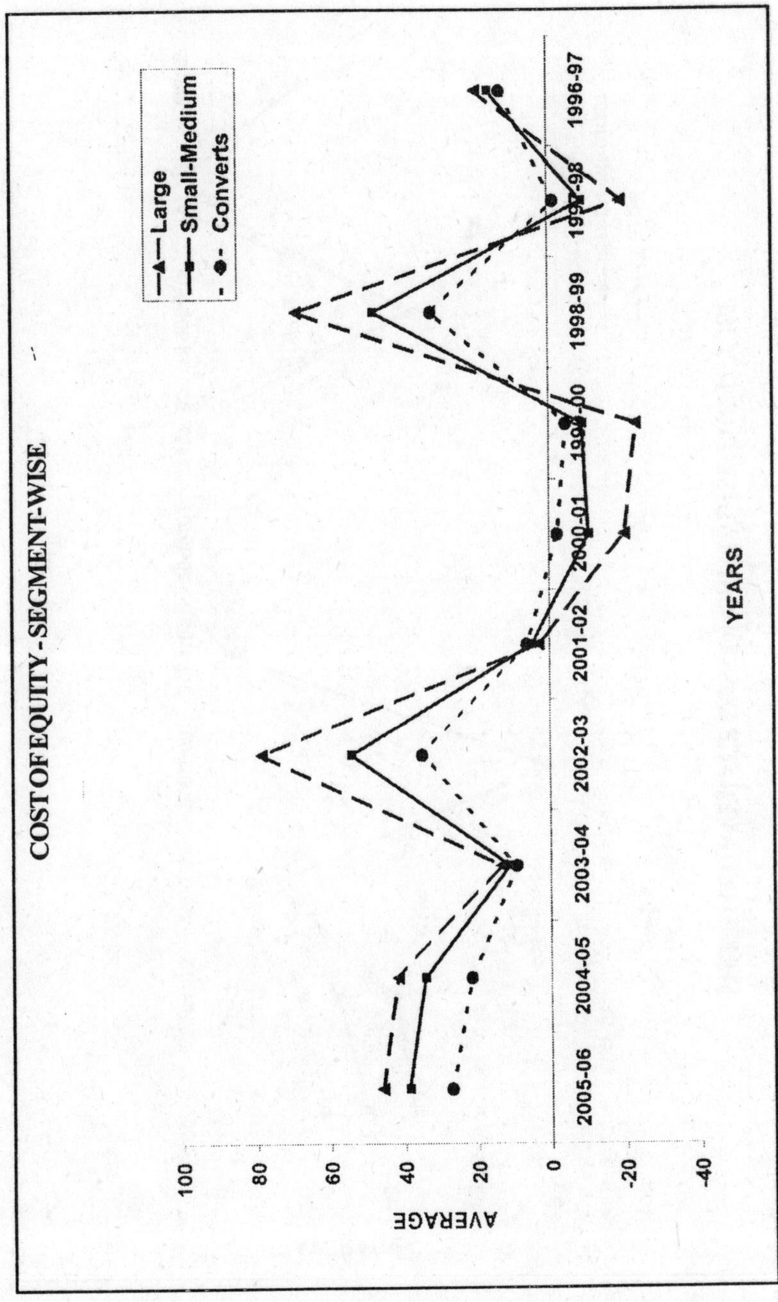
COST OF EQUITY - SEGMENT-WISE
Large
Small-Medium
Converts
AVERAGE
100
80
60
40
20
0
-20
-40
2005-06
2004-05
2003-04
2002-03
2001-02
2000-01
1999-00
1998-99
1997-98
1996-97
YEARS

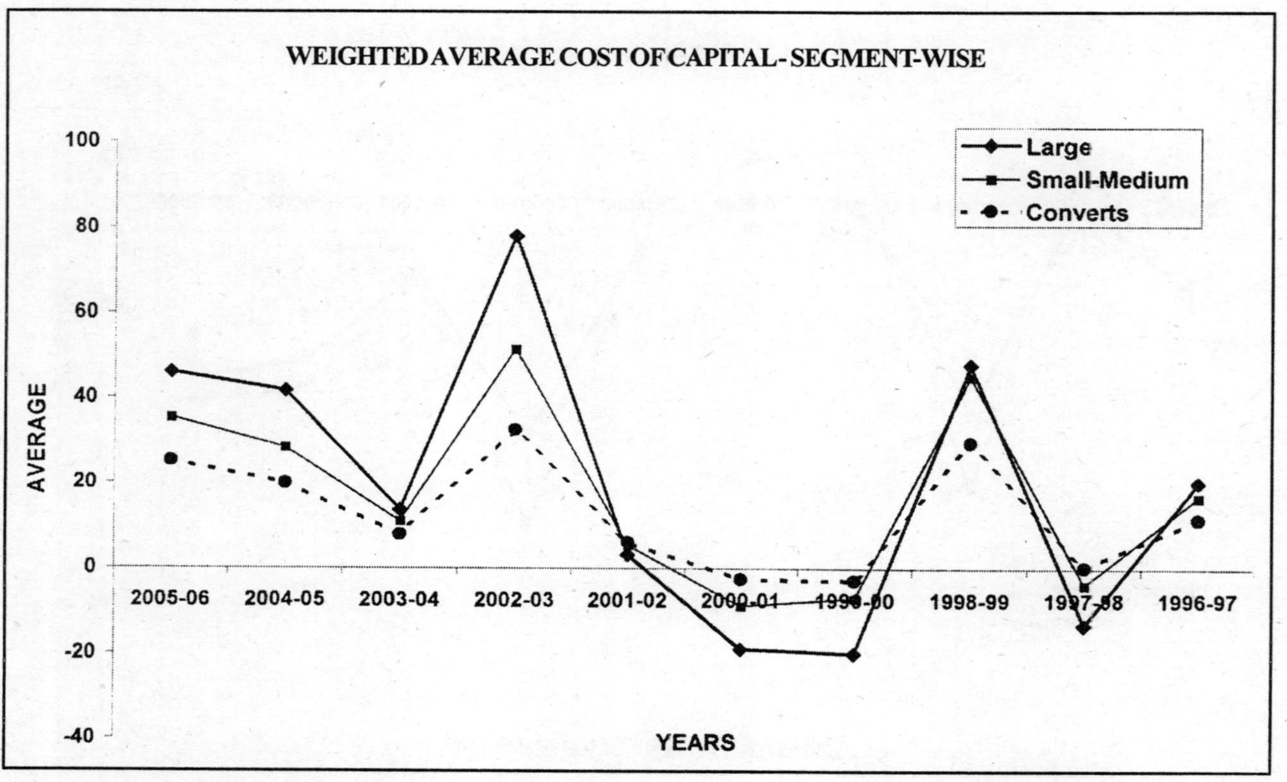
WEIGHTED AVERAGE COST OF CAPITAL - SEGMENT-WISE
Large
Small-Medium
Converts
AVERAGE
100
80
60
40
20
0
-20
-40
2005-06
2004-05
2003-04
2002-03
2001-02
2000-01
1999-00
1998-99
1997-98
1996-97
YEARS

According to Table 4.13, the calculated 'F' value is 0.884 as against the table value of 3.07. Since the calculated value being lesser than the table value, it can be concluded that there is no significant difference in average cost of debt capital of different sub groups.

Estimation of cost of equity is the most complex task. Several approaches are available to estimate the cost of equity. Capital Asset Pricing Model (CAPM) approach has been attempted as it considers the risk factor. The parameters of CAPM are risk free rate of return (r_f), market rate of return (K_m) and beta co-efficient (b).

Table 4.12 reveals that the minimum average cost of equity is -10.13 per cent and the maximum is 52.74 per cent. Since the cost of equity of sampled companies showed wide variations, an attempt is made to study the average cost of equity capital for different sub-groups.

The average cost of equity capital in Large, Small-Medium and Converts groups are found to be 20.85 per cent, 17.58 per cent and 13.91 per cent respectively (Table 4.16). To check whether cost of equity capital differs significantly in various groups of sampled companies, the ANOVA technique is used.

***H_0*:** There is no perceptible and distinctive difference in cost of equity among sub-groups of sampled companies.

Table 4.14

Cost of Equity of sub-groups – ANOVA

Source of variance	*d.f*	*SS*	*MS*	*'F' ratio*	*Sig. level at 5%*
Between Groups	2	282.261	141.1304	0.488	NS
within groups	99	28630.629	289.1983		
Total	**101**	**28912.890**			

It is obvious from Table 4.14 that 'F' ratio value is 0.488. The calculated value being less than the table value of 3.07, at 5 per cent level of significance, it can be concluded that among the sampled companies distinctive cost of equity does not exist though it varies from group to group.

The computation of overall cost of capital involves weights to specific costs and multiplying these costs by their relative weights. The overall cost of capital of sampled companies showed very wide variations and hence an attempt was made to study the average cost of capital for the different sub groups of the sampled companies.

ANOVA has been performed to ensure whether there is any pertinent and significant variation in WACC among sampled companies.

H_0: There is no significant variation in WACC among the sub groups of sampled companies.

Table 4.15

WACC among sub-groups – ANOVA

Source of variance	*d.f*	*SS*	*MS*	*'F' ratio*	*Sig. level at 5%*
Between Groups	2	338.756	169.378	0.631	NS
Within groups	99	26573.754	268.422		
Total	**101**	**26912.511**			

It is clear from the Table 4.15 that the calculated F value is 0.631 as against the table value of 3.07 at 5 per cent level of significance. Since the calculated value of WACC is less than its table value, it is concluded that the WACC among different sub groups does not show any distinctive variation.

On the whole, it can be concluded that overall cost of capital does not differ significantly from one sub-group to another sub-group of sampled companies.

The Cost of Debt, Cost of Equity and WACC for the whole sample and also for different sub-groups are summarised in Table 4.16.

Average cost of debt as well as the cost of equity were the highest for biggies followed by Small-medium segment. Converts enjoyed low cost debt and equity and hence their WACC was the lowest compared to other sub-groups.

Table 4.16

Group-wise Average Cost of Debt (K_d), Cost of Equity (K_e) & WACC (K_o)

(in percentage)

Group	*Cost of Debt*	*Cost of Equity*	*WACC*
Large	0.44	20.85	19.77
Small Medium	0.35	17.58	17.14
Converts	0.09	13.91	12.69

Table 4.17

Year-wise Average of Select Variables for the whole sample

Years	*Debt Equity (Ratio)*	*ROCE (%)*	*Turnover (Rs. in Cr.)*	*EBIT (Rs. in Cr.)*	*Total Debt (Rs. in Cr.)*	*EBIT to CE (Ratio)*
2005-06	0.131	8.857	399.74	104.013	18.131	0.106
2004-05	0.156	-15.136	255.44	64.714	12.765	-0.112
2003-04	0.123	-2.107	188.16	45.652	11.319	0.027
2002-03	0.110	-16.826	156.83	37.841	9.977	0.039
2001-02	0.095	-8.607	131.22	35.382	6.431	-0.019
2000-01	0.084	3.690	118.54	37.573	7.675	0.087
1999-00	0.083	12.713	83.88	21.295	8.777	0.149
1998-99	0.171	0.788	58.47	11.694	11.329	-0.024
1997-98	0.216	4.128	46.95	6.908	13.025	0.099
1996-97	0.217	11.308	40.79	6.659	12.145	0.130

Table 4.17 evinces the trend of certain select capital structure oriented variables. Optimal capital structure can be obtained with the proper mix of debt and equity. The Debt equity ratio was 0.217 during 1996-97, which decreased to 0.131 during 2005-06. The ratio was found to be below the standard norm of 2:1 during the entire study period. This indicates an unfavourable position to the shareholders since a very low debt equity ratio was observed deducing that firms have not been able to use low-cost outsiders funds to magnify their earnings.

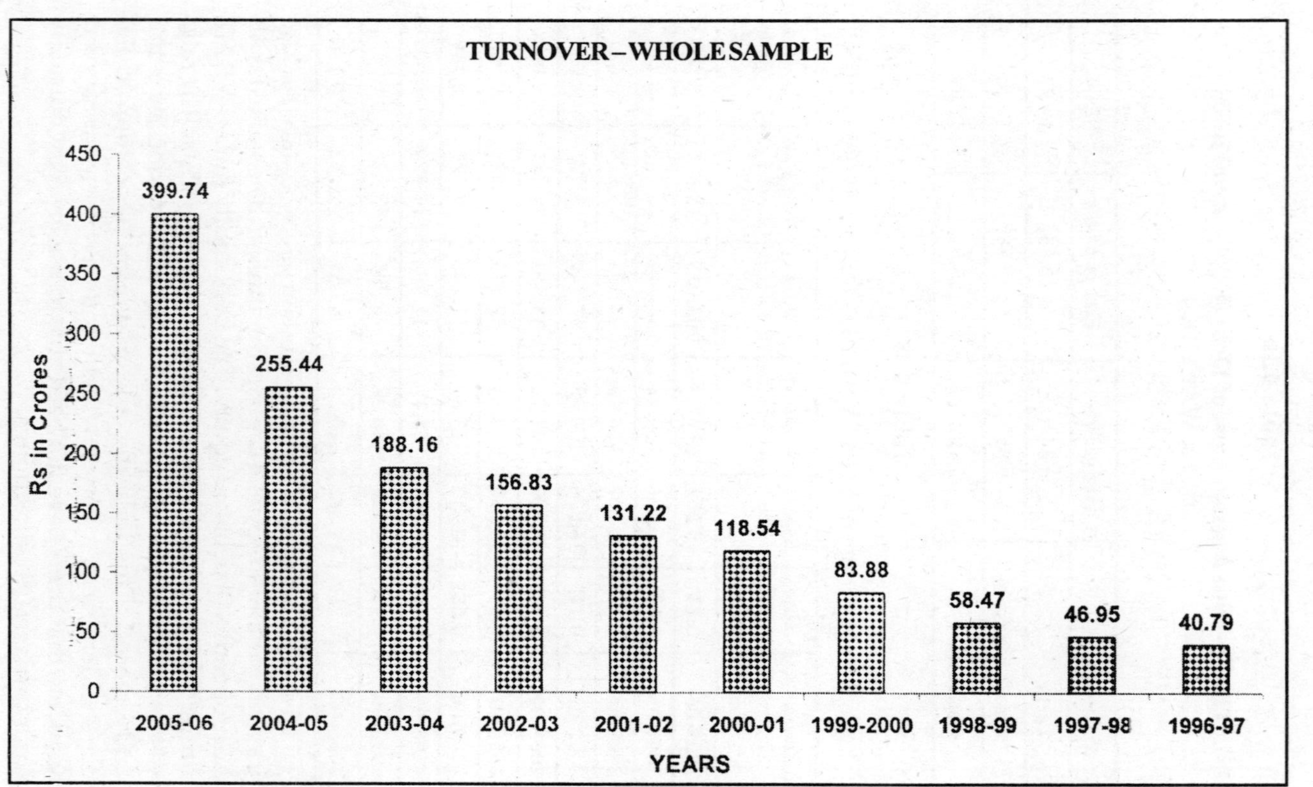
TURNOVER–WHOLESAMPLE
Rs in Crores
450
400
350
300
250
200
150
100
50
0
399.74
255.44
188.16
156.83
131.22
118.54
83.88
58.47
46.95
40.79
2005-06
2004-05
2003-04
2002-03
2001-02
2000-01
1999-2000
1998-99
1997-98
1996-97
YEARS

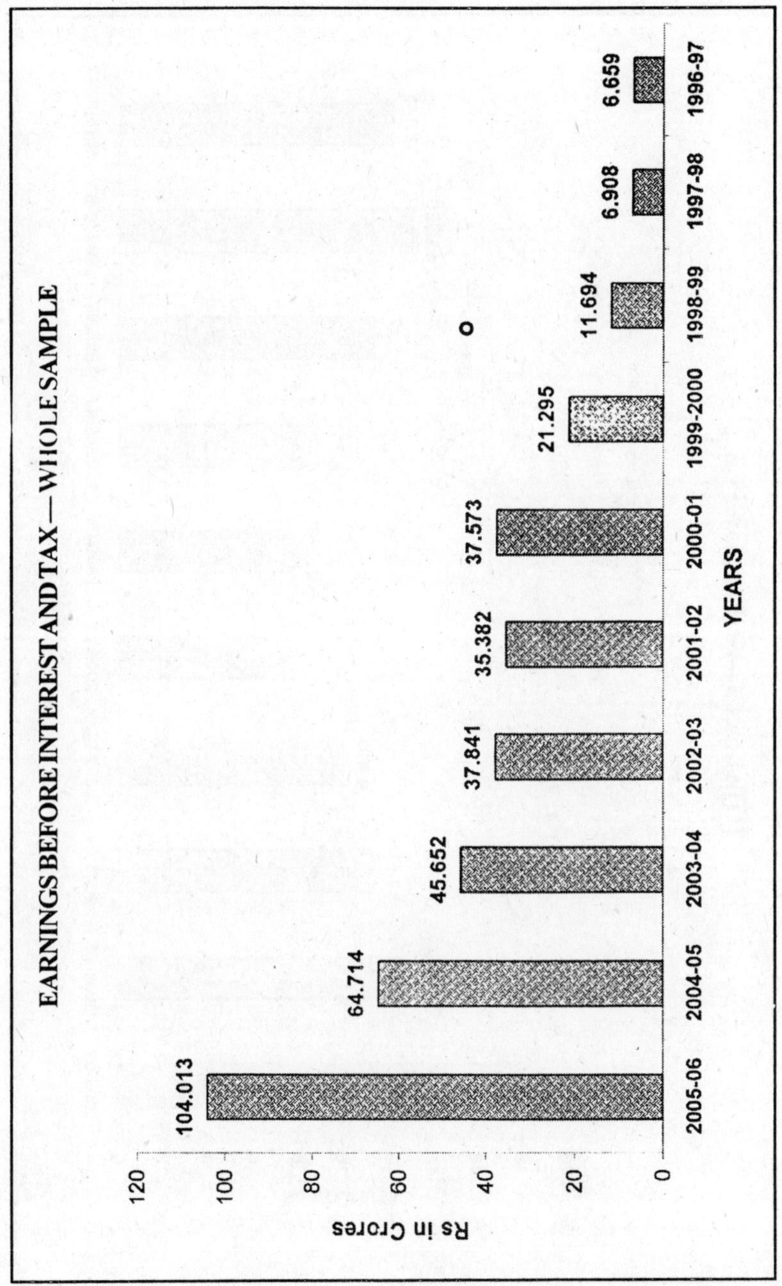
EARNINGS BEFORE INTEREST AND TAX — WHOLE SAMPLE
Rs in Crores
120
100
80
60
40
20
0
104.013
64.714
45.652
37.841
35.382
37.573
21.295
11.694
6.908
6.659
2005-06
2004-05
2003-04
2002-03
2001-02
2000-01
1999-2000
1998-99
1997-98
1996-97
YEARS

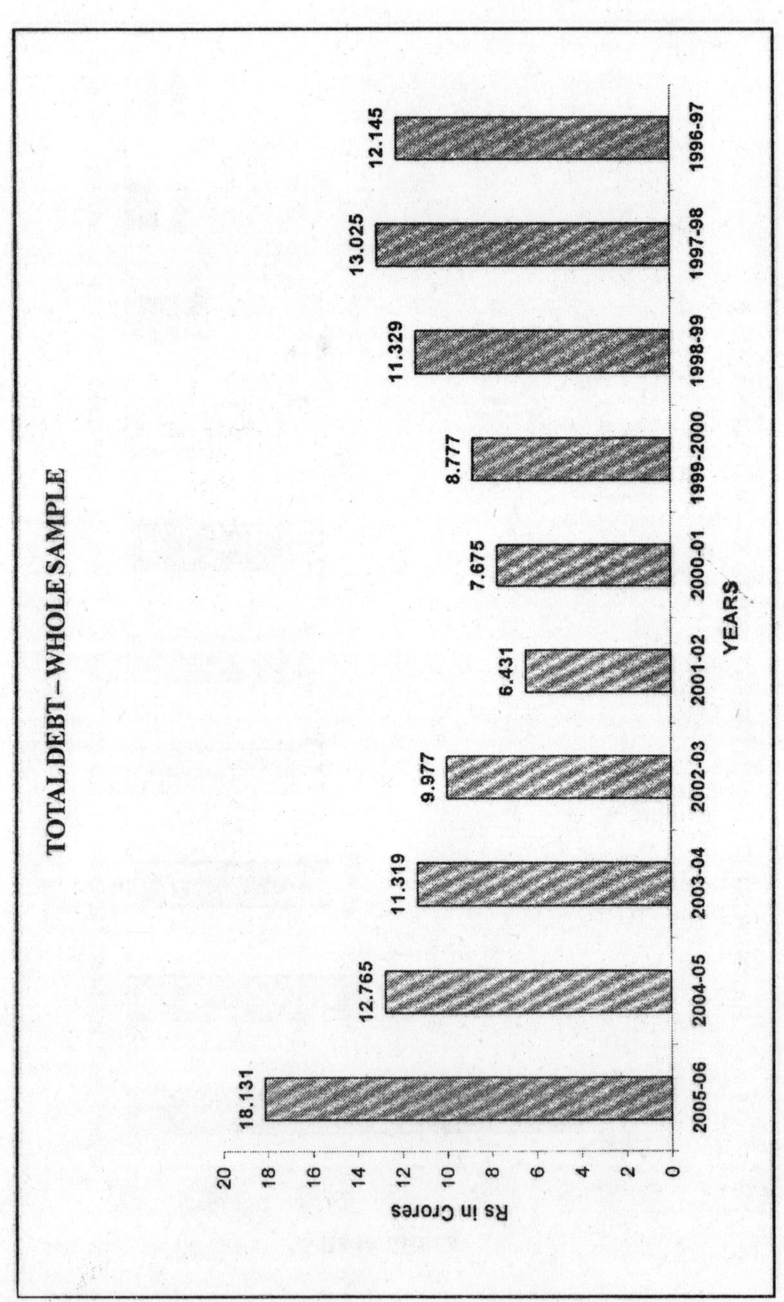

TOTAL DEBT – WHOLE SAMPLE
Rs in Crores
20
18
16
14
12
10
8
6
4
2
0
18.131
12.765
11.319
9.977
6.431
7.675
8.777
11.329
13.025
12.145
2005-06
2004-05
2003-04
2002-03
2001-02
2000-01
1999-2000
1998-99
1997-98
1996-97
YEARS

Return on Capital Employed was found to have decreased from 11.308 during 1996-97 to 8.857 during 2005-06. Decreasing trend in the debt-equity ratios exhibits less financial risk.

Turnover which has the direct impact on profitability was found to be high during 2005-06 when compared to 1996-97. An increasing trend is noticed with respect to EBIT also. Fluctuating trend is identified with respect to total debt. It ranges from Rs. 6.431 Crores to Rs. 18.131 Crores. EBIT to Capital Employed showed a decrease from 0.130 during 1996-97 to 0.106 during 2005-06.

Correlation matrix has been constructed and analysed with regard to Debt-Equity and Turnover, Total Debt and EBIT, Debt-Equity and ROCE and finally EBIT to Capital Employed and Debt-Equity (whole sample analysis).

Table exhibits an inverse relationship between Debt-Equity and Turnover. There exists positive relationship between Total Debt and EBIT in all the 10 years of the study and a high positive association is noticed during the first five years of the study period. The association between Debt-Equity and ROCE was found to be low positive during seven out of ten years of the study period as per, and the first two years exhibited a negative relationship. A high positive correlation was found during the year 2005-06 with a coefficient of 0.778.

Inverse relationship was observed in seven years of the study with regard to EBIT to capital employed and Debt-Equity ratio presented. During the remaining years of the study, a very low positive association was found.

CONCLUSION

A business firm may obtain capital by the issue of ownership securities and by the issue of creditorship securities. A company borrows capital to maximise the profits for its shareholders. A company that does not plan its capital structure may prosper in short run, but ultimately will face serious problems in raising funds to finance its activities in the long run. Hence an attempt was made to study the trends and patterns in capital structure with regard to the select Indian software companies. It can be concluded that the average amount of capitalisation of the sampled companies over the 10 year period was around Rs. 153.87 crores. With the passage of time the overall average of capital employed showed an increasing trend. In majority of the years of study, only around 10 per cent of the sampled companies had a capital employed of above Rs. 1000 crores.

Analysis reveals some significant and interesting differences among large, small-medium and converts group of companies. The average proportion of debt to total capital employed of the sampled companies showed a fluctuating trend. Significant difference in the average amount of capital employed of the sub-groups and among the average proportions of debt to total capitalization of the sampled companies were observed.

Reliance on leverage was found to be very much insignificant. There was no significant relationship between proportion of debt to total capitalisation and average capital employed in each sub-group. In contradiction to the inclination of converts towards increased debt-equity ratio, large and small-medium groups were moving towards more equity oriented capital structure.

Statistically there was no significant difference among various sub-groups with regard to cost of debt capital. Distinctive patterns were found to exist with respect to cost of equity and it varied from group to group. WACC among different sub-groups did not show any distinctive variation. Debt-equity ratio was found to be far below the standard norm in all the years under study. It establishes the fact that the share holders do not enjoy the advantages of trading on equity.

Year-wise averages of EBIT and Turnover showed an upward swing. Inverse relationship was found between debt equity and turnover and between EBIT to capital employed and debt-equity in majority of the years. Positive relationship was observed with respect to total debt and EBIT and debt-equity and ROCE. Such a positive relationship favours the proposition that the use of debt upto an optimal level could boost earnings related variables.

5

ECONOMIC VALUE ADDED PERFORMANCE

ITS EMERGENCE IN SOFTWARE INDUSTRY

"Valuation is not an exact Science – It is a sophisticated guess work"–

—**Bonbright.**

INTRODUCTION

Modern business organisations have to meet economic developments and must beat intense competition by constantly re-orienting their activities. Competitive advantage of firms depends not on cost only but also on the value created for investments made. The major responsibility of a company is to make sure that every objective meets the principle of satisfying stake holders' needs. The value created for the capital invested play a significant role in emerging as a critical dimension of stiff competition in all companies. In order to maintain the shareholders value, a company is supposed to work in all spheres of its activities. The board of directors have to play a vital role in directing and supervising the core financial objectives of the management to run the company towards shareholders wealth maximisation.

The increasing awareness among joint stock companies in respect of maximisation of shareholders value has led to a revolutionary change in the performance measure criteria of corporate entities. A new measure called Economic Value Added (EVA) is increasingly being used to understand, analyse and evaluate the financial performance of corporate entities.

EVA—its Emergence

Stern Stewart and Co, is a global consulting firm, which was established in 1982. This firm pioneered the development of its proprietary EVA framework. It has developed this tool to end inefficient use of capital. Over the past several years, the EVA measure has been gaining acceptance all over the world. It has been acknowledged by institutional firms as a creditable performance measure. In fact, the companies do not use EVA, but implement it. The wide spread adoption of EVA began in the early 1990s.

Economic value added is the financial profit performance measure most directly linked to the creation of shareholder wealth over time. A body of literature on EVA has emerged over the past decade. EVA is a measure of residual income, which focusses on the concept that a company must earn an adequate risk-adjusted return on its investment in assets. If EVA is zero, a company is earning a return from operations just sufficient to pay investors their required return for risk. Economic Value Added is a measure of surplus value created for an investment. It attempts to capture the true economic profit of an enterprise. EVA is linked to the creation of shareholders' wealth over a period.

EVA is the most accurate measure of the economic performance of the company. It can be calculated at the level of divisions and product-lines and is not a function of the market price of a company's scrip. EVA is a more accurate measure of the ability of a company to add shareholder value.

EVA will increase if:

- ➢ Operating profits can be made to grow without employing more capital, i.e., greater efficiency;
- ➢ Additional capital is invested in projects that return more than the cost of obtaining new capital i.e., profitable growth;
- ➢ Capital is curtailed in activities that do not cover the cost of capital i.e liquidate unproductive capital.

EVA is the powerful management tool that has gained international acceptance as the standard of corporate governance. Many private sector organisations around the world have found the implementation of the EVA framework a far more effective, internally – driven initiative to improve governance as compared to transaction – driven alternatives. Even public sector organisations have benefited greatly from implementing EVA in support of their privatisation process. The two important parts of EVA are efficiency and growth.

In recent years, EVA has already been garnering a following of prominent corporations that feel strongly about its ability to deliver improved company performance. Most EVA adopters allude to stock price increases as an outcome by implementing EVA performance measurement in their companies. The idea of comparing profits with the cost of capital used to produce results in a net measure showing how much value has been created or destroyed by the firm during the period. EVA is the cornerstone of focussed finance. It is both a measure of true economic performance of a company and a strategy for creating shareholder wealth.

Properly implemented, EVA frees the measurement of corporate performance from the vagaries of accounting conventions and aligns the interest of managers with those of shareholders, ending the all too common conflicts of interest.

EVA is a value-based financial performance measure; A measure reflecting the absolute amount of shareholders value created or destroyed during each year; A useful tool for choosing the most promising financial investments; An effective protection against shareholder value destruction; A tool suitable to control operations; A measure highly correlated with stock prices; A measure that can be maximised; An estimator for company's true economic value creation; A good basis for management compensation systems to motivate managers to create shareholder value.

EVA is a capital allocation tool both inside a company and whole economy. EVA sets a minimum acceptable performance level to the rate of return in the longrun. This minimum rate of return is based on the average return on the equity markets. The average return is a benchmark that should be reached. If a company cannot achieve the average return, then the shareholders would be better off if they allocated their capital to other industries or to other companies. Implementing EVA is a four – step process and Stern-Stewart calls it as the 4M process. The 4Ms are measurement, management system, motivation and mind set.

COMPONENTS OF EVA

EVA measures whether the operating profit is enough compared to the total costs of capital employed. Stewart defined EVA (1990, p.137) as Net operating profit after taxes (NOPAT) subtracted with a capital charge.

EVA= (ROIC – WACC) x Invested capital.

(or)

EVA = PAT – Cost of Equity x Equity

(or)

EVA = NOPAT – Cost of Capital x Capital employed.

— **Net Operating Profit After Tax (NOPAT)**

NOPAT represents the total pool of profits available to provide a cash return to all financial contributors of capital (equity as well as debt) to the company. NOPAT is the operating profits of the firm adjusting taxes to a cash basis.

— **Invested Capital**

Invested capital represents the total amount of capital invested in the operations of a company over its life without regard to the source of financing the capital. It does not matter whether the capital is debt or equity and the assets are working capital or fixed assets. Invested capital can be determined either from the assets side of the balance sheet or the liabilities side.

— **Return on Invested Capital (ROIC)**

The EVA of a company is just a measure of the incremental return its investment earns over the market rate of return. Companies fund their investments from equity, debt or retained earnings. The returns equity investors expect from a company are, at the very least, equal to what they will achieve by investing in the market index although the actual figure depends on the risk profile of the company. The ROIC represents the total percentage return of the company generated on its average invested capital.

ROIC = (NOPAT / Average Invested Capital) x 100.

— **Weighted Average Cost of Capital (WACC)**

Weighted average cost of capital is an opportunity cost that is equivalent to the rate of return investor could expect to earn by investing in stock of other companies of comparable risk. A company should explore projects that provide an ROIC that is greater than WACC to add wealth to its capital position, which can be distributed to its investors.

WACC = {Cost of equity x proportion of equity capital} + {Post Tax cost of debt x Proportion of debt capital}

The WACC is essentially the weighted average of the cost of debt and the cost of equity. Cost of capital or weighted average cost of capital is the average cost of both equity capital and interest bearing debt. Cost of equity capital is the opportunity return from an investment with same risk as the company has. Cost of equity is defined in Capital Asset Pricing Model (CAPM). Cost of debt includes also the tax shield due to tax allowance on interest expenses.

EVA AND PRODUCTIVITY

In the long run, productivity is the driving force behind success at every level; national, industry, firm, division, department and even at the individual level. At the national level, countries with powerful productivities continually enjoy rising standard of living and greater productive capacities. At the corporate level, productive firms generally realise rising share prices and in fact, improve performances in all of their financials. The best way to see the relationship between EVA and productivity is to distill the EVA measuring tool down to its essence shown by the general expression; EVA = $(r-k)$* capital, where r = firm's return on its capital and k is cost of that capital.

ESOPs Vs. EVA

ESOPs (Employee Stock Options) have become increasingly popular in the US and Western Europe over the last two decades.

They have encouraged firms to drive down costs of starting a company; employees can be brought on board with the promise of future growth that a share option represents. Louis Kelso, an American lawyer and investment banker was the brain behind the creation of ESOP. Contribution to ESOPs gives the company substantial tax breaks enhancing post-tax earnings. ESOP makes shareholders directly responsible for the company's profitability. Experiences across the world demonstrate that ESOPs help align employees interests with that of the company and its shareholders and attract bright talent through potentially unlimited financial awards, without committing hefty cash compensation. They help infuse a wider sense of ownership and belongingness among employees mainly in the technology sector companies.

Most US technology companies now provide most or all employees with stock options and most large and many small US companies, of any kind have broad-based employee plans of one kind or another. Employees at all levels have ideas, information and abilities that can help the company grow. EVA and ESOPs are closely linked with each other to aligning interests of employees with corporate objectives. In the case of knowledge based industries like the software sector, ESOPs would be a better instrument because:

- Companies in these sectors are less capital intensive and value creation is driven primarily by operational efficiencies in terms of employee productivity, quality of deliverables etc.;
- These companies need to attract the best and the brightest talent from across the globe.

EVA, NPV Vs. IRR, ROI

Return on capital is very common and relatively good performance measure. Different companies calculate this return with different formulae and call them by different names like Return on Investment (ROI), Return on invested capital (ROIC), Return on capital employed (ROCE), Return on Net Assets (RONA), Return on Assets (ROA) etc. The main shortcoming with all these rates of return is that maximising rate of return does not necessarily maximise the return to shareholders. The difference between EVA and ROI is actually exactly the same as with NPV (Net Present Value) and IRR (Internal Rate of Return). In the corporate control

EVA and NPV go hand in hand as also ROI and IRR. The formers tell the impacts to shareholder wealth and the latter tell the rate of return.

Implementing the EVA System

Implementing the EVA system involves several steps:

- Develop Top management commitment;
- Customize the definitions of EVA;
- Identify EVA centers;
- Analyse the Drivers of EVA;
- Tailor an incentive compensation system;
- Train all the employees.

Significance of EVA

In an era of value based competition an organisation should be at its best to emerge as a leader. EVA is relevant not only to big corporate but also to small and medium enterprises. It plays a vital role in protecting the interests of minority investors and small institutional investors. If properly implemented, EVA provides the following advantages:

- In developing economies like India, EVA meets the challenges of globalisation and competition from globalised marketing trends. It enables the companies to enhance their market shares by enhancing value;
- EVA maximises the efficiency of capital by finding ways to invest it in a most profitable way;
- In troubled enterprises where management's resources are limited, EVA is helpful in allocating the available resources in the most appropriate manner;
- EVA incentives are almost team incentives rather than individual incentives. This is aimed at the sustainability of overall performance of the firm by team work;
- EVA system provides information and motivation to make decisions that will create greatest shareholders wealth in any enterprise;

- If properly linked to a firm's operational system, EVA can be a valuable tool for changing the behaviour of employees. It can be used to educate employees in priorities to improvement;
- The use of EVA will encourage all employees to make a participative contribution in wealth creation process;
- Concept of EVA is not only useful for the shareholders but it is equally beneficial to safeguard the interests of other stake holders like employees, creditors, providers of debt capital, customers, government etc.;
- Recognizes equity cost of capital;
- EVA can be used to hold the management accountable for all expenditures whether they appear in Profit and Loss Account or in Balance sheet;
- EVA system removes all the inconsistencies resulting from the application of various financial measures for different corporate functions;
- A concept of EVA is considered to be the best corporate governance system;
- EVA can be worked out for each product brand separately over a period of time. Thus it helps in brand valuation;
- Concept of EVA is quite useful in strategy or policy formulation;
- EVA can be used to measure not only the overall performance of a company but also the divisional performance;
- EVA helps the investors in evaluating the performance of the company and monitoring their investments;
- Managers are encouraged to make profitable investment since they are being evaluated on EVA target rather than the Return on Investment;
- EVA is appealing to developing companies that need to fund their projects through satisfying the value enhancement requirements of investors;
- EVA motivates the managers as it instills both the sense of urgency and long term perspective of an owner as in EVA the cash bonus plans that cause managers to think like and act like owners because they are paid like owners;

- EVA eliminates economic distortions of GAAP to focus decisions on real economic results;
- EVA decouples bonus plans from budgetary targets;
- EVA covers all aspects of business cycle.

EVA of two merging or amalgamating companies is a very vital and interesting aspect to analyse, as it influences the earning ratios of the two corporates. EVA becomes an indicative parameter for corporate valuation for the final purpose of merger or amalgamation. EVA could also be directing factor for a firm and its owners decide on withdrawal from certain business to activity and diversify to some thing much better.

LIMITATIONS

— Financial measurements show the outcomes on the operational side. However a number of non-financial measures are also important from the point of the overall growth of the company. These must be included in the performance reports of the companies. Balance scorecard to be designed by a company to keep its performance level up.

— Companies having different divisions need to develop an entrepreneurial atmosphere as well as a spirit of common goal among its employees. EVA, though helps in promoting the former goal, is only at par with other measurements as far as encouraging a common goal in different divisions of a company is concerned.

— The measure of EVA does not seem to get well with certain industries. The new high growth companies, which have a potential to rise in the future, like those in technology and biotechnology sectors will not be able to explain the negative year-on-year changes in EVA, since the growth in these cases, many times, depends on the future cash flows.

— During times of inflation EVA fails to serve as an appropriate measure.

— The most serious shortcoming of EVA is that while it helps firms in achieving higher business unit efficiency, it does not encourage collaborative relationship between business unit managers.

— EVA is not a perfect measure. It is a better measure than conventional measures like EPS, PAT, and RONW.

— EVA is an absolute measure and so its use for comparison between firms becomes difficult.

EVA COMPUTATION IN PRACTICE

During the 1990s, EVA was promoted most heavily by Stern Stewart, a New York based consulting firm. The firm's founders Joel Stern and Bennett Stewart became the foremost evangelists for the measure. Their success spawned a whole host of imitators from other consulting firms, all of which were variants on the excess return measure. Stern Stewart, in the process of applying this measure to real firms found that it had to modify accounting measures of earnings and capital to get more realistic estimates of surplus value. Bennett Stewart, in his book titled "The Quest for Value" mentioned some of the adjustments that should be made to capital invested including adjusting for goodwill (recorded and unrecorded). He also suggested adjustments that need to be made to operating income including the conversion of operating losses into financial expenses.

Problems in Measuring EVA

- Projects with long gestation periods and uncertain return will lower EVA.
- Any new investment on assets will keep down EVA till that asset becomes fully productive. Due to this, the management will prefer to postpone such capital investment on short term thinking. This will make harmful effects on the performance of a company over a long period.
- In order to enhance value and improve EVA, the companies may go for buy back of shares or selling unproductive assets. Any iniquity of these acts, may worsen the existing position of the company.

ANALYSIS OF EVA

The concept of EVA is well established in financial economics but only recently this term has moved into the main stream of corporate finance, as more and more companies have started adopting it as the base for business planning and financial performance monitoring. There is grouping evidence that EVA, not Earnings Before Interest and Taxes (EBIT), determines the value of a firm. Effective use of capital is the key to value.

The present chapter examines in detail the EVA of sample companies. Ranking has been done with respect to EVA, NOPAT, WACC, EPS, MVA and ROCE. Trends in respect of these variables are analysed on the basis of 2005-06 data. Various statistical measures like mean, standard deviation, range, variance, skewness and kurtosis have been computed to understand the central tendency and dispersion of EVA, NOPAT and WACC of sample companies. Correlation matrices for the same have been computed for the whole sample and for the sub-groups.

Paired 't' test has been used in which the same subject experiences both levels of the variable of interest. Kendall tau-b has been used to test the association between the select financial variables. Multiple regression using backward method has been adopted to find out the best predictor from among independent variables. Discriminant analysis that creates a regression formula to maximally discriminate between levels of categorical dependent variable has been applied. Chi-square test that makes comparison between two or more samples on the observed frequency of values with the expected frequency of values have been used to estimate the relationship between observed EVA and expected EVA.

EVA based frequency distribution of sample companies is shown by Table No. 5.1 (a) and 5.1 (b). (*see on page No. 132 and 133*)

It is clear from the Table 5.1 (a) that during the first five years of the study period, 57.84 per cent in 1996-97, 28.43 per cent in 1997-98, 84.31 per cent in 1998-99, 13.73 per cent in 1999-2000 and 18.63 per cent in 2000-01 have registered negative EVA. Looking at the Table 5.1(b) it is inferred that around 55 per cent to 90 per cent of the sample companies have registered negative EVA.

Around 10 per cent to 40 per cent of the companies during the first five years of the study period and around 9 per cent to 25 per cent of the sample companies during the last five years under study are generating positive EVA, but it has been upto Rs. 3 Crores.

Table 5.1 (a)

EVA – Frequency Distribution of Sample Companies (1996-97 to 2000-01)

EVA	*No. of Companies*									
	2000-01	%	*1999-00*	%	*1998-99*	%	*1997-98*	%	*1996-97*	%
Negative	19	18.63	14	13.73	86	84.31	29	28.43	59	57.84
Upto Rs. 3 Cr	35	34.31	38	37.25	10	9.80	45	44.12	35	34.31
Rs. 3 to Rs. 6 Cr	11	10.78	13	12.75	2	1.96	11	10.78	2	1.96
Rs. 6 to Rs. 10 Cr	5	4.90	3	2.94	1	0.98	5	4.90	2	1.96
Above Rs. 10 Cr	32	31.37	34	33.33	3	2.94	12	11.76	4	3.92
	102	**100.00**	**102**	**100.00**	**102**	**100.00**	**102**	**100.00**	**102**	**100.00**

Table No. 5.1 (b)

EVA – Frequency Distribution of Sample Companies (2001-02 to 2005-06)

EVA	*No. of Companies*									
	2005-06	%	*2004-05*	%	*2003-04*	%	*2002-03*	%	*2001-02*	%
Negative	75	73.53	84	82.35	72	70.59	91	89.22	59	57.84
Upto Rs. 3 Cr	26	25.49	15	14.71	10	9.80	9	8.82	15	14.71
Rs. 3 to Rs. 6 Cr	1	0.98	1	0.98	2	1.96	0	0.00	4	3.92
Rs. 6 to Rs. 10 Cr	0	0.00	1	0.98	4	3.92	0	0.00	5	4.90
Above Rs. 10 Cr	0	0.00	1	0.98	14	13.73	2	1.96	19	18.63
	102	**100.00**	**102**	**100.00**	**102**	**100.00**	**102**	**100.00**	**102**	**100.00**

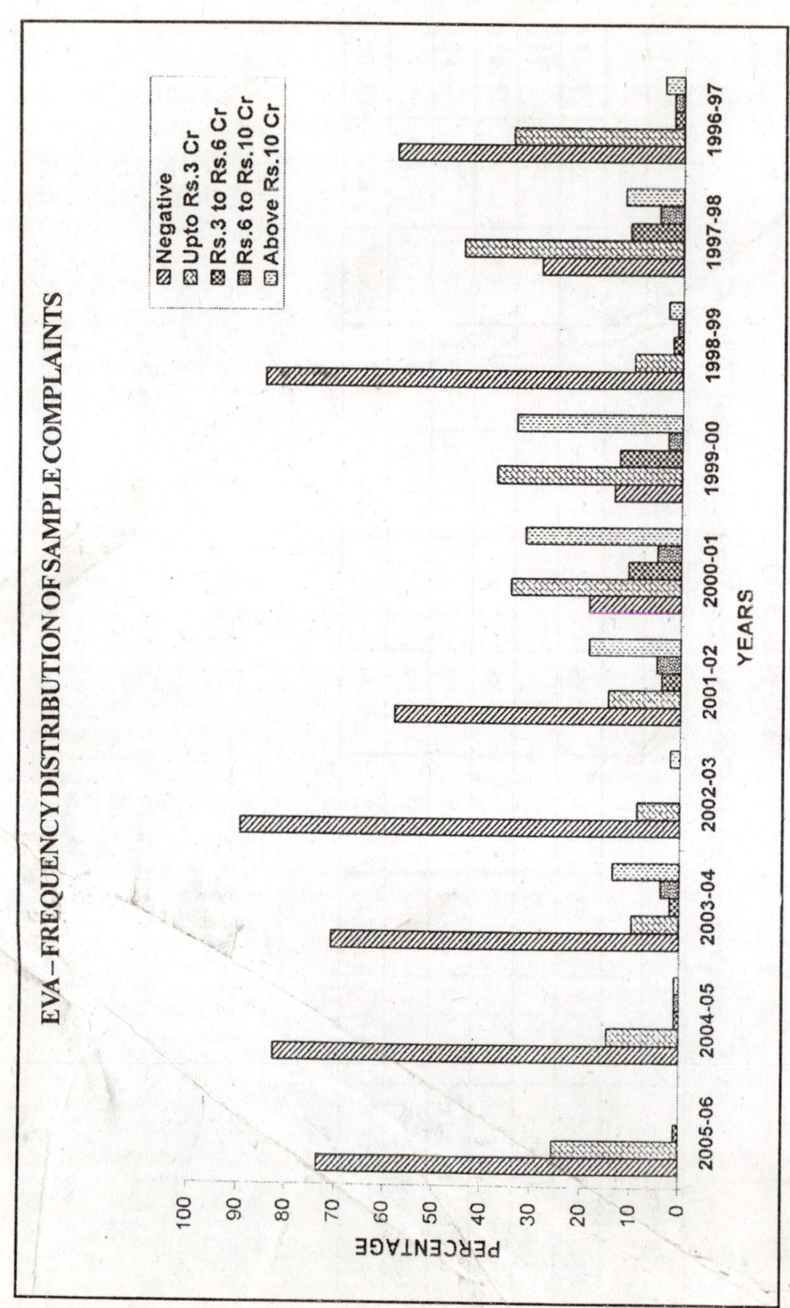
EVA – FREQUENCY DISTRIBUTION OF SAMPLE COMPLAINTS
Negative
Upto Rs.3 Cr
Rs.3 to Rs.6 Cr
Rs.6 to Rs.10 Cr
Above Rs.10 Cr
PERCENTAGE
100
90
80
70
60
50
40
30
20
10
0
2005-06
2004-05
2003-04
2002-03
2001-02
2000-01
1999-00
1998-99
1997-98
1996-97
YEARS

About 3 per cent to 33 per cent of the sample companies from 1996-97 to 2000-01 and about 1 per cent to 19 per cent of the select companies from 2001-02 to 2005-06 reported an EVA of over Rs.10 Crores. Table 5.1 (a) and 5.1 (b) (*See on page No. 132 and 133*) reveal that the number of companies generating EVA in the range of Rs.6 to Rs.10 Crores and above Rs.10 Crores has drastically come down since 2001-02.

Trends in EVA – Based Ranking

Trends in EVA of top ten and last ten (selected for the F.Y 2005-06) of the sample companies are portrayed by Table 5.2 (a) and 5.2 (b) (*see on page No. 136 and 138*) along with their EVA for the rest of the years.

The top ten companies include JETKINGQ, ICSAUIND, MANGASOF, NCCFIN, DIGITALEQP, ABACUS, BRELS, ESERVE, EUROSOFT and GTL. Out of these top ten companies, one company namely, DIGITALEQP belongs to large sector and another named ICSAIND belongs to converts and the rest are from Small – Medium sector. Among the last ten companies four companies namely, I-Flex, INFOSYS, SATYAM, WIPRO are from the large group, and one company named MASCONGLO belongs to converts and the rest belong to Small-Medium group. In four out of ten years INFOSYS, SATYAM and WIPRO have been holding the first three ranks. However in the years 2004-05 and 2005-06 their EVA performance is quite discouraging.

TRENDS IN NOPAT – BASED RANKING

Table 5.3 (a) and 5.3 (b) (*see on page No. 140 and 142*) presents the trends in the NOPAT of top ten and last ten software companies (selection on the basis of 2005-06 data).

Among the top ten companies, six companies are from the large group holding the first five and also the eighth rank and the remaining four companies belong to small-medium group; seven of the ten companies among the last ten belong to Small-Medium group. Companies namely INFOSYS, WIPRO, SATYAM, I-FLEX and TECHM come under the first eleven ranks in eight out of the ten years of the study period indicating their consistent and good performance.

Table 5.2 (a)

Trends in EVA – Leaders and Laggers

(Rs. in Crores)

Top and Last Ten Companies	*R1*	*05-06*	*R2*	*04-05*	*R3*	*03-04*	*R4*	*02-03*	*R5*	*01-02*
JETKING Q	1	3.08	5	1.51	26	1.49	7	0.72	29	1.43
ICSAIND	2	1.39	26	-0.53	44	-0.32	38	-3.37	50	-0.21
MANGASOF	3	0.82	6	0.66	41	-0.28	5	1.67	64	-0.78
NCCFIN	4	0.58	7	0.41	30	0.26	6	0.93	73	-1.26
DIGITALEQP	5	NA	9	NA	7	52.58	94	-275.54	6	92.17
ABACUS.	6	NA	10	NA	43	-0.29	19	-0.59	53	-0.24
BRELS	7	NA	64	-9.24	73	-2.84	65	-15.50	70	-1.17
ESERVE.	8	NA	11	NA	9	37.25	2	18.24	19	10.42
EUROSOFT.	9	NA	80	-32.16	87	-8.13	79	-56.83	36	0.30
GTL	10	NA	12	NA	4	126.53	1	1384.19	102	-100.03

(Contd...)

Top and Last Ten Companies	*R1*	*05-06*	*R2*	*04-05*	*R3*	*03-04*	*R4*	*02-03*	*R5*	*01-02*
MASCONGLO	93	-156.19	88	-74.55	98	-24.86	91	-207.72	14	14.68
TELEDATA	94	-212.73	4	2.31	81	-5.76	11	NA	20	9.78
MPHASIS	95	-217.70	99	-235.38	8	38.20	98	-783.67	10	27.48
AFTEK LTD	96	-218.89	93	-117.71	19	5.07	90	-183.74	9	31.18
HINDTMT	97	-252.02	98	-190.91	17	7.35	95	-335.50	8	39.48
I-FLEX	98	-357.30	100	-250.41	6	53.90	96	-383.87	5	108.32
ROLTA	99	-358.84	94	-136.80	14	10.72	93	-243.48	43	NA
INFOSYS	100	-549.23	95	-145.15	1	837.87	99	-957.96	2	726.50
SATYAM	101	-940.63	101	-714.96	3	203.01	101	-1374.40	3	389.86
WIPRO	102	-1313.28	102	-803.96	2	425.87	102	-1897.35	1	792.73

Table 5.2 (b)

Trends in EVA – Leaders and Laggers

(Rs. in Crores)

Top and Last Ten Companies	*R6*	*00-01*	*R7*	*99-00*	*R8*	*98-99*	*R9*	*97-98*	*R10*	*96-97*
JETKING Q	57	1.16	69	0.69	13	0.11	56	0.05	23	0.22
ICSAIND	56	1.49	61	1.10	58	-2.48	46	0.42	90	-1.24
MANGASOF	97	-1.49	98	-1.09	9	0.81	93	-1.08	67	-0.43
NCCFIN	98	-2.19	101	-2.25	66	-3.02	82	-0.15	52	-0.15
DIGITALEQP	11	106.31	11	61.66	93	-32.17	4	65.72	9	2.56
ABACUS.	87	-0.20	93	-0.14	32	-0.82	85	-0.24	82	-0.70
BRELS	45	3.35	43	4.76	79	-7.44	26	3.53	53	-0.16
ESERVE.	47	3.28	55	2.07	57	-2.40	96	-2.12	74	-0.59
EUROSOFT.	29	12.25	25	16.65	95	-39.49	12	13.35	16	1.43
GTL	102	-176.44	102	-110.51	2	275.75	102	-47.86	2	25.03

(Contd...)

Top and Last Ten Companies	*R6*	*00-01*	*R7*	*99-00*	*R8*	*98-99*	*R9*	*97-98*	*R10*	*96-97*
MASCONGLO	83	NA	10	88.47	48	-1.60	39	0.99	42	NA
TELEDATA	38	5.80	35	8.85	40	-1.22	40	0.88	60	-0.30
MPHASIS	6	213.17	26	16.09	85	-14.95	101	-12.65	22	0.35
AFTEK LTD	15	51.72	19	31.95	81	-10.65	23	4.17	78	-0.61
HINDTMT	10	130.04	12	60.91	100	-109.78	5	47.16	102	-28.04
I-FLEX	8	161.21	8	108.72	92	-27.38	73	NA	43	NA
ROLTA	7	178.43	5	156.63	99	-89.30	3	74.29	21	0.58
INFOSYS	2	845.21	1	444.10	102	-202.63	2	85.24	3	18.19
SATYAM	3	650.61	3	211.51	97	-42.02	7	38.49	15	1.55
WIPRO	1	1085.63	2	436.60	1	500.35	1	171.24	99	-9.12

Table 5.3 (a)

Trends in NOPAT – Leaders and Laggers

(Rs. in Crores)

Top and Last Ten Companies	*R1*	*2005-06*	*R2*	*2004-05*	*R3*	*2003-04*	*R4*	*2002-03*	*R5*	*2001-02*
INFOSYS	1	2422.00	1	1905.00	1	1244.22	1	958.68	2	808.67
WIPRO	2	2023.61	2	1500.39	2	918.04	2	816.16	1	869.00
SATYAM	3	1242.47	3	751.02	3	556.54	3	308.14	3	458.98
I-FLEX	4	240.08	4	197.64	4	175.88	4	174.37	4	127.02
TECHM	5	220.12	9	71.09	8	94.13	5	171.54	5	126.28
ROLTA	6	155.74	5	120.45	9	93.08	6	142.02	64	NA
TELEDATA	7	125.17	8	76.27	28	5.22	64	NA	24	11.03
HP	8	100.33	6	110.99	5	141.92	8	106.43	8	93.06
MPHASIS	9	78.67	13	50.27	10	89.87	10	67.86	10	49.65
CRANES.	10	75.85	12	56.79	15	39.95	18	19.63	25	10.56

(Contd...)

Top and Last Ten Companies	*R1*	*2005-06*	*R2*	*2004-05*	*R3*	*2003-04*	*R4*	*2002-03*	*R5*	*2001-02*
RAMINFO	93	-0.54	66	0	95	-3.66	94	-3.35	91	-1.82
LCCINFO	94	-0.59	98	-7.57	96	-4.32	89	-2.43	61	0.01
ODYSSEY	95	-0.69	87	-0.82	92	-2.23	87	-1.77	97	-5.32
TWINSOFT	96	-0.91	91	-1.73	88	-1.42	90	-2.75	78	-0.32
CRESSAN	97	-1.96	94	-2.28	57	0.25	51	0.14	82	-0.83
ENCORE	98	-4.48	97	-5.25	89	-1.46	49	0.34	96	-4.95
IECSOF	99	-4.68	82	-0.37	98	-7.36	88	-2.03	38	2.59
ORIENTINFO	100	-5.47	26	7.75	31	4.19	100	-21.93	101	-15.21
FRONTINF	101	-6.47	62	NA	94	-3.14	61	NA	95	-4.91
RAMCOSYS	102	-20.91	101	-28.06	101	-21.01	98	-19.88	94	-2.95

Table 5.3 (b)

Trends in NOPAT – Leaders and Laggers

(Rs. in Crores)

Top and Last Ten Companies	*R6*	*2000-01*	*R7*	*1999-00*	*R8*	*1998-99*	*R9*	*1997-98*	*R10*	*1996-97*
INFOSYS	2	629.04	1	293.94	2	135.65	2	60.65	3	38.24
WIPRO	1	674.84	2	276.93	1	147.73	1	129.06	1	125.55
SATYAM	3	520.8	4	170.65	4	99.23	6	31.19	10	24.54
I-FLEX	8	110.25	10	69.27	10	50.45	68	NA	65	NA
TECHM	9	96.58	11	63.03	9	55.24	9	28.09	12	12.12
ROLTA	7	127.44	5	109.42	5	73.91	3	52.19	4	36.83
TELEDATA	45	2.01	32	6.72	44	1.04	40	0.79	42	0.51
HP	12	54.54	16	20.98	8	56.22	8	29.68	8	27.43
MPHASIS	16	21.06	63	0.84	12	25.95	102	-12.01	13	8.74
CRANES.	72	0.08	80	0.07	71	0.04	65	0.02	63	0.03

(Contd...)

Top and Last Ten Companies	*R6*	*2000-01*	*R7*	*1999-00*	*R8*	*1998-99*	*R9*	*1997-98*	*R10*	*1996-97*
RAMINFO	58	0.87	52	1.51	43	1.07	42	0.65	49	0.04
LCCINFO	31	5.52	23	11.92	72	0.03	83	NA	84	NA
ODYSSEY	63	0.37	100	-0.08	70	0.04	89	-0.01	98	-0.66
TWINSOFT	47	1.08	40	3.76	32	3.76	31	2.00	40	0.57
CRESSAN	95	-0.50	85	0.00	77	0.00	73	NA	71	NA
ENCORE	50	1.71	39	3.86	102	-3.19	82	0.00	83	NA
IECSOF	34	4.24	46	2.48	46	0.97	45	0.04	53	0.28
ORIENTINFO	18	20.24	25	10.53	25	5.38	24	2.85	33	1.37
FRONTINF	37	3.54	45	2.94	41	1.29	35	1.03	38	0.85
RAMCOSYS	35	3.87	27	10.24	81	0.00	78	NA	78	NA

TRENDS IN WACC – BASED RANKING

Table 5.4 (a) and 5.4 (b) delineates the trends in WACC of top ten and last ten (selected as per 2005-06 data on WACC) software companies.

Table 5.4 (a)

Trends in WACC – Leaders and Laggers

(In Percentage)

Top and Last Ten Companies	*R1*	*2005-06*	*R2*	*2004-05*	*R3*	*2003-04*	*R4*	*2002-03*	*R5*	*2001-02*
ADVENT	1	369.22	1	307.31	1	67.91	1	619.49	102	-36.64
MICROTECH	2	65.17	4	59.85	5	16.11	5	101.74	94	1.29
MPHASIS	3	56.25	7	50.48	10	14.57	8	87.87	91	2.46
AFTEK LTD	4	53.77	24	38.73	7	15.19	7	93.73	92	1.99
TECHM	5	52.73	9	47.07	12	14.07	11	82.07	90	2.08
SATYAM	6	51.57	10	46.51	16	13.65	12	79.81	89	2.98
CSSOFT	7	51.38	8	47.94	8	14.91	10	82.94	88	3.09
ROLTA	8	50.32	31	36.65	46	11.3	37	56.77	98	NA
ORIENTINFO	9	50.28	11	45.53	14	13.67	13	78.78	88	3.09
INFOSYS	10	50.23	12	45.43	15	13.66	14	78.14	80	3.57

(Contd...)

Top and Last Ten Companies	R1	2005-06	R2	2004-05	R3	2003-04	R4	2002-03	R5	2001-02
SVAMSOFT	93	NA	28	37.28	32	12.02	29	63.62	68	4.35
VIRTUALS	94	NA	102	-198.93	99	2.03	94	2.55	38	6.74
CORCOMP	95	NA	100	-11.98	102	-8.19	98	-1.74	99	-0.69
MILLENCY	96	NA	96	NA	64	9.59	61	38.23	46	6.03
NETVISTA	97	NA	73	13.91	85	7.69	73	23.93	45	6.07
OMEGAIN	98	NA	83	7.93	92	6.76	91	10.12	19	8.16
SRGINFO	99	NA	61	21.14	66	9.19	64	34.27	43	6.33
TRILLENT	100	NA	97	NA	96	4.32	99	-10.02	4	11.03
CRESSAN	101	-5.26	98	-7.53	98	3.27	100	-18.81	17	8.24
MAGNUM	102	-11.99	99	-9.98	97	3.47	78	22.25	6	10.75

Table 5.4 (b)

Trends in WACC – Leaders and Laggers

(In Percentage)

Top and Last Ten Companies	*R6*	*2000-01*	*R7*	*1999-00*	*R8*	*1998-99*	*R9*	*1997-98*	*R10*	*1996-97*
ADVENT	102	-234.21	30	NA	1	499.99	102	-205.05	1	90.17
MICROTECH	98	-30.44	98	-31.42	6	85.05	29	3.94	44	15.06
MPHASIS	94	-23.73	95	-27.38	9	76.46	27	4.73	4	30.17
AFTEK LTD	96	-26.18	97	-29.85	7	82.41	93	-15.85	10	21.44
TECHM	92	-21.77	94	-25.04	10	72.01	97	-20.03	13	19.98
SATYAM	91	-20.44	84	-19.28	101	-42.58	68	-5.58	12	20.27
CSSOFT	93	-22.79	93	-24.95	96	NA	96	-18.81	94	NA
ROLTA	61	-9.68	61	-11.63	35	50.62	78	-8.58	26	17.92
ORIENTINFO	90	-20.09	92	-22.68	16	63.01	86	-10.89	35	16.54
INFOSYS	73	-13.18	48	-6.37	60	34.02	62	-3.27	25	17.96

(Contd...)

Top and Last Ten Companies	*R6*	*2000-01*	*R7*	*1999-00*	*R8*	*1998-99*	*R9*	*1997-98*	*R10*	*1996-97*
SVAMSOFT	76	-14.06	74	-15.06	30	53.11	85	-10.71	30	17.73
VIRTUALS	9	8.52	8	12.38	93	7.38	12	10.38	79	9.31
CORCOMP	36	-0.56	32	NA	94	6.07	13	9.81	80	9.03
MILLENCY	45	-4.11	15	5.15	58	34.72	60	-3.09	53	13.72
NETVISTA	34	NA	28	0.24	87	15.53	40	0.96	83	8.04
OMEGAIN	12	7.15	12	7.35	90	11.05	17	7.79	77	9.77
SRGINFO	35	NA	40	-3.35	62	31.38	57	-1.43	62	12.54
TRILLENT	7	15.13	5	17.06	97	-0.06	5	16.97	73	10.02
CRESSAN	3	20.27	3	23.81	99	-19.66	47	NA	93	NA
MAGNUM	4	20.15	4	21.51	98	-15.77	4	20.27	84	5.52

Table 5.4(a) and 5.4 (b) (*See on page No. 144 and 146*) evince that, among the top ten companies only three companies namely INFOSYS, SATYAM and TECHM belong to large group and the next seven companies belong to Small – Medium group. Six out of last ten companies belong to converts group and the rest four companies namely SVAMSOFT, VIRTUALS, CRESSAN and MAGNUM belong to Small – Medium group. Fluctuating trend was found among the companies ranked on the basis of WACC. Among the top ten companies, ADVENT (Small-Medium group) holds the first rank in six out of the ten years of the study.

Trends in EPS – Based Ranking

It is evinced from the Tables 5.5 (a) and 5.5 (b) (*See on page 149 and 151*) that the EPS of top ten and last ten (selected as per 2005-06 data) software companies showed a fluctuating trend.

From the Table 5.5(a) and 5.5(b), it is inferred that the top ten companies include six large companies, three small-medium companies and one namely ICSAIND which belong to converts group. The last ten companies comprise nine from converts group and only one from Small-Medium group. INFOSYS holds first rank in six out of the ten years of the study and remains among the top 4 in the rest of the years.

Trends in MVA – Based Ranking

Table No. 5.6 (a) and 5.6 (b) (*See on page 153 and 155*) contain the trends in the ranking of MVA of top ten and last ten companies (selected as per 2005-06 data).

Top ten companies such as INFOSYS, WIPRO and SATYAM hold the first three ranks in the last four years of the study period. Six from the large segment and four from the Small – Medium group form the top ten list. Among the last ten list, seven companies belong to Small – Medium and three belong to converts.

Trends in ROCE – Based Ranking

Table 5.7 (a) and 5.7 (b) (*See on page 157 and 159*) puts forward the trends in ROCE based ranking (selected as per 2005-06 data). Five companies among the top ten list belong to Small – Medium group and three companies from large group and only two from the converts. Nine out of the last ten category belong to Small – Medium group and only one belongs to converts.

Table 5.5 (a)

Trends in EPS – Leaders and Laggers

(Amount in Rupees)

Top and Last Ten Companies	*R1*	*2005-06*	*R2*	*2004-05*	*R3*	*2003-04*	*R4*	*2002-03*	*R5*	*2001-02*
INFOSYS	1	81.41	1	68.96	1	170.01	1	142.76	1	121.32
WIPRO	2	45.03	7	20.55	4	35.59	5	34.84	4	37.26
SATYAM	3	37.22	6	22.85	16	17.06	22	9.49	14	14.24
I-FLEX	4	30.85	5	25.69	9	23.08	2	46.04	3	37.33
HP	5	29.51	4	32.05	3	41.65	6	31.57	8	28.31
ICSAIND	6	24.68	21	6.72	43	0.76	50	0.18	97	0.00
JETKINGQ	7	21.12	16	11.02	15	17.37	17	14.65	12	15.96
TECHM	8	19.76	22	6.07	21	8.81	12	16.64	19	12.33
INFOTECENT	9	18.33	14	14.94	23	8.24	11	18.27	5	35.06
KPITCUMM	10	18.31	11	15.85	10	21.21	20	11.35	29	3.84

(Contd...)

Top and Last Ten Companies	R1	2005-06	R2	2004-05	R3	2003-04	R4	2002-03	R5	2001-02
CORCOMP	93	0	93	0	92	0	94	0	94	0
ENCORE	94	0	94	0	94	0	45	0.46	96	0
IECSOF	95	0	95	0	95	0	96	0	39	1.93
LCCINFO	96	0	96	0	96	0	97	0	98	0
MILLENCY	97	0	97	NA	98	0	99	0	99	0
NETVISTA	98	0	98	0	30	2.59	26	4.14	31	3.69
OMEGAIN	99	0	99	0	99	0	100	0	100	0
SRGINFO	100	0	100	0	100	0	101	0	101	0
TRILLENT	101	0	102	NA	102	0	102	0	102	0
SOFTSOL	102	-1.64	47	0.19	54	0.17	33	1.82	35	2.68

Table No. 5.5 (b)

Trends in EPS – Leaders and Laggers

(Amount in Rupees)

Top and Last Ten Companies	*R6*	*2000-01*	*R7*	*1999-00*	*R8*	*1998-99*	*R9*	*1997-98*	*R10*	*1996-97*
INFOSYS	2	93.73	4	43.87	3	40.54	2	37.24	1	50.94
WIPRO	7	28.06	22	10.68	11	21.16	6	18.54	2	41.33
SATYAM	10	17.17	13	22.86	7	27.68	17	7.18	18	7.06
I-FLEX	4	65.87	1	82.07	1	123.64	62	NA	65	NA
HP	16	16.34	31	8.06	18	13.96	15	8.22	15	7.56
ICSAIND	53	1.04	64	0.06	65	0.08	98	0.00	97	0.00
JETKINGQ	21	10.61	32	7.14	37	2.69	43	0.77	30	2.97
TECHM	23	9.24	9	32.29	6	28.35	1	59.46	5	24.75
INFOTECENT	8	27.92	14	17.22	20	11.39	27	4.45	17	7.02
KPITCUMM	24	8.73	91	0.00	30	6.04	25	5.01	34	2.63

(Contd...)

Top and Last Ten Companies	*R6*	*2000-01*	*R7*	*1999-00*	*R8*	*1998-99*	*R9*	*1997-98*	*R10*	*1996-97*
CORCOMP	98	0	101	NA	101	0	95	0	94	0
ENCORE	39	3.29	35	5.73	102	0	97	0	96	NA
IECSOF	33	5.07	45	3	43	1.47	47	0.51	47	0.49
LCCINFO	48	2.12	36	5.71	70	0.03	99	NA	98	NA
MILLENCY	69	0.01	69	0.34	69	0.03	100	0	100	0
NETVISTA	100	NA	43	3.48	60	0.37	61	0.01	101	0
OMEGAIN	67	0.22	24	10.52	56	0.58	55	0.01	56	0.13
SRGINFO	101	NA	76	0.17	52	0.75	48	0.47	64	0.02
TRILLENT	102	0	71	0.28	62	0.21	102	0	62	0.04
SOFTSOL	25	8.55	25	9.72	2	52.02	3	33.06	7	18.04

Table No. 5.6 (a)

Trends in MVA – Leaders and Laggers

(Rupees in Crores)

Top and Last Ten Companies	*R1*	*2005-06*	*R2*	*2004-05*	*R3*	*2003-04*	*R4*	*2002-03*	*R5*	*2001-02*
INFOSYS	1	6103.41	1	5507.72	1	11290.97	1	1299.01	3	2356.93
WIPRO	2	4497.94	2	3718.36	2	7801.46	2	1030.85	2	3159.84
SATYAM	3	2750.38	3	1809.33	3	4769.71	3	405.32	8	1379.25
CRANES	4	697.82	6	272.85	13	355.71	11	43.76	27	124.77
I-FLEX	5	471.98	4	470.03	4	1656.65	10	72.03	1	3546.1
TECHM	6	398.83	10	131.52	7	732.81	5	210.83	14	573.31
TELEDATA	7	275.91	9	155.81	28	15.05	20	NA	24	263.76
ROLTA	8	210.29	7	268.05	6	843.56	6	199.39	44	NA
HP	9	124.33	8	219.97	5	1184.88	8	120.18	5	1978.74
FINTECH	10	119.88	23	5.44	19	97.38	29	-4.89	99	-239.32

(Contd...)

Top and Last Ten Companies	R1	2005-06	R2	2004-05	R3	2003-04	R4	2002-03	R5	2001-02
CALIFSOFT	93	-51.07	90	-50.34	88	-47.14	82	-50.44	34	19.16
ORIENTINFO	94	-55.92	88	-46.51	83	-28.57	92	-90.25	102	-573.06
INFOTECENTE	95	-57.67	87	-43.46	30	10.64	85	-51.74	19	322.26
IECSOF	96	-75.91	81	-28.93	100	-150.84	80	-48.25	47	-0.97
DANLAW	97	-82.07	98	-84.77	95	-89.78	93	-92.66	97	-132.15
MICROTECH	98	-82.33	94	-58.13	90	-60.87	90	-76.06	18	379.00
VISUALSOFT	99	-89.26	93	-55.69	16	184.34	83	-50.74	12	697.05
FRONTINF	100	-90.52	35	NA	92	-66.75	19	NA	92	-90.78
RAMCO	101	-191.02	101	-252.57	101	-405.38	99	-319.02	101	-362.87
ENCORE	102	-1852.97	84	-34.21	85	-31.58	58	-16.34	94	-103.71

Table 5.6 (b)

Trends in MVA – Leaders and Laggers

(Rupees in Crores)

Top and Last Ten Companies	*R6*	*2000-01*	*R7*	*1999-00*	*R8*	*1998-99*	*R9*	*1997-98*	*R10*	*1996-97*
INFOSYS	102	-4731.03	101	-1977.45	5	95.06	95	-573.16	8	89.31
WIPRO	100	-3866.12	98	-1722.61	100	-450.72	102	-2460.95	3	461.04
SATYAM	101	-4128.83	102	-2835.04	1	240.76	100	-1148.03	6	124.12
CRANES	55	-26.45	54	-23.77	70	-16.86	64	-18.63	90	-14.75
I-FLEX	97	-895.17	92	-642.52	99	-233.57	13	NA	26	NA
TECHM	92	-568.03	88	-375.77	6	43.06	91	-249.39	12	43.94
TELEDATA	60	-40.95	66	-61.97	78	-22.84	81	-61.49	87	-12.65
ROLTA	98	-1463.59	96	-1006.68	4	109.86	96	-621.16	5	179.52
HP	96	-614.24	82	-228.23	3	114.09	97	-631.86	4	197.52
FINTECH	66	-65.82	36	-10.32	69	-16.16	67	-21.64	97	-28.71

(Contd...)

Top and Last Ten Companies	*R6*	*2000-01*	*R7*	*1999-00*	*R8*	*1998-99*	*R9*	*1997-98*	*R10*	*1996-97*
CALIFSOFT	68	-69.86	63	-53.19	83	-33.01	74	-45.42	94	-19.74
ORIENTINFO	80	-194.51	73	-108.29	68	-14.93	76	-42.61	43	-3.96
INFOTECENTE	85	-247.69	78	-168.27	74	-18.39	75	-48.57	41	-2.69
IECSOF	8	35.97	12	12.89	19	-4.09	30	-4.34	51	-7.75
DANLAW	74	-127.07	72	-102.43	48	-10.11	21	NA	37	NA
MICROTECH	71	-84.28	65	-58.62	91	-56.64	32	-4.63	64	-9.99
VISUALSOFT	90	-413.71	84	-290.08	66	-13.39	71	-33.81	58	-8.35
FRONTINF	9	25.97	11	17.19	16	-2.83	25	-2.06	44	-4.29
RAMCO	89	-403.85	91	-454.08	44	-10.00	20	NA	36	NA
ENCORE	63	-46.22	68	-70.77	49	-10.20	45	-10.00	38	NA

Table No. 5.7 (a)

Trends in ROCE—Leaders and Laggers

(in percentage)

Top and Last Ten Companies	*R1*	*2005-06*	*R2*	*2004-05*	*R3*	*2003-04*	*R4*	*2002-03*	*R5*	*2001-02*
ENCORE	1	608.97	96	-135.77	91	-16.65	43	2.73	97	-46.96
JETKINGQ	2	46.64	4	36.61	5	37.63	7	38.46	4	54.21
ICSAIND	3	46.13	5	33.33	35	6.67	48	1.69	64	0.00
TECHM	4	36.82	23	14.72	13	21.62	5	45.33	10	38.58
INFOSYS	5	35.10	3	36.32	4	38.22	9	33.49	8	38.84
DATASOFT	6	34.29	101	-352.17	86	-11.06	99	-136.36	81	-8.26
WIPRO	7	31.47	7	30.55	11	26.08	15	24.42	11	34.20
ASIANCE	8	31.00	24	14.55	30	8.81	57	0.67	90	-19.80
FINTECH	9	30.85	38	7.15	12	22.73	28	12.21	92	-28.22
TERA SOFT	10	30.46	10	26.38	22	16.89	34	6.58	49	2.95

(Contd...)

Top and Last Ten Companies	*R1*	*2005-06*	*R2*	*2004-05*	*R3*	*2003-04*	*R4*	*2002-03*	*R5*	*2001-02*
CONTECH	93	-19.15	100	-224.40	95	-25.87	92	-24.45	51	2.61
RAMCO	94	-19.41	89	-27.70	89	-13.11	89	-12.83	77	-3.61
FRONTINF	95	-23.52	64	0.00	85	-10.41	63	0.00	84	-12.74
PSI	96	-37.47	92	-38.53	100	-167.84	101	-381.01	98	-56.89
INFDS	97	-42.86	88	-24.00	96	-33.87	88	-12.05	86	-15.05
ODYSSEY	98	-47.74	98	-173.58	102	-218.45	96	-58.03	101	-114.32
IECSOF	99	-50.99	79	-3.80	97	-45.37	85	-11.80	40	5.05
CRESSAN	100	-69.59	93	-48.39	48	2.84	52	1.25	85	-12.69
MIDPOINT	101	-130.77	83	-6.67	80	-4.17	78	-7.00	78	-3.74
NCCFIN	102	-288.89	91	-32.86	93	-18.28	95	-44.34	1	129.82

Table No. 5.7 (b)

Trends in ROCE—Leaders and Laggers

(in percentage)

Top and Last Ten Companies	*R6*	*2000-01*	*R7*	*1999-00*	*R8*	*1998-99*	*R9*	*1997-98*	*R10*	*1996-97*
ENCORE	45	10.22	23	26.46	101	-238.06	68	0.00	85	0.00
JETKINGQ	3	56.28	1	60.33	14	33.33	29	14.58	3	60.00
ICSAIND	36	13.11	59	6.44	65	0.91	87	-3.89	96	-9.63
TECHM	8	41.38	8	43.19	5	59.30	3	60.91	4	54.77
INFOSYS	6	45.25	17	35.22	21	23.55	11	34.90	13	33.03
DATASOFT	96	-16.10	80	0.31	58	3.40	63	0.00	88	-0.96
WIPRO	13	35.61	11	38.76	19	27.28	23	19.80	26	17.30
ASIANCE	52	7.00	99	-22.32	99	-59.12	72	0.00	42	7.82
FINTECH	38	12.64	82	0.00	72	0.20	57	0.60	101	-51.82
TERA SOFT	46	9.67	74	1.84	41	10.81	38	10.00	70	0.00

(Contd...)

Top and Last Ten Companies	R6	2000-01	R7	1999-00	R8	1998-99	R9	1997-98	R10	1996-97
CONTECH	47	9.46	30	20.50	44	10.12	40	7.67	28	16.10
RAMCO	73	0.36	78	0.33	78	0.00	78	0.00	83	0.00
FRONTINF	51	7.16	60	5.87	51	5.59	54	1.16	58	1.06
PSI	83	0.00	4	50.96	7	52.44	10	36.81	18	23.79
INFDS	101	-124.30	87	0.00	91	-18.27	97	-32.93	81	0.00
ODYSSEY	56	6.45	97	-14.90	64	1.12	88	-7.34	100	-36.32
IECSOF	37	12.89	52	8.94	39	11.62	47	4.60	94	4.61
CRESSAN	92	-5.87	81	0.00	74	0.00	76	0.00	79	0.00
MIDPOINT	97	-33.33	98	-15.54	92	-19.19	98	-38.24	99	-30.14
NCCFIN	102	-631.43	102	-89.74	93	-19.65	90	-8.37	35	12.19

The average of the all select variables namely, EVA, NOPAT, WACC, EPS, MVA, ROCE, ROS, ROTA, SVA and Turnover have been computed for all the 102 sample companies and Table 5.8 (a) and 5.8 (b) (*See on page No. 162 and 163*) exhibits the top 10 corporates on the basis of these parameters. Except WACC all other variables have positive influence on shareholders wealth. It is found that among the biggies, INFOSYS, DIGITALEQP, TECHM, HP and WIPRO remain in the toppers list in most of the wealth related variables. It is to be noted that INFOSYS emerges as a leader, as it finds place in rank lists pertaining to all parameters barring WACC. It implies that WACC of INFOSYS is not very high considering the competitors. WIPRO, HP and DIGITALEQP are among the toppers in respect of eight out of nine positive variables. Further, it is to be noted that HP is the only company in the large category to be listed in the WACC toppers.

TECHM records its position as one among the top ten on account of seven positive variables. I-FLEX among the large group and HEXAWARE belonging to small-medium group of companies remain as a topper in six out of ten selected variables.

Table 5.9 (a) and 5.9 (b) (*See on page 164 and 165*) shows the last 10 ranks of the sampled companies with regard to the select financial variables. It is inferred from Table No. 5.9 that SRGINFO (Converts) lags in EVA, NOPAT, MVA, ROS and SVA. Among the biggies, WIPRO, IFLEX and SATHYAM occupied last ten list in terms of EVA. Eight corporates under small-medium group and two under converts group have positive effect with regard to WACC. It can be concluded that small-medium and converts group of companies find the place in the last ten list with respect to all selected financial variables except EVA.

RESULTS AND DISCUSSION ON STATISTICAL ANALYSIS

Different statistical measures have been computed for understanding the central tendency and dispersion of EVA, NOPAT and WACC of sample companies. For this purpose, statistics value of the mean, range, standard deviation, variance, skewness and kurtosis have been computed. Kurtosis and Skewness have been calculated to show about the distribution (Symmetric/Asymmetric).

Table 5.8 (a)

Ranking based on ten year average of select financial variables (Top 10 Companies)

EVA		*NOPAT*		*WACC*		*EPS*		*MVA*	
Name of the Company	*Rs. in Cr*	*Name of the Company*	*Rs. in Cr*	*Name of the Company*	*(In %)*	*Name of the Company*	*Rs.*	*Name of the Company*	*Rs. in Cr*
GTL	172.08	INFOSYS	1062.06	ADVENT	164.24	INFOSYS	85.1	INFOSYS	1946.01
INFOSYS	110.21	WIPRO	748.22	MICROTECH	28.69	I-FLEX	54.5	WIPRO	1216.09
HEXAWARE	12.52	SATYAM	416.36	MPHASIS	27.19	WIPRO	29.4	I-FLEX	555.76
DIGITALEQP	9.16	GTL	157.43	SINDUVA	26.13	GTL	28.4	GENESYS	467.32
ESERVE.	8.27	I-FLEX	114.57	ASIANCE	25.73	TECHM	21.8	SATYAM	336.66
TECHM	3.55	ROLTA	101.33	EUROSOFT	25.34	HP	21.8	HP	246.62
CRANES	3.44	TECHM	93.09	ZENSAR	24.51	GEOMETRIC	21.00	NETVISTA	211.81
HP	3.04	HP	74.16	HP	24.23	AFTEK LTD	19.6	HINDTMT	195.28
ITMICRO	1.39	DIGITALEQP	66.28	KLG	23.78	DIGITALEQP	19.5	ESERVE	177.68
JETKINGQ	1.05	HEXAWARE	42.67	AFTEK LTD	23.54	HEXAWARE	19.3	HEXAWARE	172.52

Table 5.8 (b)

Ranking based on ten year average of select financial variables (Top 10 Companies)

ROCE		*ROS*		*ROTA*		*SVA*		*TURNOVER*	
Name of the Company	*(In%)*	*Name of the Company*	*Ratio*	*Name of the Company*	*Ratio*	*Name of the Company*	*Rs. in Cr*	*Name of the Company*	*Rs. in Cr*
SOFTSOL	60.06	INFOSYS	4374.44	JETKINGQ	0.43	INFOSYS	4354	WIPRO	3965.09
JETKINGQ	43.81	WIPRO	1473.67	TECHM	0.42	WIPRO	4269	INFOSYS	3056.04
TECHM	41.66	MASTEK	1117.32	BLUESTINFO	0.04	DIGITALEQP	3399	SATYAM	1693.04
BLUESINFO	40.23	MICROTECH	988.83	ESERVE	0.38	SATYAM	1646	GTL	553.51
CORCOMP	36.69	I-FLEX	768.21	DIGITALEQP	0.35	PENTASOFT	743	TECHM	490.01
INFOSYS	35.39	AFTEK LTD	710.21	INFOSYS	0.35	TECHM	645	HP	435.55
DIGITALEQP	34.51	VISUALSOFT	618.14	HP	0.31	I-FLEX	571	DIGITALEQP	313.98
HP	30.08	DIGITALEQP	573.83	SOFTSOL	0.29	GENESYS	468	I-FLEX	295.73
SATYAM	29.16	ESERVE	494.55	MASCONGLO	0.28	HP	259	ROLTA	266.97
WIPRO	28.55	HEXAWARE	463.57	WIPRO	0.27	HINDTMT	212	HEXAWARE	253.93

Table 5.9 (a)

Ranking based on ten year average of select financial variables (Last 10 Companies)

EVA		*NOPAT*		*WACC*		*EPS*		*MVA*	
Name of the Company	*Rs. in Cr*	*Name of the Company*	*Rs. in Cr*	*Name of the Company*	*(In%)*	*Name of the Company*	*Rs.*	*Name of the Company*	*Rs. in Cr*
MASCONGLO	-45.01	CRESSAN	-0.65	CONTECH	8.33	CHOKSHIN	0.03	ORIENT INFO	-115.86
ROLTA	-45.31	SVAMSOFT	-0.77	TRILLENT	8.08	INTRAINF	0.01	CYBERTE	-136.28
PENTASOFTTE	-48.21	PAL SOFT	-0.84	EZCOM	8.01	INNOVATION	0.01	ROLTA	-142.26
SRGINFO	-49.86	VIRTUALS	-0.95	OTCO	7.02	ABACUS	0	SOFTSOL	-156.02
WIPRO	-61.13	ODYSSEY	-1.02	MAGNUM	6.62	INFDS	0	LCCINFO	-198.69
HINDTMT	-63.13	ENCORE	-1.49	GTL	2.75	MANGASOFT	0	MELSTAR	-226.27
I-FLEX	-73.35	ADVENT	-2.92	CRESSAN	0.54	MIDPOINT	0	ENCORE	-241.78
SILVERLINE	-91.62	RAMCOSYS	-7.93	CORCOMP	0.03	PIOTECH	0	RAMINFO	-299.85
MPHASIS	-96.91	SRGINFO	-19.46	PAL SOFT	-10.56	SINDUVA	0	SRGINFO	-329.75
SATYAM	-157.07	SILVERLINE	-79.47	VIRTUALS	-15.49	CORCOMP	0	GTL	-1055.2

Table 5.9 (b)

Ranking based on ten year average of select financial variables (Last 10 Companies)

ROCE		*ROS*		*ROTA*		*SVA*		*TURNOVER*	
Name of the Company	*(In%)*	*Name of the Company*	*Ratio*	*Name of the Company*	*Ratio*	*Name of the Company*	*Rs. in Cr*	*Name of the Company*	*Rs. in Cr*
MID POINT	-28.88	DYNACON	4.4814	MIDPOINT	-0.24	TRILLENT	-93.4	MILLENICY	0.495
INFDS	-37.92	VIRTUALS	4.39	VIRTUALS	-0.24	ROLTA	-124	PAL SOFT	0.353
DATASOFT	-48.69	CONTECH	4.3014	INFDS	-0.29	CYBERTE	-135	DATASOFT	0.031
PSI	-57.53	INNOVATION	3.057	NCCFIN	-0.03	SOFTSOL	-156	INNOVATION	0.288
ODYSSEY	-66.31	SRGINFO	2.668	DATASOFT	-0.41	LCCINFO	-199	ABACUS.	0.186
ADVENT	-69.89	HP	0	ENCORE	-0.42	MELSTAR	-226	CHOKSHIN	0.129
NCCFIN	-99.16	CYBERTE	0	ODYSSEY	-0.05	ENCORE	-242	INFDS	0.084
SINDUVA	-120.06	EZCOM	0	ADVENT	-0.61	RAMCOSYS	-300	MIDPOINT	0.068
SILVERLINE	-136.09	INFDS	0	PAL SOFT	-0.87	SRGINFO	-330	PIOTECH	0.039
PALSOFT	-139.02	ITMICRO	0	SINDUVA	-1.02	GTL	-1046	SINDUVA	0.016

Kurtosis is a measure of the "Peakedness" or the "flatness" of a distribution. A kurtosis value near zero (0) indicates a shape close to normal. A positive value for the kurtosis indicates a distribution more peaked than normal. A negative kurtosis indicates a shape flatter than normal. An extreme negative kurtosis (eg <-5.0) indicates a distribution where more of the values are in the tails of the distribution that around the mean. A kurtosis value between ± 1.0 is considered excellent for most psychometric purposes and a value between ± 2.0 is in many cases also acceptable.

Skewness measures to what extent a distribution of values deviates from symmetry around the mean. A value of zero (0) represents a symmetric or evenly balanced distribution. A positive skewness indicates a greater number of smaller values. A negative skewness indicates a greater number of larger values. A skewness value between ±1 is considered excellent and a value between ±2 is in many cases acceptable.

It may be observed that out of the selected one hundred and two companies, thirty one have registered negative average NOPAT, whereas INFOSYS stands first in the list with the higher average. The values of standard deviation in case of companies like INFOSYS, SATYAM, WIPRO, GTL, SILVERLINE are higher and the Skewness and Kurtosis values in case of about sixty per cent of the companies are positive which indicate that the observations cluster more and longer tails as compared to those having values zero or approximate to zero. Only one company in the sample (INFOSYS) reported zero value of Kurtosis.

The average weighted average cost of capital of only three companies has been less than five per cent during the period under study. Ten companies witnessed an average WACC of more than five but less than ten per cent and eighty seven companies registered more than ten per cent of average WACC. About major proportion of companies (82%) have shown their WACC positively skewed and only 5 per cent of the companies registered the positive values of kurtosis reflecting that the observations cluster more and with longer tails.

Company-wise statistical analysis of EVA is offered by Table 5.10, (*See on page No. 168*) where it is observed that the number of companies displaying the positive mean EVA is twelve. GTL has secured the first position with regard to the mean EVA followed by INFOSYS. The values of range show the volatility in EVA and that of standard deviation and variance display the variation scale from central tendency and dispersion. Twenty per cent companies have their EVA positively skewed and a double over this percentage indicate positive kurtosis that indicated longer tails.

In Table 5.11 (a) (*See on page No. 175*) it has been attempted to compute the relationship among EVA and NOPAT (whole sample). The correlation co-efficients between EVA and NOPAT have been observed as negative in three out of ten years. The value of correlation co-efficient has been higher in the years 1997-98, 1999-2000, 2000-01, 2001-02 and 2003-04 whereas it has been lower in case of 1996-97 (0.258) and 1998-1999(0.328)

In Table 5.11 (b) (*See on page No. 179*) the relationship among NOPAT and WACC for whole sample has been computed. As a fundamental rule, there should be inverse relationship between the cost of capital and business earnings. In tune with this, the correlation co-efficient between NOPAT and WACC are found to be inversely related in three out of ten years. In the rest of the seven years, positive but very low correlation co-efficients are found.

The relationship among EVA, WACC and NOPAT have been computed sub-group wise and are presented from Table 5.12 to Table 5.14.

Table 5.12 (a) (*See on page No. 183*) expresses the correlation co-efficient matrix of EVA and NOPAT for the large group of companies. The correlation co-efficients between EVA and NOPAT have been observed as negative for four out of ten years of the study period. Higher correlation coefficients have been found in the five years; 1997-98 (0.978), 1999-2000 (0.991), 2000-01 (0.987), 2001-02 (0.999) and 2003-04 (0.968); these correlations are significant at 1 per cent level of significance for all these five years. During the year 1998-99 the co-efficient was found to be the lowest (0.404).

Table 5.12 (b) (*See on page No. 187*) states the relationship between NOPAT and WACC for the select large group of companies during the period of study. The correlation co-efficients between NOPAT and WACC have been observed as high negative for the four years 1996-97 (-0.674), 2002-03 (-0.729), 2004-05 (-0.371) and for 2005-06 (-0.718). This negative relationship is justifiable because high WACC tends to affect the earnings. However, the remaining years registered a high positive correlation except during 1998-99.

Table 5.10

Company wise Statistical Analysis of EVA

(Rs. in Crores)

Name of the Company	*Mean*	*Range*	*SD*	*Variance*	*Skew*	*Kurt*	*Max*	*Min*
DIGITALEQP	9.16	381.85	123.62	15282.17	-2.14	4.98	106.31	-275.54
HP	3.40	232.50	77.73	6041.51	-0.90	-0.17	85.35	-147.15
I-FLEX	-73.35	545.08	222.93	49696.88	-0.54	-1.81	161.21	-383.87
INFOSYS	110.21	1803.17	606.36	367669.67	-0.31	-0.73	845.21	-957.96
SATYAM	-157.70	2025.01	641.24	411191.63	-0.87	-0.19	650.61	-1374.40
TECHM	3.55	306.61	106.66	11376.09	-0.34	-1.10	147.39	-159.22
WIPRO	-61.13	2982.98	965.65	932486.68	-0.93	-0.17	1085.63	-1897.35
ABACUS	-0.40	0.68	0.26	0.07	-0.75	-1.34	-0.14	-0.82
ABMANO	-1.15	6.45	2.05	4.19	-0.05	-0.73	2.03	-4.42
ACESOFT	-0.78	6.71	2.32	5.37	-0.29	-1.28	2.17	-4.54
ADVENT	-43.45	276.08	85.00	7225.23	-0.94	0.68	64.79	-211.29
AFTEK LTD	-40.75	270.61	96.46	9305.25	-1.12	-0.31	51.72	-218.89

(Contd...)

Name of the Company	Mean	Range	SD	Variance	Skew	Kurt	Max	Min
ASIANCE	-0.70	3.15	0.94	0.89	0.00	0.09	0.92	-2.23
AVANTELQ	-1.60	9.44	3.31	10.97	0.66	-0.60	3.52	-5.92
AZTECH	-10.01	93.41	27.55	759.08	-0.61	0.53	31.12	-62.29
B2BSOFT	-1.02	2.67	0.93	0.86	0.34	-0.86	0.44	-2.23
BLUESTINFO	1.01	31.89	12.52	156.75	-0.51	-1.61	13.25	-18.64
BRELS	-2.75	20.26	6.79	46.12	-0.79	-0.18	4.76	-15.50
CALIFSOF	-1.28	22.12	6.66	44.38	-0.74	0.42	7.39	-14.73
CGVAK	-1.31	8.35	3.04	9.21	0.14	-1.45	2.79	-5.56
CONTECH	-0.80	4.58	1.39	1.93	-1.27	1.35	0.74	-3.84
CRANES	3.44	28.61	8.14	66.24	1.41	2.09	21.66	-6.95
CRESSAN	-0.69	4.33	1.43	2.05	0.80	0.19	1.99	-2.34
CSSOFT	-1.24	10.09	3.60	12.96	-0.18	-1.21	3.30	-6.79
CYBERTE	-5.76	58.59	16.90	285.51	-0.22	0.08	22.26	-36.33
DATASOFT	-0.86	5.35	1.49	2.22	-1.68	3.70	0.89	-4.46
DYNACON	-1.74	7.22	2.54	6.43	-0.77	-0.90	0.94	-6.28

(Contd...)

Name of the Company	Mean	Range	SD	Variance	Skew	Kurt	Max	Min
ESERVE	8.27	39.65	13.67	186.79	1.64	2.45	37.25	-2.40
EUROSOFT	-10.29	73.48	26.32	692.97	-0.79	-0.79	16.65	-56.83
EZCOM	-0.35	0.41	0.11	0.01	1.79	4.21	-0.07	-0.48
FINTECH	-6.18	52.73	14.42	208.05	-1.46	3.28	12.39	-40.34
FRONTINF	-3.18	9.88	4.12	16.99	-0.76	-1.57	0.53	-9.35
GENESYS	-1.96	17.87	5.93	35.22	-0.21	-0.78	7.47	-10.40
GEOMETRIC	-4.62	72.94	24.96	622.77	-0.55	-0.79	30.00	-42.94
GOLDTECH	-0.64	20.44	5.67	32.20	-1.41	2.96	6.49	-13.95
GTL	172.08	1560.63	510.94	261056.77	2.40	6.11	1384.19	-176.44
HEXAWERE	12.52	179.97	51.40	2641.77	1.03	2.33	122.80	-57.17
HINDTMT	-63.13	465.54	152.74	23328.98	-0.67	-0.75	130.04	-335.50
INFDS	-0.46	1.58	0.51	0.26	-0.73	-0.05	0.21	-1.37
INFOTECENT	-11.99	96.77	35.22	1240.52	-0.77	-0.95	27.10	-69.67
INSOE	-0.44	1.51	0.51	0.26	-0.39	-0.78	0.20	-1.31
INTELVIS	-1.15	4.46	1.49	2.23	-0.39	-0.97	0.83	-3.63

(Contd...)

Name of the Company	*Mean*	*Range*	*SD*	*Variance*	*Skew*	*Kurt*	*Max*	*Min*
INTRAINF	-0.79	4.16	1.52	2.31	-0.57	-1.07	0.84	-3.32
ITMICRO	1.39	6.51	2.22	4.93	0.53	-0.63	5.21	-1.30
JETKINGQ	1.05	3.03	0.91	0.83	1.14	1.79	3.08	0.05
JINDONL	-0.58	1.57	0.63	0.39	-0.44	-1.69	0.05	-1.52
KASHYAP	-0.73	1.94	0.72	0.52	-0.39	-1.36	0.04	-1.90
KEDIN	-0.28	1.53	0.49	0.24	-1.82	3.47	0.10	-1.43
KLG	-7.61	37.56	12.65	160.02	-0.10	-1.25	11.41	-26.15
KPITCUMM	-0.70	17.26	5.24	27.46	-0.05	-0.34	8.15	-9.11
LEENEE	-1.18	9.95	3.28	10.73	-0.24	-0.70	3.59	-6.36
MARRSOF	-12.02	75.73	26.08	680.41	0.49	-0.65	34.74	-40.99
MAGNUM	-0.72	2.82	0.99	0.99	-0.54	-1.06	0.56	-2.26
MANGASOF	-0.12	3.16	1.05	1.10	0.38	-1.14	1.67	-1.49
MASTEK	-3.31	94.52	30.38	922.97	-0.09	-0.82	43.30	-51.22
MELSTAR	-1.00	25.64	8.52	72.51	0.32	-0.06	12.36	-13.28
MICROTECH	-12.01	75.08	24.52	601.11	-0.97	-0.09	15.88	-59.20

(Contd...)

Name of the Company	*Mean*	*Range*	*SD*	*Variance*	*Skew*	*Kurt*	*Max*	*Min*
MIDPOINT	-0.61	2.17	0.71	0.50	-0.67	-0.61	0.29	-1.88
MINDTEK	-3.32	17.35	4.41	19.46	-0.19	2.32	5.04	-12.31
MPHASIS	-96.91	996.84	273.12	74591.82	-1.98	4.81	213.17	-783.67
NCCFIN	-0.68	3.95	1.39	1.93	-0.60	-1.25	0.93	-3.02
NUCLEUSSOFT	-2.62	38.61	10.94	119.71	-0.92	1.36	12.55	-26.06
ODYSSEY	-1.46	6.41	1.85	3.43	-1.28	1.83	0.84	-5.57
ONWARD	-6.65	42.89	14.49	209.86	-0.44	-0.65	12.27	-30.62
ORIENTINFO	-13.31	122.76	36.04	1298.93	-0.36	0.10	42.57	-80.19
OTCO	0.19	1.52	0.50	0.25	1.85	2.97	1.32	-0.20
PALSOFT	-1.18	7.02	1.94	3.75	-0.06	1.34	2.31	-4.71
PENTASOFTTE	-48.21	852.10	232.07	53858.66	-1.45	3.81	246.72	-605.38
PIOTECH	-1.40	2.48	0.90	0.81	-0.70	-0.88	-0.40	-2.88
PSI	-2.63	40.49	12.19	148.52	0.45	0.43	20.49	-20.00
RAMINFO	-4.41	16.21	5.35	28.65	-0.87	0.12	0.91	-15.30
RAMCOSYS	-44.12	202.22	72.11	5200.39	-0.21	-1.14	44.70	-157.52

(Contd...)

Name of the Company	*Mean*	*Range*	*SD*	*Variance*	*Skew*	*Kurt*	*Max*	*Min*
ROLTA	-45.31	537.27	179.68	32283.34	-0.50	-0.54	178.43	-358.84
SANRASOF	-0.70	3.28	1.16	1.35	-0.72	-0.81	0.51	-2.77
SILVERLINE	-91.62	1401.93	387.30	150004.62	-2.83	8.63	237.74	-1164.19
SINDUVA	-0.04	0.55	0.16	0.03	0.83	1.32	0.29	-0.26
SOFTSOL	-6.97	50.31	16.93	286.57	-0.63	-0.82	13.32	-36.99
SONATA	-13.63	147.19	46.97	2206.46	-0.48	-0.58	50.90	-96.29
SVAMSOFT	-3.57	19.56	6.72	45.17	-0.37	-1.03	4.77	-14.79
TELEDATA	-21.38	222.51	71.93	5173.73	-2.97	8.88	9.78	-212.73
TERASOFT	-0.80	8.74	2.54	6.46	-1.16	1.32	2.51	-6.23
TWINSOFT	-1.74	9.63	2.75	7.56	-0.45	0.57	2.46	-7.17
VIRTUALS	-0.75	6.29	1.75	3.05	1.30	3.03	3.14	-3.15
VISUALSOFT	-13.21	200.40	66.45	4415.68	-0.37	-0.73	88.46	-111.94
VJIL	-2.60	20.99	6.83	46.71	-0.42	-0.61	6.41	-14.58
ZENSAR	-7.83	74.84	23.90	571.36	-1.00	0.11	22.09	-52.75
CHOKSHIN	-0.36	0.92	0.26	0.07	-1.19	2.02	-0.02	-0.94

(Contd...)

Name of the Company	*Mean*	*Range*	*SD*	*Variance*	*Skew*	*Kurt*	*Max*	*Min*
CORCOMP	-0.22	0.53	0.24	0.06	-0.28	-2.33	0.01	-0.52
DANLAW	-3.72	19.75	6.71	45.00	-0.26	-0.57	5.04	-14.71
ENCORE	-2.19	11.70	4.09	16.69	0.90	-0.51	5.14	-6.56
ICSAIND	-0.38	4.86	1.62	2.62	-0.69	-0.29	1.49	-3.37
IECSOF	-2.24	10.92	3.68	13.57	-0.82	-0.77	2.11	-8.81
INFOTREK	-0.56	3.99	1.19	1.43	-0.38	-0.27	1.26	-2.73
LCCINFO	-6.45	38.87	13.36	178.44	0.05	-1.10	13.01	-25.86
MASCONGLO	-45.10	296.19	96.73	9356.33	-0.61	-0.23	88.47	-207.72
MILLENCY	-0.38	1.58	0.56	0.31	-0.65	-0.56	0.24	-1.34
NETVISTA	-1.12	19.19	6.01	36.08	-2.15	5.27	4.16	-15.03
OMEGAIN	-0.84	10.48	2.66	7.09	-0.22	3.51	4.24	-6.24
SRGINFO	-49.86	200.76	67.62	4572.83	-1.33	1.44	13.84	-186.92
SYNLOG	-2.53	16.02	4.29	18.38	-0.65	1.79	4.40	-11.62
TRILLENT	-0.77	2.94	1.00	0.99	-0.35	-0.78	0.52	-2.42
VAKRANG	-6.69	51.61	15.94	254.21	-0.82	0.05	13.56	-38.05

The correlation between EVA and its main components NOPAT and WACC have been analysed and presented in Table 5.11 (a) and 5.11 (b).

Table 5.11 (a)

Correlation Matrix between EVA and NOPAT– for the Whole Sample (1997–2006)

	EVA06	*EVA05*	*EVA04*	*EVA03*	*EVA02*	*EVA01*	*EVA00*	*EVA99*	*EVA98*	*EVA97*
EVA06	1									
EVA05	.956(**)	1								
EVA04	-.666(**)	-.502(**)	1							
EVA03	.868(**)	.857(**)	-.461(**)	1						
EVA02	-.887(**)	-.763(**)	.890(**)	-.753(**)	1					
EVA01	-.920(**)	-.856(**)	.776(**)	-.883(**)	.958(**)	1				
EVA00	-.840(**)	-.721(**)	.735(**)	-.826(**)	.907(**)	.947(**)	1			
EVA99	-.440(**)	-.439(**)	0.126	-0.08	.271(**)	.240(*)	0.108	1		
EVA98	-.811(**)	-.705(**)	.612(**)	-.760(**)	.855(**)	.842(**)	.865(**)	.230(*)	1	
EVA97	0.065	0.145	.284(**)	0.183	0.062	0.012	0.127	0.067	-0.059	1

(Contd...)

	EVA06	*EVA05*	*EVA04*	*EVA03*	*EVA02*	*EVA01*	*EVA00*	*EVA99*	*EVA98*	*EVA97*
NOPAT06	**-.841(**)**	-.720(**)	.946(**)	-.773(**)	.987(**)	.941(**)	.903(**)	.246(*)	.801(**)	**0.228**
NOPAT05	-.814(**)	**-.659(**)**	.961(**)	-.743(**)	.980(**)	.925(**)	.892(**)	.241(*)	.790(**)	0.202
NOPAT04	-.818(**)	-.687(**)	**.961(**)**	-.642(**)	.968(**)	.908(**)	.863(**)	0.187	.737(**)	0.199
NOPAT03	-.634(**)	-.513(**)	.768(**)	**-.266(**)**	.749(**)	.606(**)	.572(**)	.201(*)	.519(**)	0.062
NOPAT02	-.892(**)	-.777(**)	.901(**)	-.705(**)	**.980(**)**	.951(**)	.899(**)	.338(**)	.812(**)	0.158
NOPAT01	-.906(**)	-.829(**)	.819(**)	-.566(**)	.856(**)	**.857(**)**	.792(**)	.395(**)	.647(**)	.278(*)
NOPAT00	-.859(**)	-.732(**)	.760(**)	-.429(**)	.752(**)	.750(**)	**.754(**)**	.380(**)	.599(**)	.441(**)
NOPAT99	-.854(**)	-.756(**)	.754(**)	-.529(**)	.797(**)	.789(**)	.780(**)	**.328(**)**	.731(**)	.436(**)
NOPAT98	-.836(**)	-.712(**)	.666(**)	-.525(**)	.791(**)	.767(**)	.777(**)	.507(**)	**.848(**)**	.282(**)
NOPAT97	-.835(**)	-.743(**)	.603(**)	-.488(**)	.715(**)	.715(**)	.674(**)	.636(**)	.758(**)	**.258(*)**

(Contd...)

	NOPAT 06	NOPAT 05	NOPAT 04	NOPAT 03	NOPAT 02	NOPAT 01	NOPAT 00	NOPAT 99	NOPAT 98	NOPAT 97
EVA06										
EVA05										
EVA04										
EVA03										
EVA02										
EVA01										
EVA00										
EVA99										
EVA98										
EVA97										
NOPAT06	1									
NOPAT05	.995(**)	1								
NOPAT04	.992(**)	.993(**)	1							
NOPAT03	.743(**)	.751(**)	.778(**)	1						
NOPAT02	.987(**)	.978(**)	.977(**)	.725(**)	1					

(Contd...)

	NOPAT 06	NOPAT 05	NOPAT 04	NOPAT 03	NOPAT 02	NOPAT 01	NOPAT 00	NOPAT 99	NOPAT 98	NOPAT 97
NOPAT01	.963(**)	.945(**)	.897(**)	.614(**)	.937(**)	1				
NOPAT00	.932(**)	.914(**)	.817(**)	.551(**)	.859(**)	.958(**)	1			
NOPAT99	.890(**)	.858(**)	.828(**)	.556(**)	.877(**)	.918(**)	.936(**)	1		
NOPAT98	.811(**)	.785(**)	.755(**)	.524(**)	.848(**)	.840(**)	.864(**)	.923(**)	1	
NOPAT97	.754(**)	.743(**)	.691(**)	.465(**)	.789(**)	.817(**)	.835(**)	.881(**)	.958(**)	1

** Correlation is significant at the 0.01 level (2-tailed).

* Correlation is significant at the 0.05 level (2-tailed).

Table No. 5.11(b)

Correlation Matrix between NOPAT & WACC – for the Whole Sample (1997–2006)

	NOPAT 06	*NOPAT 05*	*NOPAT 04*	*NOPAT 03*	*NOPAT 02*	*NOPAT 01*	*NOPAT 00*	*NOPAT 99*	*NOPAT 98*	*NOPAT 97*
NOPAT06	1									
NOPAT05	.995(**)	1								
NOPAT04	.992(**)	.993(**)	1							
NOPAT03	.743(**)	.751(**)	.778(**)	1						
NOPAT02	.987(**)	.978(**)	.977(**)	.725(**)	1					
NOPAT01	.963(**)	.945(**)	.897(**)	.614(**)	.937(**)	1				
NOPAT00	.932(**)	.914(**)	.817(**)	.551(**)	.859(**)	.958(**)	1			
NOPAT99	.890(**)	.858(**)	.828(**)	.556(**)	.877(**)	.918(**)	.936(**)	1		
NOPAT98	.811(**)	.785(**)	.755(**)	.524(**)	.848(**)	.840(**)	.864(**)	.923(**)	1	
NOPAT97	.754(**)	.743(**)	.691(**)	.465(**)	.789(**)	.817(**)	.835(**)	.881(**)	.958(**)	1

(Contd…)

	NOPAT 06	*NOPAT 05*	*NOPAT 04*	*NOPAT 03*	*NOPAT 02*	*NOPAT 01*	*NOPAT 00*	*NOPAT 99*	*NOPAT 98*	*NOPAT 97*
WACC06	0.06	0.045	0.065	0.061	0.058	0.058	.253(*)	0.088	0.036	0.023
WACC05	0.059	0.06	0.074	0.068	0.07	0.071	0.132	0.094	0.055	0.05
WACC04	0.044	0.047	0.063	0.062	0.055	-0.002	-0.018	0.03	0.011	-0.013
WACC03	0.046	0.045	0.062	0.067	0.05	-0.018	-0.051	0.012	-0.006	-0.033
WACC02	-0.056	-0.04	-0.057	-0.042	-0.051	0.013	0.036	-0.016	0.003	0.032
WACC01	-0.03	-0.021	-0.041	-0.028	-0.037	0.025	0.061	-0.006	0.012	0.039
WACC00	-0.073	-0.057	-0.075	-0.044	-0.074	0.02	0.065	-0.051	-0.045	-0.009
WACC99	-0.072	-0.055	-0.039	-0.018	-0.041	-0.097	-0.118	-0.039	-0.015	-0.027
WACC98	-0.006	-0.001	-0.02	-0.017	-0.022	0.01	-0.015	-0.02	-0.019	0.01
WACC97	0.028	0.033	0.054	0.025	0.056	0.027	0.021	0.037	0.004	0.052

(Contd...)

	WACC 06	WACC 05	WACC 04	WACC 03	WACC 02	WACC 01	WACC 00	WACC 99	WACC 98	WACC 97
NOPAT06										
NOPAT05										
NOPAT04										
NOPAT03										
NOPAT02										
NOPAT01										
NOPAT00										
NOPAT99										
NOPAT98										
NOPAT97										

(Contd...)

	WACC 06	*WACC 05*	*WACC 04*	*WACC 03*	*WACC 02*	*WACC 01*	*WACC 00*	*WACC 99*	*WACC 98*	*WACC 97*
WACC06	1									
WACC05	.993(**)	1								
WACC04	.986(**)	.868(**)	1							
WACC03	.987(**)	.855(**)	.969(**)	1						
WACC02	-958(**)	-.774(**)	-.863(**)	-.938(**)	1					
WACC01	-.983(**)	-.845(**)	-.954(**)	-.990(**)	.966(**)	1				
WACC00	-.876(**)	-.679(**)	-.946(**)	-.963(**)	.883(**)	.988(**)	1			
WACC99	.955(**)	.828(**)	.945(**)	.966(**)	-.911(**)	-.968(**)	-.911(**)	1		
WACC98	-.951(**)	-.816(**)	-.930(**)	-.955(**)	.917(**)	.961(**)	.864(**)	-.953(**)	1	
WACC97	.884(**)	.764(**)	.867(**)	.879(**)	-.833(**)	-.884(**)	-.661(**)	.872(**)	-.864(**)	1

** Correlation is significant at the 0.01 level (2-tailed).

* Correlation is significant at the 0.05 level (2-tailed).

Table 5.12 (a)

Correlation Matrix between EVA and NOPAT – Large Group (1997-2006)

	EVA06	*EVA05*	*EVA04*	*EVA03*	*EVA02*	*EVA01*	*EVA00*	*EVA99*	*EVA98*	*EVA97*
EVA06	1									
EVA05	.944(**)	1								
EVA04	-0.489	-0.2	1							
EVA03	.977(**)	.897(**)	-0.563	1						
EVA02	-.819(*)	-0.606	.877(**)	-.870(*)	1					
EVA01	-.902(**)	-0.737	.791(*)	-.943(**)	.983(**)	1				
EVA00	-.773(*)	-0.55	.901(**)	-.827(*)	.990(**)	.962(**)	1			
EVA99	-0.626	-0.653	-0.04	-0.577	0.391	0.454	0.325	1		
EVA98	-0.695	-0.532	0.504	-0.732	0.782	0.768	0.754	0.778	1	
EVA97	0.582	0.713	0.298	0.579	-0.199	-0.332	-0.127	-.857(*)	-0.575	1

(Contd…)

	EVA06	*EVA05*	*EVA04*	*EVA03*	*EVA02*	*EVA01*	*EVA00*	*EVA99*	*EVA98*	*EVA97*
NOPAT06	**-0.718**	-0.454	.927(**)	-0.8	.980(**)	.950(**)	.981(**)	0.184	0.692	-0.11
NOPAT05	-0.665	**-0.371**	.956(**)	-0.747	.971(**)	.922(**)	.979(**)	0.165	0.7	-0.042
NOPAT04	-0.687	-0.434	**.968(**)**	-0.753	.961(**)	.917(**)	.968(**)	0.138	0.623	0.062
NOPAT03	-0.671	-0.412	.949(**)	**-0.729**	.969(**)	.911(**)	.985(**)	0.25	0.725	0.01
NOPAT02	-.827(*)	-0.619	.877(**)	-.877(**)	**.999(**)**	.986(**)	.989(**)	0.376	0.763	-0.192
NOPAT01	-.881(**)	-0.717	.819(*)	-.923(**)	.967(**)	**.987(**)**	.949(**)	0.323	0.651	-0.226
NOPAT00	-.805(*)	-0.601	.893(**)	-.849(*)	.984(**)	.971(**)	**.991(**)**	0.278	0.681	-0.108
NOPAT99	-.834(*)	-0.632	.859(*)	-.888(**)	.995(**)	.987(**)	.973(**)	**0.404**	0.778	-0.232
NOPAT98	-0.78	-0.63	0.524	-0.784	.825(*)	.821(*)	0.791	0.806	**.978(**)**	-0.561
NOPAT97	-0.771	-0.653	0.385	-0.766	0.731	0.748	0.678	.882(*)	.966(**)	**-0.674**

(Contd...)

	NOPAT 06	NOPAT 05	NOPAT 04	NOPAT 03	NOPAT 02	NOPAT 01	NOPAT 00	NOPAT 99	NOPAT 98	NOPAT 97
EVA06										
EVA05										
EVA04										
EVA03										
EVA02										
EVA01										
EVA00										
EVA99										
EVA98										
EVA97										

(Contd...)

	NOPAT 06	NOPAT 05	NOPAT 04	NOPAT 03	NOPAT 02	NOPAT 01	NOPAT 00	NOPAT 99	NOPAT 98	NOPAT 97
NOPAT06	1									
NOPAT05	.993(**)	1								
NOPAT04	.991(**)	.998(**)	1							
NOPAT03	.969(**)	.985(**)	.976(**)	1						
NOPAT02	.983(**)	.973(**)	.964(**)	.965(**)	1					
NOPAT01	.965(**)	.931(**)	.934(**)	.900(**)	.975(**)	1				
NOPAT00	.992(**)	.980(**)	.970(**)	.966(**)	.988(**)	.976(**)	1			
NOPAT99	.974(**)	.959(**)	.952(**)	.948(**)	.996(**)	.974(**)	.973(**)	1		
NOPAT98	0.67	0.674	0.655	0.755	0.81	0.715	0.736	.823(*)	1	
NOPAT97	0.571	0.572	0.539	0.631	0.716	0.631	0.622	0.74	.979(**)	1

** Correlation is significant at the 0.01 level (2-tailed).

* Correlation is significant at the 0.05 level (2-tailed).

Table 5.12 (b)

Correlation Matrix between NOPAT and WACC – Large Group (1997-2006)

	NOPAT 06	*NOPAT 05*	*NOPAT 04*	*NOPAT 03*	*NOPAT 02*	*NOPAT 01*	*NOPAT 00*	*NOPAT 99*	*NOPAT 98*	*NOPAT 97*
WACC06	**-0.718**	-0.454	.927(**)	-0.8	.980(**)	.950(**)	.981(**)	0.184	0.692	-0.11
WACC05	-0.665	**-0.371**	.956(**)	-0.747	.971(**)	.922(**)	.979(**)	0.165	0.7	-0.042
NOPAT06	1									
NOPAT05	.944(**)	1								
NOPAT04	-0.489	-0.2	1							
NOPAT03	.977(**)	.897(**)	-0.563	1						
NOPAT02	-.819(*)	-0.606	.877(**)	-.870(*)	1					
NOPAT01	-.902(**)	-0.737	.791(*)	-.943(**)	.983(**)	1				
NOPAT00	-.773(*)	-0.55	.901(**)	-.827(*)	.990(**)	.962(**)	1			
NOPAT99	-0.626	-0.653	-0.04	-0.577	0.391	0.454	0.325	1		
NOPAT98	-0.695	-0.532	0.504	-0.732	0.782	0.768	0.754	0.778	1	
NOPAT97	0.582	0.713	0.298	0.579	-0.199	-0.332	-0.127	-.857(*)	-0.575	1

(Contd...)

	NOPAT 06	*NOPAT 05*	*NOPAT 04*	*NOPAT 03*	*NOPAT 02*	*NOPAT 01*	*NOPAT 00*	*NOPAT 99*	*NOPAT 98*	*NOPAT 97*
WACC06	**-0.718**	-0.454	.927(**)	-0.8	.980(**)	.950(**)	.981(**)	0.184	0.692	-0.11
WACC05	-0.665	**-0.371**	.956(**)	-0.747	.971(**)	.922(**)	.979(**)	0.165	0.7	-0.042
WACC04	-0.687	-0.434	**.968(**)**	-0.753	.961(**)	.917(**)	.968(**)	0.138	0.623	0.062
WACC03	-0.671	-0.412	.949(**)	**-0.729**	.969(**)	.911(**)	.985(**)	0.25	0.725	0.01
WACC02	-.827(*)	-0.619	.877(**)	-.877(**)	**.999(**)**	.986(**)	.989(**)	0.376	0.763	-0.192
WACC01	-.881(**)	-0.717	.819(*)	-.923(**)	.967(**)	**.987(**)**	.949(**)	0.323	0.651	-0.226
WACC00	-.805(*)	-0.601	.893(**)	-.849(*)	.984(**)	.971(**)	**.991(**)**	0.278	0.681	-0.108
WACC99	-.834(*)	-0.632	.859(*)	-.888(**)	.995(**)	.987(**)	.973(**)	**0.404**	0.778	-0.232
WACC98	-0.78	-0.63	0.524	-0.784	.825(*)	.821(*)	0.791	0.806	**.978(**)**	-0.561
WACC97	-0.771	-0.653	0.385	-0.766	0.731	0.748	0.678	.882(*)	.966(**)	**-0.674**

(Contd...)

	WACC 06	*WACC 05*	*WACC 04*	*WACC 03*	*WACC 02*	*WACC 01*	*WACC 00*	*WACC 99*	*WACC 98*	*WACC 97*
NOPAT06										
NOPAT05										
NOPAT04										
NOPAT03										
NOPAT02										
NOPAT01										
NOPAT00										
NOPAT99										
NOPAT98										
NOPAT97										

(Contd...)

	WACC 06	WACC 05	WACC 04	WACC 03	WACC 02	WACC 01	WACC 00	WACC 99	WACC 98	WACC 97
WACC06	1									
WACC05	.993(**)	1								
WACC04	.991(**)	.998(**)	1							
WACC03	.969(**)	.985(**)	.976(**)	1						
WACC02	.983(**)	.973(**)	.964(**)	.965(**)	1					
WACC01	.965(**)	.931(**)	.934(**)	.900(**)	.975(**)	1				
WACC00	.992(**)	.980(**)	.970(**)	.966(**)	.988(**)	.976(**)	1			
WACC99	.974(**)	.959(**)	.952(**)	.948(**)	.996(**)	.974(**)	.973(**)	1		
WACC98	0.67	0.674	0.655	0.755	0.81	0.715	0.736	.823(*)	1	
WACC97	0.571	0.572	0.539	0.631	0.716	0.631	0.622	0.74	.979(**)	1

** Correlation is significant at the 0.01 level (2-tailed).

* Correlation is significant at the 0.05 level (2-tailed).

Considering the small-medium and converts groups of companies it is evinced from the Table 5.13 (a) and 5.14 (a) (*See on page No. 192 and 200*) that the correlation coefficients between EVA and NOPAT are found to be a high positive in the seven out of ten years of the study period. Such a strong positive relationship between EVA and NOPAT proves that NOPAT has favourable effect on EVA. From Table 5.13 (b) and 5.14 (b) (See on page No. *196 and 204)* it could be seen that in three out of ten years in case of Small-Medium group and in four out of ten years in case of converts group of companies, negative relationship exist between NOPAT and WACC. In the remaining years of the study period low positive relationship is registered. The overall analysis implies that increase in cost of capital over the earnings, resulted in wealth reduction with regard to many software companies in the study period.

t-test has been applied to test the paired differences between EVA, WACC and NOPAT. The following hypothesis has been framed and tested.

H_0: There exist no significant differences in the paired samples.

While testing through *t* hypothesis at 5 per cent level of significance it is reported that the results of the paired sample test are insignificant. i.e., there exist no significant differences in the paired samples.

EVA vis-à-vis Select Financial Variables

Various statistical tools like Mean, Standard Deviation, Variance, Range and the Paired Sample Test show inconsistent results to get a grip over EVA's behaviour. Supplementary information based on statistical analysis is considered necessary to understand the behaviour patterns of the EVA Measure.

The generic research task of this part is to observe and assess how the EVA measure is related with the long established but traditional financial measures. In this section, an attempt has been made to bring out the basic analysis of relationship between select financial measures and EVA of selected companies for a period of ten years from 1996-97 to 2005-06. These measures include Turnover, ROS, ROTA, ROCE, EPS, Market Price, MVA and SVA. These measures are mainly used to appraise the financial performance of a corporate. Kendall's tau-b has been considered appropriate tool to measure the relationship of EVA with the select financial variables, since it is based on the ranked variables.

Table 5.13 (a)

Correlation Matrix between EVA and NOPAT –Small-Medium (1997-2006)

	EVA06	*EVA05*	*EVA04*	*EVA03*	*EVA02*	*EVA01*	*EVA00*	*EVA99*	*EVA98*	*EVA97*
EVA06	1									
EVA05	.830(**)	1								
EVA04	-0.01	0.073	1							
EVA03	.452(**)	.627(**)	.679(**)	1						
EVA02	-.670(**)	-.569(**)	-.299(**)	-.599(**)	1					
EVA01	-.624(**)	-.766(**)	-.590(**)	-.890(**)	.504(**)	1				
EVA00	-.560(**)	-.493(**)	-.653(**)	-.688(**)	.371(**)	.829(**)	1			
EVA99	.584(**)	.520(**)	.518(**)	.707(**)	-.768(**)	-.584(**)	-.598(**)	1		
EVA98	-.626(**)	-.430(**)	-.368(**)	-.558(**)	.523(**)	.612(**)	.767(**)	-.774(**)	1	
EVA97	.334(*)	.323(**)	.270(*)	.335(**)	-.626(**)	-.258(*)	0.009	.598(**)	-.261(*)	1

(Contd...)

	EVA06	*EVA05*	*EVA04*	*EVA03*	*EVA02*	*EVA01*	*EVA00*	*EVA99*	*EVA98*	*EVA97*
NOPAT06	**-.760(**)**	-.471(**)	0.231	-.359(**)	.479(**)	.419(**)	.338(**)	-.342(**)	.490(**)	-0.053
NOPAT05	-.780(**)	**-.475(**)**	.332(**)	-0.207	.528(**)	.349(**)	.417(**)	-.345(**)	.549(**)	0.09
NOPAT04	-.763(**)	-.699(**)	**.605(**)**	.240(*)	-0.01	0.104	0.066	0.191	0.092	0.135
NOPAT03	-0.193	-0.073	.391(**)	**.536(**)**	0.113	-.388(**)	-.257(*)	0.064	-0.194	-0.114
NOPAT02	-.608(**)	-.660(**)	0.159	0.047	**-0.182**	.289(*)	0.19	.444(**)	-0.17	.269(*)
NOPAT01	-.528(**)	-.531(**)	.296(**)	.338(**)	-.646(**)	**0.034**	0.052	.623(**)	-0.135	.454(**)
NOPAT00	-.521(**)	-.361(**)	.298(**)	.348(**)	-.662(**)	0.014	**0.168**	.585(**)	0	.613(**)
NOPAT99	-.612(**)	-.442(**)	.335(**)	0.169	-.569(**)	0.159	.275(*)	**.375(**)**	0.193	.610(**)
NOPAT98	-.518(**)	-.251(*)	0.232	0.159	-.525(**)	0.125	.387(**)	0.193	**.441(**)**	.508(**)
NOPAT97	-.517(**)	-.382(**)	.389(**)	0.216	-.564(**)	0.073	0.167	.385(**)	0.177	**.551(**)**

(Contd...)

	NOPAT 06	NOPAT 05	NOPAT 04	NOPAT 03	NOPAT 02	NOPAT 01	NOPAT 00	NOPAT 99	NOPAT 98	NOPAT 97
EVA06										
EVA05										
EVA04										
EVA03										
EVA02										
EVA01										
EVA00										
EVA99										
EVA98										
EVA97										

(Contd...)

	NOPAT 06	*NOPAT 05*	*NOPAT 04*	*NOPAT 03*	*NOPAT 02*	*NOPAT 01*	*NOPAT 00*	*NOPAT 99*	*NOPAT 98*	*NOPAT 97*
NOPAT06	1									
NOPAT05	.920(**)	1								
NOPAT04	.671(**)	.813(**)	1							
NOPAT03	0.047	0.216	.474(**)	1						
NOPAT02	.469(**)	.481(**)	.638(**)	-0.122	1					
NOPAT01	.416(**)	.375(**)	.529(**)	-0.122	.851(**)	1				
NOPAT00	.446(**)	.521(**)	.553(**)	-0.065	.789(**)	.950(**)	1			
NOPAT99	.603(**)	.618(**)	.613(**)	-0.124	.743(**)	.846(**)	.935(**)	1		
NOPAT98	.492(**)	.589(**)	.501(**)	-0.146	.581(**)	.717(**)	.851(**)	.912(**)	1	
NOPAT97	.526(**)	.613(**)	.579(**)	-0.158	.705(**)	.819(**)	.882(**)	.927(**)	.896(**)	1

** Correlation is significant at the 0.01 level (2-tailed).

* Correlation is significant at the 0.05 level (2-tailed).

Table 5.13 (b)

Correlation Matrix between NOPAT and WACC –Small-Medium (1997-2006)

	NOPAT 06	*NOPAT 05*	*NOPAT 04*	*NOPAT 03*	*NOPAT 02*	*NOPAT 01*	*NOPAT 00*	*NOPAT 99*	*NOPAT 98*	*NOPAT 97*
NOPAT06	1									
NOPAT05	.920(**)	1								
NOPAT04	.671(**)	.813(**)	1							
NOPAT03	0.047	0.216	.474(**)	1						
NOPAT02	.469(**)	.481(**)	.638(**)	-0.122	1					
NOPAT01	.416(**)	.375(**)	.529(**)	-0.122	.851(**)	1				
NOPAT00	.446(**)	.521(**)	.553(**)	-0.065	.789(**)	.950(**)	1			
NOPAT99	.603(**)	.618(**)	.613(**)	-0.124	.743(**)	.846(**)	.935(**)	1		
NOPAT98	.492(**)	.589(**)	.501(**)	-0.146	.581(**)	.717(**)	.851(**)	.912(**)	1	
NOPAT97	.526(**)	.613(**)	.579(**)	-0.158	.705(**)	.819(**)	.882(**)	.927(**)	.896(**)	1

(Contd…)

	NOPAT 06	*NOPAT 05*	*NOPAT 04*	*NOPAT 03*	*NOPAT 02*	*NOPAT 01*	*NOPAT 00*	*NOPAT 99*	*NOPAT 98*	*NOPAT 97*
WACC06	**0.086**	-0.052	0.082	0.036	0.053	0.019	0.166	0.057	-0.005	0.01
WACC05	0.074	**0.007**	0.1	0.035	0.092	0.04	0.077	0.05	0.014	0.034
WACC04	0.06	-0.047	**-0.031**	0.029	-0.068	-0.155	-.254(*)	-0.114	-0.108	-0.132
WACC03	0.065	-0.05	-0.037	**0.028**	-0.084	-0.178	-.309(**)	-0.133	-0.125	-0.152
WACC02	-0.088	0.065	0.073	0.015	**0.079**	0.17	.291(*)	0.139	0.137	0.154
WACC01	-0.068	0.054	0.056	0.01	0.076	**0.166**	.278(*)	0.121	0.117	0.146
WACC00	-.303(*)	-0.232	-0.003	0.02	0.048	.237(*)	**.238(*)**	0.161	0.117	0.163
WACC99	0.055	-0.057	-0.011	-0.001	-0.019	-0.098	-0.152	**-0.064**	-0.062	-0.086
WACC98	-0.025	0.103	0.05	0.005	0.054	0.082	0.115	0.066	**0.046**	0.088
WACC97	0.081	-0.079	-0.002	-0.018	0.01	-0.058	-0.132	-0.077	-0.119	**-0.021**

(Contd...)

	WACC 06	WACC 05	WACC 04	WACC 03	WACC 02	WACC 01	WACC 00	WACC 99	WACC 98	WACC 97
NOPAT06										
NOPAT05										
NOPAT04										
NOPAT03										
NOPAT02										
NOPAT01										
NOPAT00										
NOPAT99										
NOPAT98										
NOPAT97										

(Contd...)

	WACC 06	*WACC 05*	*WACC 04*	*WACC 03*	*WACC 02*	*WACC 01*	*WACC 00*	*WACC 99*	*WACC 98*	*WACC 97*
WACC06	1									
WACC05	.995(**)	1								
WACC04	.988(**)	.880(**)	1							
WACC03	.990(**)	.853(**)	.989(**)	1						
WACC02	-.963(**)	-.795(**)	-.940(**)	-.958(**)	1					
WACC01	-.987(**)	-.844(**)	-.984(**)	-.991(**)	.978(**)	1				
WACC00	-.901(**)	-.670(**)	-.948(**)	-.966(**)	.882(**)	.991(**)	1			
WACC99	.988(**)	.849(**)	.987(**)	.990(**)	-.954(**)	-.990(**)	-.975(**)	1		
WACC98	-.959(**)	-.817(**)	-.956(**)	-.959(**)	.939(**)	.963(**)	.856(**)	-.968(**)	1	
WACC97	.896(**)	.770(**)	.886(**)	.886(**)	-.863(**)	-.892(**)	-.653(**)	.895(**)	-.876(**)	1

** Correlation is significant at the 0.01 level (2-tailed).

* Correlation is significant at the 0.05 level (2-tailed).

Table 5.14 (a)

Correlation Matrix between EVA and NOPAT—Converts (1997-2006)

	EVA06	*EVA05*	*EVA04*	*EVA03*	*EVA02*	*EVA01*	*EVA00*	*EVA99*	*EVA98*	*EVA97*
EVA06	1									
EVA05	.976(**)	1								
EVA04	.916(**)	.866(**)	1							
EVA03	.998(**)	.644(*)	.868(**)	1						
EVA02	-.902(**)	0.465	0.151	-0.304	1					
EVA01	-.843(**)	-.856(**)	-.697(**)	-.848(**)	-0.45	1				
EVA00	-.996(**)	-0.398	-.717(**)	-.957(**)	.539(*)	.766(**)	1			
EVA99	0.013	.911(**)	.636(**)	0.32	.709(**)	0.33	-0.044	1		
EVA98	-0.306	-.635(*)	-.593(*)	-0.435	-0.294	0.122	0.319	-0.517	1	
EVA97	.902(*)	.683(*)	.739(**)	.870(**)	.669(*)	-.757(*)	-.885(**)	0.569	-.616(*)	1

(Contd...)

	EVA06	*EVA05*	*EVA04*	*EVA03*	*EVA02*	*EVA01*	*EVA00*	*EVA99*	*EVA98*	*EVA97*
NOPAT06	**-.813(**)**	-.796(**)	-.643(*)	-.830(**)	.853(**)	0.055	.819(**)	0.046	0.411	-0.528
NOPAT05	-.948(**)	**.823(**)**	0.493	0.097	.843(**)	-0.284	0.188	.963(**)	-0.488	0.588
NOPAT04	-.649(*)	-0.051	**-0.019**	-0.453	.619(*)	-0.181	.545(*)	0.17	0.042	0.07
NOPAT03	.989(**)	0.288	.616(*)	**.902(**)**	-.637(**)	0.247	-.973(**)	-0.045	-0.186	-0.025
NOPAT02	-.980(**)	-0.271	-.587(*)	-.880(**)	**.699(**)**	0.096	.951(**)	0.069	0.162	0.175
NOPAT01	-0.321	-0.42	-.818(**)	-0.445	-.556(*)	**.735(**)**	0.424	0.046	-0.205	0.002
NOPAT00	-.994(**)	-0.294	-.649(**)	-.917(**)	.617(*)	.620(*)	**.992(**)**	0.066	0.252	-0.584
NOPAT99	-.915(**)	-.811(**)	-.875(**)	-.883(**)	0.066	-0.004	.741(**)	**-.603(*)**	0.368	-.592(*)
NOPAT98	-0.432	-.831(**)	-.749(**)	-0.475	-0.474	-0.186	0.285	-.769(**)	**.873(**)**	-0.563
NOPAT97	0.783	0.01	0.091	0.241	-0.068	-0.451	-0.598	-0.156	-.583(*)	**.595(*)**

(Contd...)

	NOPAT 06	NOPAT 05	NOPAT 04	NOPAT 03	NOPAT 02	NOPAT 01	NOPAT 00	NOPAT 99	NOPAT 98	NOPAT 97
EVA06										
EVA05										
EVA04										
EVA03										
EVA02										
EVA01										
EVA00										
EVA99										
EVA98										
EVA97										

(Contd...)

	NOPAT 06	*NOPAT 05*	*NOPAT 04*	*NOPAT 03*	*NOPAT 02*	*NOPAT 01*	*NOPAT 00*	*NOPAT 99*	*NOPAT 98*	*NOPAT 97*
NOPAT06	1									
NOPAT05	.894(**)	1								
NOPAT04	.793(**)	0.306	1							
NOPAT03	-.807(**)	-0.29	-.553(*)	1						
NOPAT02	.827(**)	0.3	.591(*)	-.970(**)	1					
NOPAT01	-0.438	-0.591	-.733(**)	-0.246	0.157	1				
NOPAT00	.805(**)	0.292	.541(*)	-.980(**)	.961(**)	0.461	1			
NOPAT99	.784(**)	-0.408	0.308	-.702(**)	.721(**)	0.102	.676(**)	1		
NOPAT98	0.351	-.722(**)	-0.15	-0.177	0.152	-0.138	0.207	.569(*)	1	
NOPAT97	-0.515	-0.105	-0.226	-0.265	-0.115	0.228	-.769(**)	0.209	-0.249	1

** Correlation is significant at the 0.01 level (2-tailed).

* Correlation is significant at the 0.05 level (2-tailed).

Table 5.14 (b)

Correlation Matrix between NOPAT and WACC – Converts (1997-2006)

	NOPAT 06	*NOPAT 05*	*NOPAT 04*	*NOPAT 03*	*NOPAT 02*	*NOPAT 01*	*NOPAT 00*	*NOPAT 99*	*NOPAT 98*	*NOPAT 97*
NOPAT06	1									
NOPAT05	.894(**)	1								
NOPAT04	.793(**)	0.306	1							
NOPAT03	-.807(**)	-0.29	-.553(*)	1						
NOPAT02	.827(**)	0.3	.591(*)	-.970(**)	1					
NOPAT01	-0.438	-0.591	-.733(**)	-0.246	0.157	1				
NOPAT00	.805(**)	0.292	.541(*)	-.980(**)	.961(**)	0.461	1			
NOPAT99	.784(**)	-0.408	0.308	-.702(**)	.721(**)	0.102	.676(**)	1		
NOPAT98	0.351	-.722(**)	-0.15	-0.177	0.152	-0.138	0.207	.569(*)	1	
NOPAT97	-0.515	-0.105	-0.226	-0.265	-0.115	0.228	-.769(**)	0.209	-0.249	1

(Contd...)

	NOPAT 06	*NOPAT 05*	*NOPAT 04*	*NOPAT 03*	*NOPAT 02*	*NOPAT 01*	*NOPAT 00*	*NOPAT 99*	*NOPAT 98*	*NOPAT 97*
WACC06	**.671(*)**	0.436	0.569	-0.259	0.343	-0.282	0.283	0.407	0.168	-0.56
WACC05	0.622	**0.051**	0.344	-0.206	0.211	0.103	0.229	0.208	0.03	-0.341
WACC04	.756(*)	-0.005	**0.213**	-0.229	0.231	0.257	0.414	0.223	0.088	-0.191
WACC03	0.35	0.051	0.241	**-0.06**	0.054	0.196	0.087	0.023	0.015	-0.44
WACC02	-0.193	-0.026	-0.189	-0.166	**0.149**	0.119	0.106	0.155	0.101	0.27
WACC01	-.728(*)	-0.336	-0.388	-.562(*)	0.066	**-0.132**	-0.159	0.177	0.068	0.463
WACC00	-0.583	-0.146	-0.344	0.235	-0.226	-0.16	**-0.287**	-0.141	-0.08	0.443
WACC99	.638(*)	0.11	0.334	-0.349	0.294	0.194	0.356	**0.213**	0.108	-0.292
WACC98	-0.619	-0.076	-0.397	0.344	-0.322	-0.058	-0.386	-0.188	**-0.266**	0.492
WACC97	-0.019	-0.069	-0.101	-0.174	-0.341	0.248	-.765(**)	0.197	-0.209	**.635(*)**

(Contd...)

	WACC 06	WACC 05	WACC 04	WACC 03	WACC 02	WACC 01	WACC 00	WACC 99	WACC 98	WACC 97
NOPAT06										
NOPAT05										
NOPAT04										
NOPAT03										
NOPAT02										
NOPAT01										
NOPAT00										
NOPAT99										
NOPAT98										
NOPAT97										

(Contd...)

	WACC 06	WACC 05	WACC 04	WACC 03	WACC 02	WACC 01	WACC 00	WACC 99	WACC 98	WACC 97
WACC06	1									
WACC05	.898(**)	1								
WACC04	.843(**)	.894(**)	1							
WACC03	.642(*)	.929(**)	.730(**)	1						
WACC02	-0.548	0.157	0.374	-0.318	1					
WACC01	-.691(*)	-.767(**)	-0.458	-.934(**)	.649(*)	1				
WACC00	-.727(*)	-.955(**)	-.918(**)	-.940(**)	.816(**)	.954(**)	1			
WACC99	0.608	.875(**)	.711(**)	.917(**)	-0.242	-.902(**)	-.916(**)	1		
WACC98	-0.553	-.790(**)	-.648(*)	-.872(**)	0.266	.866(**)	.886(**)	-.936(**)	1	
WACC97	-0.008	0.361	0.346	0.317	0.051	-0.228	-0.218	0.512	-0.233	1

** Correlation is significant at the 0.01 level (2-tailed).

* Correlation is significant at the 0.05 level (2-tailed).

KENDALL'S TAU-B

It is a non parametric measure of association for ordinal or ranked variables that takes ties into account. The sign of the coefficient indicates the direction of the relationship, and its absolute value indicates the strength, with large absolute values indicating stronger relationships. The relationship of EVA with the select financial variables has been analysed and are presented in the Table 5.15 (*See on Page No. 209*)

H_0: There is no significant relationship between EVA and Selected financial variables.

Glancing all the way through the Table 5.15, it is noticed that the correlation between EVA and Turnover is found at above moderate level in the years 1999-00 and 2000-01. On the other hand, the correlation between these variables in 1998-99, 2002-03, 2004-05 and 2005-06 recorded negative trend but significant at 1 per cent level.

Below moderate level of relationship was found during the entire study period with regard to EVA with ROS and EVA with market price. The correlation coefficient explaining the relationship between EVA and ROTA reveals that moderate relationship exists during 1996-97, 1997-98, 2000-01 and 2001-02. Comparing the year 1996-97 with the year 2005-06 an adverse relationship is noticed.

The table further reveals that there exists moderate degree but positive correlation in six out of ten years as regards EVA and ROCE. The degrees of negative correlation observed are -0.107 in 1998-99, -0.116 in 2002-03, -0.124 in 2004-05 and -0.243 in 2005-06. It is noticed that the degree of correlation is superior in 1996-97, 1997-98, 2000-01 and 2001-02 to that of the rest of the study period. There existed high degree positive correlation between EVA and EPS over the period of five out of ten years, with 1 per cent level of significance.

The relationship of EVA with MVA shows that though the result is positive in seven out of ten years of the study, there was above moderate level of significance in two years only (i.e. 2001-02 and 2003-04). Compared to other variables, the association between EVA and MVA holds top with major positive relationship.

The correlation between EVA and SVA is though positive in six out of ten years of the study period, the strength is moderate/ low in all the years under study except during 2001-02.

Table 5.15

EVA with Select Financial Variables (Whole Sample) – Kendall's tau b

Variables / *Years*	*2005-06*	*2004-05*	*2003-04*	*2002-03*	*2001-02*	*2000-01*	*1999-00*	*1998-99*	*1997-98*	*1996-97*
Turnover	-.619(**)	-.438(**)	.135(*)	-.486(**)	.288(**)	.654(**)	.600(**)	-.312(**)	.467(**)	.335(**)
ROS	-.288(**)	-.215(**)	.353(**)	-.170(*)	.498(**)	.423(**)	.299(**)	-.183(**)	.341(**)	.272(**)
ROTA	-.264(**)	-.180(*)	.415(**)	-.198(**)	.538(**)	.525(**)	.439(**)	-.136(*)	.524(**)	.541(**)
ROCE	-.243(**)	-0.124	.456(**)	-0.116	.564(**)	.504(**)	.460(**)	-0.107	.545(**)	.524(**)
EPS	-.373(**)	-.264(**)	.451(**)	-.251(**)	.570(**)	.608(**)	.616(**)	-.209(**)	.585(**)	.489(**)
Market Price	-.316(**)	-.219(**)	.209(**)	-.283(**)	.251(**)	.345(**)	.363(**)	-.181(*)	.228(**)	0.117
MVA	0.055	0.117	.552(**)	.292(**)	.660(**)	-.538(**)	-.531(**)	0.064	-.302(**)	.398(**)
SVA	-0.089	0.043	.553(**)	.254(**)	.669(**)	-.485(**)	-.447(**)	0.007	-.309(**)	.382(**)

* Correlation is significant at the .05 level (2-tailed).

** Correlation is significant at the .01 level (2-tailed).

The analysis of the relationship of EVA with the select financial variables with regard to the whole sample reveals that, the first year of the study (1996-97) indicates a positive figure whereas the year 2005-06 explains negative relationship among all the other variables except MVA. Hence it can be concluded that during the year 2005-06 there is significant relationship between EVA and select financial variables. The wealth indicators MVA and SVA showed insignificant results.

The analysis of relationship of EVA with the select financial variables has been made segment wise and the results are depicted in Table 5.15 (a) through Table 5.15 (c). (*See on page No. 211, 212 & 213*) The co-efficients may resonance whether there subsists some statistical rapport between the variables. Accordingly, in order to evaluate the significance of such relationship the Kendall Tau-b values are being considered.

Table 5.15 (a) puts forward the synoptic description of the relationship of EVA with select financial variables as regards large group of companies over the period of ten years from 1996-97 to 2005-06. Considering all the selected financial variables, the variables such as ROS, ROTA, ROCE and Market Price showed insignificant association with EVA throughout the period of study. The rest of the variables namely Turn over, EPS, MVA and SVA showed significant association in some of the years under study. The variables EPS and MVA showed significant relationship during the year 2005-06 at 5 per cent level. It can be concluded that EPS dominates EVA as the co-efficients during the ten years show minimum negative values among the select financial variables in the large group of companies.

The association between EVA and select financial variables regarding small-medium group of companies are observed in Table 5.15 (b). The variables such as ROS, Market Price had very little relationship with EVA over the ten year period of study. Variables such as Turnover, ROTA, ROCE, MVA and EVA had moderate relationship in most of the years under study. EPS showed strong relationship in five out of the ten years of the study. Among the small-medium group of companies, MVA and SVA dominate EVA by showing minimum negative values during the study period.

Table 5.15 (a)

EVA with Select Financial Variables (Large) – Kendall's tau b

Years / *Variables*	*2005-06*	*2004-05*	*2003-04*	*2002-03*	*2001-02*	*2000-01*	*1999-00*	*1998-99*	*1997-98*	*1996-97*
Turnover	-0.467	-0.333	0.488	-.683(*)	.976(**)	.878(**)	.781(*)	-0.098	0.276	-0.276
ROS	-0.2	-0.067	0.293	0.293	-0.293	0	-0.488	-0.143	-0.138	0.276
ROTA	-0.067	-0.2	0.238	0.333	-0.333	0	0.488	0.195	0	0.069
ROCE	-0.067	-0.2	0.238	0.333	-0.39	0.098	0.39	0.195	0	0.069
EPS	-.733(*)	0.467	0.39	-0.195	0.195	0.488	0.39	-0.293	0.276	0.276
Market Price	-0.067	0	0.39	-0.586	0.488	0.552	0.69	-0.276	0.552	-0.913
MVA	-.714(*)	-0.524	.810(*)	-0.429	0.619	-0.619	-.714(*)	-0.333	-0.333	-0.143
SVA	-0.6	-0.333	.810(*)	-0.429	0.619	-0.619	-.714(*)	-0.333	-0.067	-0.467

Table 5.15 (b)

EVA with Select Financial Variables (Small-Medium) – Kendall's tau b

Years / Variables	2005-06	2004-05	2003-04	2002-03	2001-02	2000-01	1999-00	1998-99	1997-98	1996-97
Turnover	-.617(**)	-.379(**)	0.075	-.408(**)	.177(*)	.595(**)	.542(**)	-.315(**)	.441(**)	.337(**)
ROS	-.260(**)	-.182(*)	.288(**)	-0.12	.454(**)	.440(**)	.368(**)	-.184(*)	.321(**)	.265(**)
ROTA	-.239(**)	-0.129	.361(**)	-0.101	.497(**)	.453(**)	.402(**)	-0.118	.502(**)	.576(**)
ROCE	-.229(**)	-0.086	.407(**)	-0.061	.519(**)	.468(**)	.429(**)	-0.094	.520(**)	.544(**)
EPS	-.337(**)	-.195(*)	.383(**)	-.166(*)	.525(**)	.557(**)	.612(**)	-.207(**)	.553(**)	.509(**)
Market Price	-.283(**)	-.245(**)	.209(**)	-.255(**)	.245(**)	.328(**)	.425(**)	-.238(**)	.262(**)	0.18
MVA	.165(*)	.209(**)	.448(**)	.446(**)	.607(**)	-.497(**)	-.491(**)	.214(**)	-.233(**)	.391(**)
SVA	0.05	0.136	.451(**)	.398(**)	.619(**)	-.414(**)	-.376(**)	0.14	-.230(**)	.392(**)

Table 5.15 (c)

EVA with Select Financial Variables (Converts) – Kendall's tau b

Years / Variables	2005-06	2004-05	2003-04	2002-03	2001-02	2000-01	1999-00	1998-99	1997-98	1996-97
Turnover	-0.378	-.429(*)	-.383(*)	-.460(*)	0.159	.667(**)	.619(**)	-0.075	0.056	0.061
ROS	-0.022	-0.055	.377(*)	0.092	.393(*)	0.154	-0.086	-0.008	0.313	0.229
ROTA	0.022	0.121	0.192	-0.2	.367(*)	0.359	.410(*)	-0.1	.411(*)	0.321
ROCE	0.2	0.253	0.326	0.117	.450(*)	0.103	.486(*)	-0.083	.433(*)	.443(*)
EPS	0.024	-0.127	0.298	-0.032	.411(*)	.536(*)	.524(**)	-0.12	0.365	0.259
Market Price	-0.192	-0.077	-0.128	-0.231	-0.055	.398(*)	0.143	0.231	-0.219	0.212
MVA	0.39	.613(**)	.667(**)	.633(**)	.667(**)	-.402(*)	-.450(*)	-.367(*)	-0.118	0.263
SVA	0.111	.582(**)	.667(**)	.633(**)	.667(**)	-0.41	-.467(*)	-.367(*)	-0.155	0.121

Table 5.15 (c) implies the relationship of EVA with the select eight financial variables in case of converts group of companies. It displays that there exists poor relationship between EVA and most of the select financial variables under the study. Only the pair of wealth indicators namely MVA and SVA shows strong relationship during the last five years of the study. The state of affairs of ROTA, ROCE, EPS and Market Price is quite watery as the table evidence diverse trend and insignificant results during the last four years of the study i.e., 2002-03, 2003-04, 2004-05 and year 2005-06. ROCE dominates EVA since it holds only one negative co-efficient among the ten years of the study.

Among the three sub-groups namely, Large, Small-Medium and Converts, only in the small-medium group, though EVA had negative and below moderate relationship with all the variables selected for the study, such relationship remained significant in most of the years.

Sample Based Regression Analysis of Select Financial Variables

The present chapter makes an attempt to find the relevance of Stern and Stewarts claim and the hypothesis that EVA of the firm is positively associated with the select financial variables. The multiple regression analysis between the dependent variable (EVA) and independent variables (MVA, SVA, ROCE, ROS, ROTA, EPS, Turnover and Market Price) is carried out to study the relationship between EVA and other select financial variables to bump into the simple most significant explanatory variable. The *Backward* mode of regression analysis to select the best predictor has been considered appropriate for this analysis. Backward method begins with all independent variables in the model, and at each step the least predictor is removed. Variables are removed until an established criterion for the *F*-statistics and adjusted *R*-square no longer holds good. Accordingly under this method the un-removed variable(s) is the best predictor of the dependent variable.

Durbin-Watson model allows to establish the auto-correlation, if any between the dependent and independent variable (the desirable value is two and any value more than two signifies negative auto-correlation and vice versa); values of adjusted R^2 indicate the extent of variation in the dependent variable which may be explicated by independent variables and the standard error speaks about the limits within which the estimated value of the dependent variable is expected to lie.

It is evident from Table (5.16) that the values of correlation co-efficients are coming down and that of the adjusted R-Square is going up till the 4th model is reached, where the estimated standard error is also minimum. This shows that market price, ROS, ROCE, ROTA and MVA are the best determinants of EVA. The 5th model of regression discloses that both coefficients of correlation and adjusted *R*-square have revealed the downward trend in their values. The Durbin–Watson model rules out any positive auto-correlation between the dependent and independent variables. Table 5.18 presents the results of ANOVA analysis. The *F*-statistics shows that the value of the residual is the minimum in 4th model, and the 5th model supports the observation of Table 5.16.

Table 5.16

EVA and other independent variables (Average): Durbin-Watson Analysis Whole Sample - Model Summary[f]

Model	*R*	*R Square*	*Adjusted R Square*	*Std. Error of the Estimate*	*Durbin-Watson*
1.	.549[a]	.301	.241	28.417	
2.	.549[b]	.301	.249	28.266	
3.	.548[c]	.300	.256	28.126	2.353
4.	.541[d]	.293	.256	28.123	
5.	.529[e]	.280	.250	28.236	

a. *Predictors:* (Constant), Market Price, ROS, ROCE, SVA, ROTA, EPS, MVA, Turnover

b. *Predictors:* (Constant), Market Price, ROS, ROCE, ROTA, EPS, MVA, Turnover

c. *Predictors:* (Constant), Market Price, ROS, ROCE, ROTA, MVA, Turnover

d. *Predictors:* (Constant), Market Price, ROS, ROCE, ROTA, MVA

e. *Predictors:* (Constant), Market Price, ROCE, ROTA, MVA

f. *Dependent Variable:* EVA.

In Table 5.17 (*See on next page*) the significance of the values are tested through F-statistics at 1 per cent level of significance. Table 5.18 (*See on page No. 217*) highlights the most exploratory independent variable. Tested with t statistics the table brings out that the ROS is significant if tested at 18.5 per cent level. MVA and Market Price are observed to be quite significant even at 1 per cent level of significance. The overall conclusion of Tables 5.16 to 5.18 throws light on four important variables i.e, Market Price, ROCE, ROTA and MVA.

Table 5.17

EVA and other independent variables (Average): ANOVA[f]

Model		*Sum of Squares*	*df*	*Mean Square*	*F*	*Sig.*
1.	Regression	32328.345	8	4041.043	5.004	.000[a]
	Residual	75100.550	93	807.533		
	Total	**107428.895**	**101**			
2.	Regression	32326.898	7	4618.128	5.780	.000[b]
	Residual	75101.998	94	798.957		
	Total	**107428.895**	**101**			
3.	Regression	32278.981	6	5379.830	6.801	.000[c]
	Residual	75149.914	95	791.052		
	Total	**107428.895**	**101**			
4.	Regression	31500.140	5	6300.028	7.965	.000[d]
	Residual	75928.756	96	790.925		
	Total	**107428.895**	**101**			
5.	Regression	30091.230	4	7522.807	9.435	.000[e]
	Residual	77337.666	97	797.296		
	Total	**107428.895**	**101**			

a. *Predictors:* (Constant), Market Price, ROS, ROCE, SVA, ROTA, EPS, MVA, Turnover

b. *Predictors:* (Constant), Market Price, ROS, ROCE, ROTA, EPS, MVA, Turnover

c. *Predictors:* (Constant), Market Price, ROS, ROCE, ROTA, MVA, Turnover

d. *Predictors:* (Constant), Market Price, ROS, ROCE, ROTA, MVA

e. *Predictors:* (Constant), Market Price, ROCE, ROTA, MVA

f. *Dependent Variable:* EVA

Table 5.18

EVA and other independent variables (Average): Coefficient[a]

Model		Unstandardized Coefficients		Standardised Coefficients	t	Sig.
		B	Std. Error Beta			
1.	(Constant)	-11.525	3.671		-3.140	.002
	Turnover	-.009	.011	-.138	-.786	.434
	SVA	.000	.009	.008	.042	.966
	EPS	-.118	.489	-.042	-.242	.809
	ROCE	.325	.133	.327	2.431	.017
	ROS	1.139	.944	.130	1.207	.231
	ROTA	-58.561	23.125	-.414	-2.532	.013
	MVA	-.074	.020	-.626	-3.614	.000
	Market Price	.057	.013	.847	4.412	.000
2.	(Constant)	-11.524	3.651		-3.156	.002
	Turnover	-.008	.009	-.134	-.942	.349
	EPS	-.119	.486	-.042	-.245	.807
	ROCE	.325	.133	.327	2.445	.016
	ROS	1.137	.937	.130	1.213	.228
	ROTA	-58.499	22.955	-.413	-2.548	.012
	MVA	-.073	.018	-.622	-4.141	.000
	Market price	.057	.013	.848	4.441	.000
3.	(Constant)	-11.829	3.414		-3.465	.001
	Turnover	-.009	.009	-.139	-.992	.324
	ROCE	.325	.132	.328	2.459	.016
	ROS	1.144	.932	.131	1.228	.222
	ROTA	-59.957	22.060	-.424	-2.718	.008
	MVA	-.073	.018	-.621	-4.156	.000
	Market Price	.055	.010	.818	5.545	.000
4.	(Constant)	-12.097	3.403		-3.555	.001
	ROCE	.322	.132	.324	2.436	.017
	ROS	1.237	.927	.141	1.335	.185
	ROTA	-61.564	21.999	-.435	-2.799	.006
	MVA	-.080	.016	-.684	-5.066	.000
	Market Price	.051	.009	.768	5.544	.000

(Contd...)

	Model	Unstandardized Coefficients		Standardized Coefficients	t	Sig.
		B	Std. Error Beta			
5.	(Constant)	-13.695	3.198		-4.283	.000
	ROCE	.284	.130	.287	2.195	.031
	ROTA	-46.309	18.872	-.327	-2.454	.016
	MVA	-.079	.016	-.671	-4.961	.000
	Market Price	.051	.009	.753	5.436	.000

a *Dependent Variable:* EVA

The four best predictors observed in the regression using backward method are further analysed and it is found that market price contributes an R^2 of 20.3 per cent, while MVA contributes an R^2 of 28.8 per cent. This reveals that among the select financial variables, MVA contributes the maximum towards the shareholders wealth maximization.

General Loglinear Analysis using multinomial model has been used to study the influence of EVA components on EVA. Co-variances of parameter estimates are being considered to evaluate the results obtained. Any variable whose co-variance is minimum is said to be more consistent whereas those with maximum co-variance show greater variability.

It is observed from the Table 5.19 to 5.22 (*See on page No. 219 to 222*) that beta coefficient has maximum covariance among whole sample, large, and small-medium group of companies which shows greater variability whereas cost of debt found to be maximum in converts group. Minimum covariance observed regarding whole sample is the cost of debt, debt to total capitalisation in case of large group, cost of equity in case of small-medium group and equity to total capitalization in case of converts group stating their consistency.

Table 5.19

Logit Analysis – Whole Sample

Covariances of Parameter Estimates (a, b, c)

Variables	*Beta*	*CE*	*COCE*	*COE*	*COD*	*DE*	*ECE*
Beta	884.972	-2.531	0.039	1.291	-585.108	-34.206	-59.803
CE	-2.531	0.011	0.000	-0.006	2.418	0.283	0.425
COCE	0.039	0.000	0.001	-0.001	0.088	0.209	0.226
COE	1.291	-0.006	-0.001	0.004	-1.403	-0.209	-0.296
COD	-585.108	2.418	0.088	-1.403	558.463	63.846	96.282
DE	-34.206	0.283	0.209	-0.209	63.846	124.032	133.096
ECE	-59.803	0.425	0.226	-0.296	96.282	133.096	144.619

a. *Model:* Multinomial

b. *Design:* Constant + Beta + CE + COCE + COE + COD + DE + ECE + EVA + NOPAT + PAT + WACC

c. Constants and redundant parameters are not displayed.

Table 5.20

Logit Analysis – Large Group

Covariances of Parameter Estimates (a, b, c)

Variables	*Beta*	*CE*	*COCE*	*COD*	*COE*	*DCE*
Beta	164.491	0.107	-0.199	-102.447	-15.783	-349.426
CE	0.107	0.000	0.000	-0.066	-0.010	-0.219
COCE	-0.199	0.000	0.001	0.121	0.017	0.388
COD	-102.447	-0.066	0.121	64.503	9.971	217.997
COE	-15.783	-0.010	0.017	9.971	1.574	33.260
DCE	-349.426	-0.219	0.388	217.997	33.260	779.120

a. *Model:* Multinomial

b. *Design:* Constant + Beta + CE + COCE + COD + COE + DCE + ECE + EVA + NOPAT + PAT + WACC

c. Constants and redundant parameters are not displayed.

Table 5.21

Logit Analysis – Small-Medium

Covariances of Parameter Estimates (a, b, c)

Variables	*Beta*	*CE*	*COCE*	*COD*	*COE*	*DCE*	*ECE*
Beta	307.058	0.344	-4.802	24.451	-9.945	224.385	-1.475
CE	0.344	0.000	-0.005	0.027	-0.011	0.253	-0.002
COCE	-4.802	-0.005	0.077	-0.530	0.152	-3.540	0.025
COD	24.451	0.027	-0.530	21.746	-0.507	15.632	-0.379
COE	-9.945	-0.011	0.152	-0.507	0.335	-7.032	0.047
DCE	224.385	0.253	-3.540	15.632	-7.032	185.474	-0.801
ECE	-1.475	-0.002	0.025	-0.379	0.047	-0.801	0.020

a. *Model:* Multinomial.

b. *Design:* Constant + Beta + CE + COCE + COD + COE + DCE + ECE + EVA + NOPAT + PAT + WACC

c. Constants and redundant parameters are not displayed.

Table 5.22

Logit Analysis – Converts

Covariances of Parameter Estimates (a, b, c)

Variables	*Beta*	*CE*	*COCE*	*COD*	*COE*	*DCE*	*ECE*
Beta	3.826	-0.074	1.454	4.984	-0.198	-3.967	-3.982
CE	-0.074	0.013	-0.115	0.059	0.012	-0.009	-0.009
COCE	1.454	-0.115	1.556	1.563	-0.182	-1.893	-1.898
COD	4.984	0.059	1.563	33.161	-0.349	-15.152	-15.188
COE	-0.198	0.012	-0.182	-0.349	0.028	0.232	0.233
DCE	-3.967	-0.009	-1.893	-15.152	0.232	21.848	21.882
ECE	-3.982	-0.009	-1.898	-15.188	0.233	21.882	21.916

a. *Model:* Multinomial

b. *Design:* Constant + Beta + CE + COCE + COD + COE + DCE + ECE + EVA + NOPAT + PAT + WACC

c. Constants and redundant parameters are not displayed.

(*CE:* Capital Employed; *DE:* Debt Equity; *COCE:* Cost of Capital Employed; *COD:* Cost of Debt; *COE:* Cost of Equity; *DCE:* Debt to Capital Employed; *ECE:* Equity to Capital Employed)

DISCRIMINANT FUNCTION ANALYSIS

Discriminant analysis is a statistical technique which allows to study the differences between two or more groups with respect to several variables simultaneously and provide a means of classifying any object/individual into the group with which it is most closely associated and to infer the relative importance of each variable used to discriminate between different groups. A linear combination of predictor variables, weighted in such a way that it will best discriminate among groups with the least error is called a linear discriminant function and is given by:

$D = L_1.X_1 + L_2.X_2 + \ldots\ldots\ldots\ldots + L_K.X_K$, where X_is are predictor variables, L_is represent the discriminant coefficients, and D is the value of the discriminant function of a particular individuals/element such that if this value is greater than a certain critical value D*, the individual would be classified in group I ; otherwise the individual would be classified in Group II. In the present study there are two groups: Group I (Wealth Destroyers – companies with negative EVAs for more than 5 years) and Group II (Wealth Creators). Predictor variables considered for the analysis include the following:

X_1- Turnover, X_2-ROS, X_3-ROTA, X_4-ROCE, X_5 – EPS X_6-Market Price, X_7- SVA, and X_8-MVA,

Table 5.23

Group Mean Score

Variables	*Wealth Destroyers* (N_1=80)	*Wealth Creators* (N_2=22)
	Mean score	
X_1	26.133	542.832
X_2	2.731	48.710
X_3	-.025	.242
X_4	-7.186	24.005
X_5	3.215	18.220
X_6	105.483	478.438
X_7	-13.908	676.872
X_8	-24.931	186.921

Table 5.24
Tests of Equality of Group Means
Univariate ANOVAs

Variable	*Wilk's Lambda*	*F (DF=1, 100)*	*Sig*
X_1	.831	20.288	.000
X_2	.974	2.657	.106
X_3	.770	29.862	.000
X_4	.846	18.144	.000
X_5	.713	40.275	.000
X_6	.900	11.165	.000
X_7	.846	18.215	.000
X_8	.900	11.061	.000

**- Significant at 1 per cent level.

Connanical Discriminant Function Fitted:

$$D = -.520 + .001\ X_1 + .001\ X_2 + 1.447\ X_3 + .006\ X_4 + .113\ X_6$$

Table 5.25
Test Functions

Eigen Value	*Percentage of variation explained*	*Wilks Lambda*	*Chi-Square*	*DF*	*P*	*Canonical Correlation*
0.786	100	0.560	55.66	8	0.000	0.663

Classification of Individual

Using the discriminant function fitted and the observed predictor variables of the individual companies, the sample companies are classified and the correct percentage of classification is presented in Table 5.26.

Table 5.26

Determination of Percentage of Correct Classification by using Discriminant Function on the Data

Companies	*Using the Dis. Function fitted Companies are classed as*		*Total*
	Group I	*Group II*	
Group I	**75**	5	80
Group II	7	**15**	22

From Table 5.26, it is observed that out of the 102 companies under study, out of 80 companies in Group I (Wealth Destroyers), 75 (93.8%) were correctly classified; out of 22 companies in Group II (Wealth Creators), 15 (68.2%) were correctly classified. Thus out of total 102 companies, 90 companies were correctly classified. Hence the percentage of correct classification is (90/102)*100 per cent or 88.2 per cent.

RELATIVE IMPORTANCE OF PREDICTOR VARIABLE

The relative importance of each predictor variable in discriminating between the two groups are obtained and the results are presented in Table 5.27.

Table 5.27

The Relative importance of characters in Discriminating between the groups

Variables	*Importance value of the variable (Ij)*	*Relative Importance (Rj)*	*Rank*
X_1	0.5167	14.37	3
X_2	0.0460	1.279	6
X_3	0.3864	10.74	4
X_4	0.1872	5.205	5
X_5	1.6956	47.16	1
X_6	0.7639	21.25	2
Total	**3.5957**	**100.00**	

Among the variables under study, three variables namely EPS, Market Price and Turnover are substantially important variables in discriminating between groups.

CHI-SQUARE ANALYSIS

The regression analysis (Table 5.28) reveals that in the years 1999-2000, 2000-01, 2001-02 and 2003-04 the companies were able to generate more economic value than what was expected. In the remaining years of the study period, the companies on the whole generated less economic value than what was expected. In four out of the ten years, negative EVAs were found which adversely affected the shareholders wealth. To test the significance of the differences between actual figures of EVA and expected figure of EVA, Chi-Square test has been applied.

Table 5.28

Regression Analysis of EVA (1996-07 to 2005-06)

Years	*NOPAT (X)*	*EVA (Y)*	Y_c
2005-06	720.09	-594.10	-387.99
2004-05	511.40	-407.47	-318.91
2003-04	377.32	140.30	-249.84
2002-03	188.26	-866.93	-180.76
2001-02	305.97	220.45	-111.68
2000-01	333.18	445.42	-42.61
1999-00	195.03	257.43	26.47
1998-99	104.12	-31.69	95.54
1997-98	55.39	62.89	164.62
1996-97	49.89	2.22	233.70
	$\sum X = 2840.64$	**$\sum Y = 771.47$**	**$\sum Yc-771.47$**

Regression Line y on x : $y = -0.64x + 103.65$

H_0: There is no significant difference between actual EVA and expected EVA.

Table 5.29

χ^2 Analysis of EVA

Years	*EVA (Y)*	*Expected EVA* (Y_C)	$(Y-Y_C)^2$	$(Y-Y_C)^2/Y_C$
2005-06	-594.10	-387.99	42481.04	-109.49
2004-05	-407.47	-318.91	7842.218	-24.5905
2003-04	140.30	-249.84	152205.9	-609.221
2002-03	-866.93	-180.76	470831.1	-2604.72
2001-02	220.45	-111.68	110316.2	-987.747
2000-01	445.42	-42.61	238173	-5589.77
1999-00	257.43	26.47	53344.23	2015.477
1998-99	-31.69	95.54	16187.04	169.421
1997-98	62.89	164.62	10349.26	62.86783
1996-97	2.22	233.70	53578.96	229.2685
	Σ Y = -771.47	**Σ Yc-771.47**	**Σ (Y-Yc)²= 1155308.91**	$\Sigma \frac{(Y-Y_c)^2}{Y_c}$ = **-7448.51**

It can be seen from Table 5.29 that the calculated value of Chi-Square comes to -7448.51 while the table value of Chi-Square at 5 per cent level of significance for 9 degrees of freedom is 16.92. Since the calculated value is much lesser than the table value of χ^2 it can be concluded that the differences between the expected and actual figures of EVA were insignificant. The companies should make efforts either to reduce cost of capital employed or to increase the amount of NOPAT in order to have positive and pretty good figure of EVA in future years.

CONCLUSION

In this chapter, EVA has been analysed with the select financial variables and the results are outlined below:

Around 10 to 40 per cent of the companies during the first five years of the study and around 9 to 25 per cent of the sample companies in the last five years generated positive EVA. EVAs of over Rs.10 crores have been reported by about 3 per cent to 33 per cent of the sample companies from 1996-97 to 2000-01 and by about 1 to 19 per cent of the companies from 2001-02 to 2005-06.

The average of all the select financial variables computed and ranked revealed that except WACC all other variables had positive influence on shareholders wealth. Among the biggies, INFOSYS, DIGITALEQP, TECHM, HP and WIPRO remained in the toppers list in most of the wealth related variables. HP (Large group) is the only company to be listed in the WACC toppers. SRGINFO (Converts) lags in five variables namely EVA, NOPAT, MVA, ROS and SVA. Eight corporates under small-medium and two under converts have positive effect with respect to WACC.

Out of the select 102 software companies, thirty one have registered negative average NOPAT. The values of skewness and kurtosis in case of 60 per cent of the companies are found to be positive which indicate longer tails. Only INFOSYS reported zero value of kurtosis.

Ten companies registered an average WACC of greater than five but less than ten per cent and eighty seven companies registered more than ten per cent of average WACC. A meager over three companies registered less than five per cent of average WACC. Eighty two per cent of companies have shown their WACC, positively skewed and only 5 per cent registered positive value of kurtosis.

The number of companies registered positive mean EVA is found to be twelve. Twenty per cent companies have their EVA positively skewed and a double over this percentage indicate positive kurtosis. The correlation coefficients between EVA and NOPAT (Whole sample) have been observed as negative in three years, high in five years, whereas low in two years. NOPAT and WACC are found to be inversely related in three years and a very low positive relationship is observed in the rest seven years.

As regards large group of companies, the correlation coefficients between EVA and NOPAT have been observed as negative in four years, high in five years and lowest during one year (1998-99). The relationship between NOPAT and WACC have been observed as high negative in four years and high positive during the remaining years except during 1998-99.

A favourable effect of NOPAT on EVA is observed in case of small-medium and converts group of companies, Negative relationship is found between NOPAT and WACC in three out of ten years in small-medium group and in four out of ten years in case of converts.

't' test analysis exhibit that there exist no significant difference in the paired samples. Though in actual content differences are being observed, statistically those differences are not significant.

Kendall tau-b results show that the association of EVA with the select financial variables with regard to the whole sample during 1996-97 indicate a positive figure whereas the year 2005-06 explained inverse relationship among all the other variables expect MVA. The variables such as ROS, ROTA, ROCE and Market Price showed insignificant association with EVA (Large group) throughout the study period. Remaining variables exhibited significant results in some of the years under study.

Among the small-medium group, the variables such as ROS and Market Price had very little relationship with EVA over the ten year period. EPS showed strong relationship in five out of ten years. MVA and SVA dominate EVA with minimum negative values during the study period.

Poor relationship between EVA and most of the select financial variables is observed in case of converts group of companies. Only the twin wealth indicators namely MVA and SVA show strong relationship during the last five years of the study period. ROCE dominates EVA, holding only one negative coefficient among the ten years of the study. Among the sub groups only in small-medium group though EVA had negative and below moderate relationship with all the select variables, such relationship remained significant in most of the years.

Logit loglinear relationship reveals that beta coefficient has maximum covariance among whole sample, large, and small-medium group of companies which shows greater variability whereas cost of debt is found to be maximum in converts group. Minimum covariance observed in case of whole sample is cost of debt, debt to total capitalisation in case of large group, cost of equity in case of small-medium group and equity to total capitalisation in case of converts group stating their consistency.

Discriminant analysis reveals that the three variables namely EPS, Market Price and Turnover are substantially important variables in discriminating between groups.

Chi-Square analysis concludes that the differences between the expected and actual figures of EVA were insignificant.

6

MEASURE OF VALUE CREATION

MARKET VALUE ADDED

"You are never given a wish without being given the power to make it come true; you may have to work for it".

—Richard Bach

INTRODUCTION

Value Based Management (VBM) has been referred to as the "fastest and hottest ticket" to shareholder wealth. Incorporating such techniques as Economic Value Added (EVA), Return on Operating Invested Capital (ROIC), and Market Value Added (MVA), VBM is a complete financial management and incentive compensation system that guides decision-making at every level. Adopting companies use VBM as a guide in financial planning, monitoring and controlling operations. Shareholder value creation is represented by the difference between the market value of the firm's equity and the equity capital invested by shareholders. Former reflects the value imputed by financial market on the equity of the firm and latter reflects the actual amount of money contributed by equity share holders by way of capital and retained earnings.

The market value of a business at a point in time is an approximation of the fair value of the business entire debt and equity capitalisation. This can be arrived at by taking the number of shares and multiplying by the share price and adding the book value of long and short term loans net of any cash deposits.

Market value at a point in time is equal to the total capital employed plus or minus the net present value of all future economic profits. Therefore, market value is maximised by maximising the present value of future economic profits. In order to measure shareholder's wealth Stewart invented the term Market Value Added. MVA is defined as excess of market value of a company over its invested capital. MVA is a cumulative measure of the value created by management in excess of the capital invested by shareholders. According to Ehrbar and Hamel (1997), "...there is one measure, Market Value Added (MVA), that captures all the dynamics of corporate performance"

MVA is the value added by the management to the equity capital and debt entrusted to it by the company's share holders. MVA is a market-generated number calculated by subtracting the capital invested in a firm (C) from the sum (V) of the total market value of the firm's equity and the book value of its debt: $MVA_t = V_t - C_t$. While this measure of value depends on a book value of capital which is subject to inflation influences, it may provide a useful market indication of present and future value creation by representing the difference between the capital invested and the present value of the cash flows expected from that capital. It is an accomplishment of a firm with a high level of MVA just to maintain that level, as this requires the satisfaction of both present and future earning expectations.

Market Value Added is identical by meaning with the market-to-book-ratio. The difference is only that MVA is an absolute measure and market-to-book-ratio is a relative measure. If MVA is positive means the market-to-book-ratio is more than one. Negative MVA means market-to-book-ratio less than one. According to Stewart, Market Value Added tells us how much value company has added to or subtracted from, its shareholders investment. Successful companies add their MVA and thus increase the value of capital invested in the company. Whether a company succeeds in creating MVA (increasing shareholders value) or not, depends on its rate of return. If a company's rate of return exceeds its cost of capital, the company will sell on the stock markets with premium compared to the original capital (has positive MVA). On the other hand, companies that have rate of return smaller than their cost of capital sell with discount compared to the original capital invested in company. The company's positive or negative MVA entirely depends on the level of rate of return compared to cost of capital. This applies to EVA also. Hence, positive EVA implies positive MVA and vice versa. Market value Added is equal to present value of all future EVAs. Increasing EVA of a company increases its Market Value Added.

MVA—The Basic Premise

The basic premise of the method is that, from a shareholders perspective, the extra value created by the use of capital is one of the major measures of success for a company's management. When shareholder buy stock, they are hiring a company to create value for them. If a company does that, it is successful and the measure of its success is determined by subtracting the total amount of money invested from the total market value of the company. The Total Market Value (TMV) of a company is the value of its stock and debt. Total invested capital (IC) includes all stock and debt offerings, retained earnings, bank loans and certain investments in future earnings like R & D. TMV minus IC equals MVA. The greater the difference, the more a company's management has succeeded.

The basic problem with using this system is that it doesn't rely on a true market value but on a subjective market value. True market value is pretty hard to figure because it is more than what something actually sells for, on a given day.

MVA is the perfect measure of the company's ability to create wealth, which can be calculated only at the level of the entire company and is as volatile as any market index. To determine whether management has created or destroyed value, the market value of the firm's capital (both equity and debt capital) may be compared to the capital invested by shareholders and lenders (the capital employed in the firm). The difference between the market value of capital and capital employed is called Market Value Added (MVA).

MVA = Market Value of Capital – Capital Employed.

MVA can also be computed with the following formula:

MVA = Market Value of the firm – Book Value of the firm

$$\text{Market Value of the firm} = \frac{\text{EBIT}}{K_o}$$

Where EBIT = Earnings Before Interest and Taxes

K_o = Weighted Average cost of Capital (WACC)

Book Value of the firm = Equity share capital + Revaluation reserves + Miscellaneous Expenses.

Properties of MVA

The importance of MVA stems from the following properties:

- MVA increases when the firm undertakes positive NPV projects.

  NPV = Present value of cash inflows from the project – Capital employed in the project.
- Maximising MVA is consistent with maximizing shareholder value.

EVA and Market Value Added

- The relationship between EVA and Market Value Added is more complicated than the one between EVA and Firm Value.
- The market value of a firm reflects not only the expected EVA of Assets in Place but also the Expected EVA from Future Projects.
- To the extent that the actual Economic Value Added is smaller than the expected EVA, the market value can decrease even though the EVA is higher.

MVA ANALYSIS

MVA is one of the external indicators which gives the utmost satisfaction to the investors. From the investors perspective, increase of the share price is always desirable. The most reliable measure of a management's long term success in adding value is known as

"Market Value Added". MVA is the best internal performance indicator as it indicates the market assessment of the effectiveness with which companies managers have used the scarce resources under their control. Hence, it turns out to be very significant and important to analyze and identify the internal indicators that relate well with MVA.

In the present chapter, Karl Pearson's correlation model has been adopted to establish the relationship between EVA and MVA. Nine variables have been selected which signify the wealth maximisation. Factor analysis has been done to test which among these variables contribute much towards maximizing shareholders wealth. Multiple regression analysis has been carried out to find out the extent of relationship between the dependent variable (MVA) with the select financial variables (independent).

Accordingly under this method the unremoved variable(s) is the best predictor of the dependent variable. The analysis of variance and the Durbin-Watson test have been applied to examine the impact of variables. In this way, it is determined whether the given classification is important in affecting the results. This can be done via the mechanism of the F and T tests. To test whether EVA, MVA and SVA are correlated or not, 't' test has been applied and the results discussed. It is evinced that among the biggies, in the last five out of the ten years of the study period, MVA has registered a positive trend. There have been some fluctuations during the first five years of the study period. It is observed from the figures of small-medium group of companies that a majority of 73 companies (92.47%) during the year 1998-99 have registered negative MVA. It tinkles that the book value of shares of these companies has been dominating over the market value.

Among the 16 converts companies selected for the study, 14 companies have registered a negative MVA during 1997-98, 1998-99, 2002-03 and 2003-04. The overall analysis implies that in most of the years of the study, wealth destruction has been found mainly in case of small-medium and converts group of companies. Further, it can be concluded that large group of companies show favourable wealth creation compared to the other two groups. MVA based Frequency Distribution of Sample Companies has been displayed for first five years and last five years in Table 6.1 (a) and (b) respectively.

Table 6.1 (a)

MVA Based Frequency Distribution of Sample Companies (1996-97 to 2000-01)

	No. of Companies									
MVA	*2000-01*	%	*1999-00*	%	*1998-99*	%	*1997-98*	%	*1996-97*	%
Negative	81	79.41	84	82.35	89	87.25	80	78.43	62	60.78
Upto Rs. 1000 Cr.	20	19.61	16	15.69	13	12.75	21	20.59	39	38.24
Rs. 1000 to Rs. 2000 Cr.	1	0.98	1	0.98	0	0.00	0	0.00	0	0.00
Rs. 2000 to Rs. 5000 Cr.	0	0.00	1	0.98	0	0.00	1	0.98	1	0.98
Above Rs. 5000 Cr.	0	0.00	0	0.00	0	0.00	0	0.00	0	0.00
	102	**100.00**	**102**	**100.00**	**102**	**100.00**	**102**	**100.00**	**102**	**100.00**

Table 6.1 (b)

MVA Based Frequency Distribution of Sample Companies (2001-02 to 2005-06)

	No. of Companies									
MVA	*2005-06*	%	*2004-05*	%	*2003-04*	%	*2002-03*	%	*2001-02*	%
Negative	52	50.98	61	59.80	66	64.71	82	80.39	58	56.86
Upto Rs. 1000 Cr	47	46.08	38	37.25	31	30.39	18	17.65	35	34.31
Rs. 1000 to Rs. 2000 Cr	0	0.00	1	0.98	2	1.96	2	1.96	5	4.90
Rs. 2000 to Rs. 5000 Cr.	2	1.96	1	0.98	1	0.98	0	0.00	4	3.92
Above Rs. 5000 Cr.	1	0.98	1	0.98	2	1.96	0	0.00	0	0.00
	102	100.00	102	100.00	102	100.00	102	100.00	102	100.00

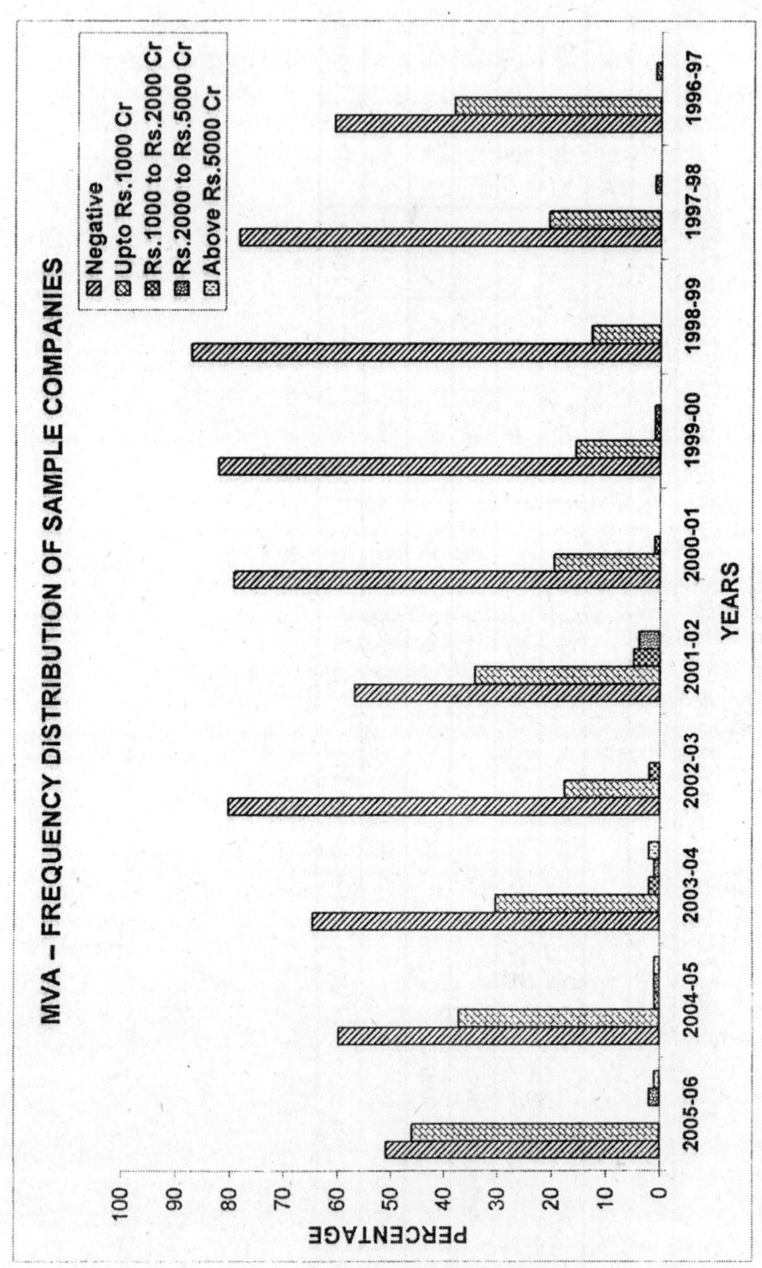
MVA – FREQUENCY DISTRIBUTION OF SAMPLE COMPANIES
Negative
Upto Rs.1000 Cr
Rs.1000 to Rs.2000 Cr
Rs.2000 to Rs.5000 Cr
Above Rs.5000 Cr
PERCENTAGE
100
90
80
70
60
50
40
30
20
10
0
2005-06
2004-05
2003-04
2002-03
2001-02
2000-01
1999-00
1998-99
1997-98
1996-97
YEARS

CORRELATION BETWEEN EVA AND MVA

Karl Pearson's Correlation Model has been adopted in order to establish the relationship between the two most important wealth creators of a corporate – EVA and MVA. The association between these two variables has been analysed for the industry as a whole as also with the sub groups. To test the association of EVA with MVA the following hypothesis has been framed.

H_0: There is no significant relationship between EVA and MVA.

Considering the whole sample, Table 6.2 detects that the relationship between these two variables is seen as significant and high positive during the three years of the study namely 1996-97 (0.591), 2001-02 (0.872) and 2003-04 (0.708). Though negative correlations have been observed in the rest of the years of study they also remain significant at 1 per cent level of significance. Adverse trend has been noticed in 2005-06 comparing with the year 1996-97.

The association between EVA and MVA is significant and positive during the latter two years of the study i.e, 2001-02 (0.708) and 2003-04 (0.974) among the large group of companies. The year 1996-97 registered a negative value of -0.542 and a similar trend is noticed during the year 2005-06 (-0.714). It is apparent from the table that insignificant relationship is found in six out of the ten years of the study. There exists positive relationship at 1 per cent level of significance during 1996-97, 2000-01 and 2001-02 among the small-medium group of companies. Negative relationship is observed during the seven out of ten years of the period under study. Strong, positive relationship has been observed during the year 2000-01 (0.715).

It is found that there exists above moderate relationship between EVA and MVA in six out of the ten years of the study period in case of convert group of companies. It is further deduced that the association between the variables is not significant in the other four years of the study period i.e., 1998-99 with -0.348, 1999-2000 with -0.398, 2003-04 with 0.327 and 2004-05 with 0.467.

All the financial variables considered in the study have their own significance in the shareholders wealth maximisation. EVA and MVA, the major indicators of wealth maximisation have been correlated using Karl Pearsons co-efficient of correlation and the results are presented in the Table 6.2.

Table 6.2

Correlation between EVA and MVA

Years	Whole Sample		Large		Small-Medium		Converts	
	Correlation Coefficient	*Sig. (2-tailed)*	*Correlation Coefficient*	*Sig. (2-tailed)*	*Correlation Coefficient*	*Sig. (2-tailed)*	*Correlation Coefficient*	*Sig. (2-tailed)*
2005-06	-0.784**	0	-0.714	0.072	-0.257*	0.022	0.518**	0
2004-05	-0.592**	0	-0.387	0.392	-0.014	0.218	0.467	0.068
2003-04	0.708**	0	0.974**	0	-0.543**	0	0.327	0.217
2002-03	-0.633**	0	-0.715	0.071	-0.247*	0.028	0.868**	0
2001-02	0.872**	0	0.708	0.075	0.403**	0	0.686**	0.003
2000-01	-0.925**	0	-0.927**	0.003	0.715**	0	-0.616*	0.011
1999-00	-0.616**	0	-0.071	0.074	-0.466**	0	-0.398	0.127
1998-99	-0.523**	0	-0.781*	0.038	-0.716**	0	-0.348	0.186
1997-98	-0.484**	0	-0.836*	0.019	-0.092	0.417	-0.552*	0.027
1996-97	0.591**	0	-0.542	0.208	0.0679**	0	0.588*	0.017

* Correlation is significant at the 0.5 level.

** Correlation is significant at the 0.1 level.

Nine functional parameters which signify the wealth maximisation of shareholders have been considered for the study, viz., MVA, Turn Over, NOPAT, ROS, ROTA, ROCE, EPS Market Price and SVA. In order to disclose which among these factors contribute much towards shareholders wealth maximisation, Factor analysis has been done.

FACTORANALYSIS

Factor analysis attempts to identify underlying variables, or factors, that explain the pattern of correlations within a set of observed variables. Factor analysis is often used in data reduction to identify a small number of factors that explain most of the variance observed in a much larger number of manifest variables. Factor analysis can also be used to generate hypotheses regarding causal mechanisms or to screen variables for subsequent analysis (for example, to identify collinearity prior to performing a linear regression analysis). Factor analysis is primarily used for data reduction or structure detection. The purpose of data reduction is to remove redundant (highly correlated) variables from the data file, perhaps replacing the entire data file with smaller number of uncorrelated variables. The purpose of structure detection is to examine the underlying (or latent) relationships between the variables.

Factor analysis has been done in the present study for the industry as a whole and for all the three groups. Communalities table, one of the outputs of this analysis, represents the proportion of the variance explained by the component or factor. In general any variable having communality less than 0.5 has little in common with the rest of the variables and cannot be explained by other components.

Results of factor analysis are tabled (*Tables 6.4 to 6.9 on pages 243 to 250*). For extraction, Principle Component Method is used. Looking at the factor analysis results for whole sample, in the communality table (Table 6.4) all factors have values higher than 0.5 and can be considered in the analysis. It is easier to visualise the variables that make up the factors by rotating the matrix of factors. An orthogonal rotation is performed using varimax with Kaiser Normalisation. Table 6.3 exhibits the çorrelation matrix among the variables.

Table 6.3

Correlation Matrix of select financial variables

Variables	*MVA*	*Turnover*	*NOPAT*	*ROS*	*ROTA*	*ROCE*	*EPS*	*Market Price*	*SVA*
MVA	1.000	.745	.792	.145	.215	.134	.646	.769	.826
Turn over	.745	1.000	.953	.094	.266	.207	.671	.733	.852
NOPAT	.792	.953	1.000	.089	.255	.237	.767	.849	.842
ROS	.145	.094	.089	1.000	.553	.296	.220	.144	.109
ROTA	.215	.266	.255	.553	1.000	.751	.468	.306	.268
ROCE	.134	.207	.237	.296	.751	1.000	.354	.231	.200
EPS	.646	.671	.767	.220	.468	.354	1.000	.833	.642
Market Price	.769	.733	.849	.144	.306	.231	.833	1.000	.731
SVA	.826	.852	.842	.109	.268	.200	.642	.731	1.000

Table 6.4

Results of Factor Analysis—Whole Sample and Large Group

Functional Parameters	*Whole Sample*						*Large Group*							
	Communalities		*Component Matrix*		*Rotated Component Matrix*		*Communalities*		*Component Matrix*			*Rotated Components Matrix*		
	Initial	*Extr-action*	*1.00*	*2.00*	*1.00*	*2.00*	*Initial*	*Extr-action*	*1.00*	*2.00*	*3.00*	*1.00*	*2.00*	*3.00*
MVA	1.00	0.79	0.85	-0.24	0.88	0.06	1.00	0.98	0.98	-0.09	0.13	**0.98**	-0.06	0.15
Turn over	1.00	0.85	0.90	-0.22	0.92	0.08	1.00	0.93	0.87	-0.06	-0.42	0.86	-0.25	-0.37
NOPAT	1.00	0.93	0.94	-0.22	**0.96**	0.10	1.00	0.97	0.98	0.01	-0.12	0.98	-0.07	-0.12
ROS	1.00	0.51	0.26	0.66	0.03	0.71	1.00	0.93	-0.18	-0.71	0.63	-0.18	-0.38	**0.87**
ROTA	1.00	0.88	0.48	0.81	0.19	**0.92**	1.00	0.98	-0.07	0.92	0.37	-0.04	**0.99**	-0.04
ROCE	1.00	0.69	0.39	0.74	0.13	0.82	1.00	0.98	-0.05	0.96	0.22	-0.02	0.97	-0.20
EPS	1.00	0.75	0.86	0.08	0.79	0.35	1.00	0.99	0.75	-0.15	0.64	0.75	0.11	0.64
Market Price	1.00	0.82	0.90	-0.13	0.89	0.17	1.00	0.98	0.94	0.09	0.29	0.95	0.18	0.22
SVA	1.00	0.83	0.88	-0.21	0.91	0.09	1.00	0.79	0.82	0.17	-0.30	0.82	0.01	-0.35

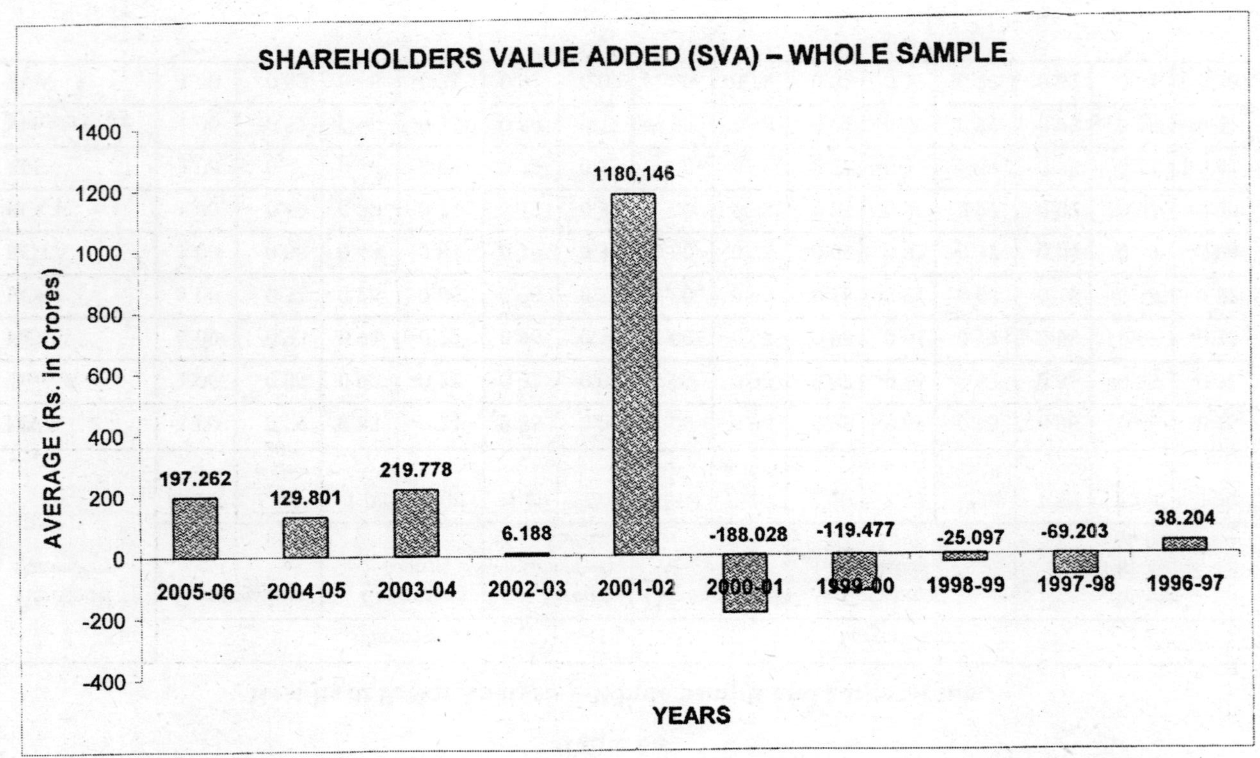
SHAREHOLDERS VALUE ADDED (SVA) – WHOLE SAMPLE
AVERAGE (Rs. in Crores)
1400
1200
1000
800
600
400
200
0
-200
-400
197.262
129.801
219.778
6.188
1180.146
-188.028
-119.477
-25.097
-69.203
38.204
2005-06
2004-05
2003-04
2002-03
2001-02
2000-01
1999-00
1998-99
1997-98
1996-97
YEARS

Table 6.5

Whole Sample Result of Factor Analysis: Total Variance Explained

Component	*Initial Eigen values of Squared Loadings*			*Extraction Sums*			*Rotation Sums of Squared Loadings*		
	Total	*% of Variance*	*Cumulative %*	*Total*	*% of Variance*	*Cumulative %*	*Total*	*% of Variance*	*Cumulative %*
1.	5.19	57.663	57.663	5.19	57.663	57.663	4.834	53.716	53.716
2.	1.853	20.585	78.249	1.853	20.585	78.249	2.208	24.533	78.249
3.	0.732	8.137	86.386						
4.	0.452	5.027	91.413						
5.	0.291	3.232	94.645						
6.	0.204	2.264	96.91						
7.	0.134	1.49	98.4						
8.	0.123	1.369	99.768						
9.	0.021	0.232	100						

Table 6.6

Large Sample Result of Factor Analysis: Total Variance Explained

Component	*Initial Eigen values*			*Extraction Sums of Squared Loadings*			*Rotation Sums of Squared Loadings*		
	Total	*% of Variance*	*Cumulative %*	*Total*	*% of Variance*	*Cumulative %*	*Total*	*% of Variance*	*Comulative %*
1.	4.816	53.511	53.511	4.816	53.511	53.511	4.814	53.487	53.487
2.	2.335	25.94	79.451	2.334	25.94	79.451	2.174	24.153	77.64
3.	1.385	15.391	94.842	1.385	15.391	94.843	1.548	17.202	94.843
4.	0.285	3.172	98.015						
5.	0.138	1.538	99.553						
6.	0.04	0.447	100						
7.	2.50E-16	2.78E-15	100						
8.	1.58E-17	1.76E-16	100						
9.	-3.43E-17	-3.80E-16	100						

The rotated component matrix is shown in Table 6.4 for whole sample and for large companies, Table 6.7 for small-medium companies and for Converts. The factorial analysis of the whole sample (*See Table 6.5 on page 245*) has shown that 78.25 per cent of the total effect can be represented by 2 factors by grouping the nine parameters. Factor 1 groups MVA, Turnover, NOPAT, EPS, Market Price and SVA. ROS, ROTA, ROCE are grouped together as factor 2. NOPAT and ROTA are found to have a stronger relationship.

Similarly in the case of large companies, all the 9 variables are grouped under 3 factors only (*See Table 6.6 on page 246*) with 94.84 per cent of variance. MVA, Turnover, NOPAT, EPS, Market Price and SVA are grouped as Factor 1. ROS represents Factor 3, & ROTA and ROCE together are grouped as Factor 2. MVA, ROS and ROTA are found to have stronger relationship.

In the case of Small-Medium companies all the 9 variables are grouped under 3 factors only (Table 6.8). Factor 2 groups MVA and SVA. Turnover, NOPAT, EPS and Market Price are grouped under Factor 1, and the remaining variables are grouped under Factor 3. Stronger relationship between variables are noticed with regard to EPS, MVA and ROTA.

Tables 6.7 & 6.9 (*See on pages 248 and 250*) signify the factor analysis results for the converts group of companies. Three factors are defined in the rotated component matrix. MVA, NOPAT, ROS, ROTA and SVA are grouped under factor 1 and Turnover and EPS under factor 2 and ROCE and Market Price under factor 3. Stronger relationship between variables are identified with regard to MVA, ROCE and EPS.

In this chapter, the result of the statistical analysis made on the data obtained from the three sub-groups is presented and useful inferences are obtained. Based on the correlation analysis it can be understood that EVA and MVA have insignificant association between 1996-97 and 2005-06 in case of large group of companies. The relationship sounds good in the other two sub-groups during these two years.

The major contributor towards the wealth maximisation of shareholders is confirmed in the factor analysis with only 2 factors (NOPAT and ROTA as strong contributors) in whole sample and 3 factors each in all the sub-groups represent all the nine variables i.e

Table 6.7

Results of Factor Analysis - Small-Medium and Converts

Components	Small-Medium								Converts							
	Communalities		Components Matrix			Rotated Components Matrix			Communalities		Components Matrix			Rotated Components Matrix		
	Initial	Extr-action	1	2	3	1	2	3	Initial	Extr-action	1	2	3	1	2	3
MVA	1	0.931	-0.05	0.78	0.27	-0.01	0.954	0.012	1	0.91	0.78	-0.5	-0.01	0.94	-0.011	0.125
Turnover	1	0.869	0.85	-0.02	0.32	0.83	-0.415	0.011	1	0.85	0.35	0.85	0.09	-0.01	0.915	-0.009
NOPAT	1	0.754	0.79	-0.03	0.19	0.69	-0.512	0.118	1	0.76	0.81	-0.01	0.32	0.65	0.357	0.449
ROS	1	0.051	0.44	0.46	-0.03	0.13	0.062	0.007	1	0.82	0.84	-0.01	-0.03	0.87	0.233	-0.012
ROTA	1	0.876	0.65	0.54	-0.04	0.24	0.014	0.905	1	0.89	0.84	0.38	-0.02	0.61	0.712	-0.014
ROCE	1	0.778	0.6	0.42	-0.05	0.14	-0.098	0.865	1	0.83	-0.00	-0.05	0.75	0.02	-0.034	0.844
EPS	1	0.882	0.85	0.16	0.38	0.89	-0.073	0.298	1	0.93	0.54	0.74	0.31	0.07	0.946	0.182
Market Price	1	0.625	0.53	0.37	0.46	0.72	0.264	0.197	1	0.51	0.28	-0.00	0.66	0.07	0.231	0.671
SVA	1	0.867	-0.4	0.77	0.35	-0.00	0.931	0.011	1	0.91	0.78	-0.05	-0.01	0.94	-0.011	0.125

Table 6.8

Small-Medium Sample Results of Factor Analysis: Total Variance Explained

Component	*Initial Eigen values*			*Extraction Sums of Squared Loadings*			*Rotation Sums of Squared Loadings*		
	Total	*% of Variance*	*Cumulative %*	*Total*	*% of Variance*	*Cumulative %*	*Total*	*% of Variance*	*Cumulative %*
1.	3.702	41.13	41.13	3.702	41.13	41.13	2.583	28.696	28.696
2.	2.193	24.366	65.496	2.193	24.366	65.496	2.3	25.551	54.247
3.	1.199	13.326	78.821	1.199	13.326	78.821	2.212	24.574	78.821
4.	0.699	7.771	86.592						
5.	0.639	7.1	93.693						
6.	0.003	3.339	97.031						
7.	0.015	1.665	98.697						
8.	0.077	0.852	99.549						
9.	0.041	0.451	100						

Table 6.9

Converts Sample Results of Factor Analysis: Total Variance Explained

Component	*Initial Eigen values*			*Extraction Sums of Squared Loadings*			*Rotation Sums of Squared Loadings*		
	Total	*% of Variance*	*Cumulative %*	*Total*	*% of Variance*	*Cumulative %*	*Total*	*% of Variance*	*Cumulative %*
1.	3.764	41.823	41.823	3.764	41.823	41.823	3.319	36.873	36.873
2.	2.287	25.407	67.23	2.287	25.407	67.23	2.611	29.012	65.885
3.	1.348	14.983	82.213	1.348	14.983	82.213	1.469	16.328	82.213
4.	0.933	10.363	92.576						
5.	0.381	4.236	96.813						
6.	0.228	2.532	99.345						
7.	0.05	0.555	99.899						
8.	0.009	0.101	100						
9.	9.27E-08	1.03E-06	100						

MVA, ROS and ROTA in case of large sample, EPS, MVA and ROTA in case of Small-medium group and MVA, ROCE and EPS in case of converts group of companies. All the variables got selected in all the rotations providing scope for further analysis.

REGRESSION ANALYSIS

Multiple Regression Analysis has been carried out to explore the extent of relationship existed among dependent and independent variables incase of selected companies, and also to find out whether a particular independent variable emerges as the most explanatory variable. MVA is taken as the dependent variable and Market Price, ROS, ROCE, SVA, ROTA, EPS, Turnover and NOPAT are taken as the independent variables. The results witness the positive auto correlation as per the result of Durbin Waston model as depicted in Table 6.10.

Table 6.10

MVA and other independent variables (Average): Durbin-Watson Analysis for the Whole Sample - Model Summary (h)

Model	*R*	*R Square*	*Adjusted R Square*	*Std. Error of the Estimate*	*Durbin-Watson*
1.	.868(a)	.754	.732	143.460	1.832
2.	.868(b)	.754	.735	142.701	
3.	.868(c)	.753	.737	142.118	
4.	.866(d)	.750	.737	142.334	
5.	.865(e)	.748	.738	142.083	
6.	.863(f)	.745	.737	142.117	
7.	.861(g)	.741	.736	142.506	

a. ***Predictors:*** (Constant), Market Price, ROS, ROCE, SVA, ROTA, EPS, Turnover, NOPAT

b. *Predictors:* (Constant), Market Price, ROS, ROCE, SVA, EPS, Turnover, NOPAT

c. *Predictors:* (Constant), Market Price, ROS, ROCE, SVA, Turnover, NOPAT

d. *Predictors:* (Constant), Market Price, ROS, ROCE, SVA, NOPAT

e. *Predictors:* (Constant), Market Price, ROS, ROCE, SVA

f. *Predictors:* (Constant), Market Price, ROCE, SVA

g. *Predictors:* (Constant), Market Price, SVA

h. *Dependent Variable:* MVA

It is evident from Table 6.10 that the value of correlation coefficients are coming down and that of the adjusted R-Square are going uptill the 5th model is reached wherein the estimated standard error is also minimum. This shows that Market Price, ROS, ROCE and SVA are the best determinants of MVA. The 6th and 7th models of regression disclose that both the coefficients of correlation and adjusted R-square have revealed the downward trend in their values. The Durbin-Watson model testifies the positive auto-correlation in the variables as the value is below two.

Table 6.11 (*See on page 253*) presents the results ANOVA analysis. The F-statistics shows that the value of the residual is minimum in the 5th model. Table 6.12 (*See on page 255*) is used to find the most explanatory independent variable or set of variables of MVA.

Tested with t-statistics, the Table 6.12 brings out that ROCE is found significant if tested at 14.4 per cent level whereas SVA and Market Price are observed quite significant even at 1 per cent level of significance. The overall conclusion of Table 6.10 to 6.12 throws light on three most important variables i.e., Market Price, ROCE and SVA where in ROCE stands third and Market Price is the best one.

Analysis of Correlation Between Variants of Value Added of the Companies Under Study

Different variants of corporate value added viz., Economic Value Added (EVA), Market Value Added (MVA) and Shareholders Value Added (SVA) have been computed separately for each company under study. It would be fruitful if it is examined whether these variants are correlated or not. With this intention coefficient of correlation in between EVA and MVA, EVA and SVA and MVA and SVA have been calculated separately for all the companies under study. To test the significance of observed correlation coefficient (*r*), 't'-test has been applied with the following hypothesis:

H_0: The different variants of value added in the Indian Software Companies under study are uncorrelated.

Table 6.11

MVA and other independent variables (Average): ANOVA (h)

Model		*Sum of Squares*	*Df*	*Mean Square*	*F*	*Sig.*
1.	Regression	5853995.135	8	731749.392	35.555	.000(a)
	Residual	1914002.319	93	20580.670		
	Total	**7767997.454**	**101**			
2.	Regression	5853817.773	7	836259.682	41.066	.000(b)
	Residual	1914179.681	94	20363.614		
	Total	**7767997.454**	**101**			
3.	Regression	5849235.610	6	974872.602	48.267	.000(c)
	Residual	1918761.844	95	20197.493		
	Total	**7767997.454**	**101**			
4.	Regression	5823136.889	5	1164627.378	57.487	.000(d)
	Residual	1944860.565	96	20258.964		
	Total	**7767997.454**	**101**			
5.	Regression	5809797.703	4	1452449.426	71.948	.000(e)
	Residual	1958199.751	97	20187.626		
	Total	**7767997.454**	**101**			

(Contd...)

Model		*Sum of Squares*	*Df*	*Mean Square*	*F*	*Sig.*
6.	Regression	5788666.468	3	1929555.489	95.536	.000(f)
	Residual	1979330.986	98	20197.255		
	Total	**7767997.454**	**101**			
7.	Regression	5757510.548	2	2878755.274	141.755	.000(g)
	Residual	2010486.906	99	20307.949		
	Total	**7767997.454**	**101**			

a. *Predictors:* (Constant), Market Price, ROS, ROCE, SVA, ROTA, EPS, Turnover, NOPAT

b. *Predictors:* (Constant), Market Price, ROS, ROCE, SVA, EPS, Turnover, NOPAT

c. *Predictors:* (Constant), Market Price, ROS, ROCE, SVA, Turnover, NOPAT

d. *Predictors:* (Constant), Market Price, ROS, ROCE, SVA, NOPAT

e. *Predictors:* (Constant), Market Price, ROS, ROCE, SVA

f. *Predictors:* (Constant), Market Price, ROCE, SVA

g. *Predictors:* (Constant), Market Price, SVA

h. *Dependent Variable:* MVA

Table 6.12

MVA and other independent variables (Average): Coefficients (a)

Model		*Unstandardised Coefficients*		*Standardised Coefficients*	*t*	*Sig.*
		B	*Std. Error*	*Beta*		
1.	(Constant)	-30.305	19.348		-1.566	.121
	Turnover	-.126	.118	-.236	-1.065	.290
	SVA	.217	.040	.566	5.483	.000
	EPS	-1.060	2.553	-.044	-.415	.679
	ROCE	-.648	.708	-.077	-.915	.362
	NOPAT	.728	.561	.355	1.299	.197
	ROS	5.410	4.734	.073	1.143	.256
	ROTA	-11.620	125.171	-.010	-.093	.926
	Market Price	.156	.074	.274	2.107	.038
2.	(Constant)	-30.370	19.233		-1.579	.118
	Turnover	-.129	.111	-.242	-1.160	.249
	SVA	.217	.039	.566	5.512	.000
	EPS	-1.138	2.399	-.047	-.474	.636
	ROCE	-.696	.480	-.083	-1.452	.150
	NOPAT	.747	.519	.364	1.440	.153
	ROS	5.192	4.093	.070	1.269	.208
	Market Price	.156	.073	.273	2.122	.036

(Contd...)

Model		*Unstandardised Coefficients*		*Standardised Coefficients*	*t*	*Sig.*
		B	*Std. Error*	*Beta*		
3.	(Constant)	-34.434	17.149		-2.008	.047
	Turnover	-.126	.111	-.236	-1.137	.259
	SVA	.217	.039	.567	5.551	.000
	ROCE	-.752	.463	-.089	-1.624	.108
	NOPAT	.710	.511	.346	1.390	.168
	ROS	4.924	4.037	.066	1.220	.226
	Market Price	.140	.065	.245	2.149	.034
4.	(Constant)	-41.412	16.038		-2.582	.011
	SVA	.201	.036	.524	5.517	.000
	ROCE	-.712	.462	-.084	-1.540	.127
	NOPAT	.205	.253	.100	.811	.419
	ROS	4.427	4.020	.059	1.101	.273
	Market Price	.178	.056	.313	3.205	.002
5.	(Constant)	-43.110	15.872		-2.716	.008
	SVA	.219	.029	.571	7.638	.000
	ROCE	-.678	.460	-.080	-1.475	.144
	ROS	4.082	3.990	.055	1.023	.309
	Market Price	.207	.043	.363	4.810	.000

(Contd...)

Model		Unstandardised Coefficients		Standardised Coefficients	t	Sig.
		B	Std. Error	Beta		
6.	(Constant)	-47.586	15.261		-3.118	.002
	SVA	.218	.029	.570	7.628	.000
	ROCE	-.549	.442	-.065	-1.242	.217
	Market Price	.210	.043	.368	4.882	.000
7.	(Constant)	-45.853	15.239		-3.009	.003
	SVA	.217	.029	.566	7.557	.000
	Market Price	.203	.043	.356	4.751	.000

a. *Dependent Variable:* MVA.

Table 6.13

Variants of value added in the sample companies (1996-97 to 2005-06)

(Rs. in Crores)

Variables	*2005-06*	*2004-05*	*2003-04*	*2002-03*	*2001-02*	*2000-01*	*1999-00*	*1998-99*	*1997-98*	*1996-97*
EVA	-75.202	-44.290	14.270	-89.449	22.967	48.005	26.626	-3.456	7.550	0.285
MVA	164.876	117.586	201.453	0.511	238.068	-235.799	-155.980	-29.766	-71.337	38.523
SVA	197.262	129.801	219.778	6.188	1180.146	-188.028	-119.477	-25.097	-69.203	38.204

It is clear from Table 6.13 that inspite of negative EVA found during the latter years of the study, MVA is good and SVA is good too. This is mainly due to some exogenous factors causing the fluctuations in the Market Price. Analysis of observed values of coefficient of correlation (r) of different variants of value added of Software Companies are shown in the Table 6.14.

Table 6.14

Analysis of observed Correlation Coefficient (*r*) of different Variants of Value Added

Particulars	*EVA-SVA*	*EVA-MVA*	*MVA-SVA*
Pearson Correlation coefficient (r)	0.058	-0.357	0.744*
Standard Deviation (SD)	116.166	286.800	301.739
Value of t statistic $\left(\frac{\lvert r \rvert}{\sqrt{1-r^2}} \times \sqrt{n-2}\right)$	0.164	1.080	3.150

* 5% level of significance.

Table 6.14 infers that the coefficient of correlation was negative in between EVA-MVA, while it was positive but very low in between EVA and SVA. However, between MVA and SVA it is highly positive indicating strong relationship.

The value of '*t*' statistic was 0.164 in EVA-SVA, 1.080 in EVA-MVA, 3.150 in MVA-SVA whereas the table value of $t_{0.05}$ for 8 degrees of freedom was 2.31. It can be seen from the table that the value of '*r*' is significant in MVA-SVA at 5 per cent level of significance. Thus, the null hypothesis of uncorrelated variance stands rejected. Therefore it may be concluded that these two variants are correlated. However, the coefficient of correlation in EVA-MVA was negative. Since the value of '*t*' statistics in EVA-SVA was lower than the value of '*t*' at 5 degrees of freedom, the *r* was not significant. Hence, the hypothesis of uncorrelated variants is accepted in case of these variants.

CONCLUSION

An attempt has been made in this chapter to find out the whole sample-wise and sub-group wise trends in the independent variables that affect MVA.

- *MVA Analysis* shows that in most of the years under study, wealth reduction has been observed mainly in the case of small-medium and converts group of companies. Favourable wealth creation climate is noticed in case of large group of companies.
- *Correlation Analysis* has been done in order to test whether there exist any significant relationship between EVA and MVA with regard to the whole sample as well as for the sub-groups for the ten-year period from 1996-97 to 2005-06. Significant and high positive relationship has been observed during 1996-97, 2001-02 and 2003-04 with regard to the whole sample.

Among the large group of companies, significant and positive relationship has been observed in only two years of the study i.e., 2001-02 and 2003-04. Insignificant relationship has been found in six out of ten years of the study. Negative but significant relationship was found during 1997-98 and 1998-99.

Positive relationship at 1 per cent level of significance was noticed during 1996-97, 2000-01 and 2001-02 with regard to small-medium group of companies. Strong relationship has been observed during 2000-01 and in seven out of ten years of the study, negative relationship has been observed.

In case of converts group of companies, above moderate positive relationship has been found in four and negative relationship has been found in two out of ten years of the study period. The association between the variables has been found to be insignificant in the remaining four years of the study.

- *Factor Analysis* can be used either for the purpose of data reduction or structure detection. In the present study, analysis has been made to examine the underlying relationship between the variables.

The whole sample result of factor analysis reveals that NOPAT and ROTA have stronger relationship, whereas in case of large group of companies, three variables namely, MVA, ROS andROTA; in case of small-medium group, EPS, MVA and ROTA; and in case of converts, MVA, ROCE and EPS exhibit strong relationships. All the variables taken for the study got selected in all the rotations.

- ***Multiple Regression analysis*** using backward method has been adopted in order to explore the extent of relationship between dependent and independent variables. The Durbin-Watson model exhibits positive auto-correlation among the variables. Three most important variables namely, Market Price, ROCE and SVA remained after the least predictors got eliminated. ROCE stands third and Market Price as per the overall analysis stands in high merit. This implies that wealth creation is strongly influenced by the market forces.

- ***'t' test*** has been applied in order to examine whether or not EVA, MVA and SVA are correlated. High positive relationship between MVA and SVA, very low positive relationship between EVA and SVA and negative relationship between EVA and MVA have been observed.

Finally it can be concluded that MVA, the best indicator of wealth is influenced by exogenous factors apart from the Market Price.

7

SUMMARY OF FINDINGS AND RECOMMENDATIONS

INTRODUCTION

Making steady addition to the value of shareholders has turned out to be the new-fangled corporate practice in India. Those corporates, which were once bestowing the ordinary feel to the shareholders curiosity are now conferring the utmost preference for it. The shareholders wealth is measured in terms of the returns they receive on their investment. The returns may take any form namely dividend or capital appreciation or with both. Capital appreciation in turn depends on the subsequent changes in the market value of the shares. The market value in turn is influenced by a number of factors, which may either be company specific or industry specific.

The financial performance evaluation measure used in any corporate needs to be accurate, consistent and globally analogous and should lead to goal similitude between the owners and managers. Leading Multinational companies, worldwide have already adopted EVA-based system of financial management that put the system ahead of its rivals. Business majors like Cola-Cola, AT&T, IBM, General Electric, Proctor and Gamble, Johnson and Johnson, Microsoft and many other globally reputed corporate giants have already become the ardent followers of the EVA concept. The Indian corporates simply may not stay behind for understanding and implementing the concept. The corporates in India need to be fully equipped with the ifs along with the buts of EVA not just for the reason of global competition but for their long standing persistent survival.

The EVA analysis has captivated much attention in the western countries both as a management innovation as well as stock market analysis. The recognition of such a technique in the Indian context shows diverse trends to some extent. Some corporate houses have started publishing EVA in their financial statements. Majority of companies are still not prepared to put in the EVA technique for evaluating their financial performance due to certain inherent difficulties associated with regard to the computation.

EVA is a measure that should be used by top management to evaluate investment centre managers because it considers goal semblance between the shareholders and corporate managers. EVA as a model for corporate financial disclosure in India is on the rise. The use of EVA as an alternative of turnover –based analysis crosses all industrial and commercial boundaries. Value added indicates the net wealth created by the production of goods or services during a specified period in a corporate, hence, the concept is superior to the existing methods. No enterprise can survive or glow if it fails to generate wealth for ultimate stake holders. An enterprise may exist without making profit but cannot survive without adding value.

Economic value added is basically a broader financial measure of judging the output of a corporate in particular and the industry in which such corporate works in general to economic growth and development of nation. Hence the mounting significance of the EVA concept has necessitated the investigators to undergo a self-regulating study for throwing light on some of myths and realities of it. The corporate procedures have undergone through a deep-seated change in the modern time and hence the use of traditional financial variables to explain the behaviour of the present capital market is not an appropriate move toward.

Methodology in a Nutshell

As the corporate's most vital objective at this moment is to maximise share holder value, establishing a relationship between financial variables and the corporate objective is imperative. With this objective in mind, the present study intends to examine the relationship between shareholders wealth and financial variables; EVA, MVA, SVA, the measures of shareholder wealth along with the financial variables such as turnover, ROS, ROTA, ROCE, Market Price, EPS through variable- wise, year-wise, industry-wise and segment-wise have been considered for the study. For carrying out the study, the specific objectives have been set and analysed.

Hypothesis means the researcher must choose from the intricacy of observed events such considerable and pertinent facts that would most effectively elucidate the problem under study. It gives an idea about indispensable associations that exist between the different fundamentals within the complexity. Hypotheses for the present study have been stated in Chapter I and also in the specific context in different chapters. It is not possible in practice for an individual research work to approach all the bits and pieces in the universe. Only a small amount of bits and pieces from the universe for the purpose of the study on the basis of stratified sampling has been selected. The sample so selected constitutes sample design for the purpose.

The data used in this study relate to those software companies listed in the Bombay Stock Exchange (BSE) for which the data are available in the Capitaline database. The analysis is confined to the BSE listed Indian software companies only. Capitaline database contained data relating to 465 BSE listed software companies. Stratified sampling technique was used and hence the total population was sub-divided into three standard sub-groups namely Large (Turnover greater than Rs.900 Crores), Small-Medium (Turnover less than Rs.900 Crores) and Converts (diversified companies), in such a way that each strata is more homogeneous than the total population. For selection of sample companies in each stratum, companies for which data were available for minimum of eight years were identified. The researcher selected all those companies from each stratum which fulfilled the above condition. Thus the final sample consisted of 102 software companies.

For the purpose of this study, both primary as well as secondary data have been used. The primary data have been collected through a well administered questionnaire to examine the extent of awareness and adaptability of EVA among the corporate managers of sample companies. The relevant secondary data have been collected from BSE Stock Exchange Official Directory, CMIE publications, Business Newspapers, through internet, etc. The study required variety of data. Therefore, websites like http://indiainfoline.com and www.indiastat.com have been widely groped around for the purpose. The information relating to bank interest rates have been collected from banks.

In order to comprehend the level of awareness and adaptability of EVA in the minds of Indian corporate managers, the sample companies were served a well structured questionnaire. Out of 102 only 11 companies responded; due to poor response, no further analysis could be made in this regard and it has been specified in the limitations of the study. Secondary data was collected in raw form from different sources and then made suitable for analysis as per the methodology defined for the purpose.

The role of statistical tools is important in analyzing the data and drawing inferences there from. In order to derive the open-handed results from the information collected through secondary data various statistical tools like mean, standard deviation, variance, kurtosis, skewness, correlation and regression have been accomplished through EXCEL and SPSS software. Some of these statistical techniques particularly Correlation Coefficients, The Paired-Samples, Durbin-Watson Test, The Independent Sample t-test, Kendall's Test, Discriminant Analysis, Logit Loglinear Analysis and the Chi-Square Test have been used to interpret the sense of mathematical relationship amongst values of different variables computed in the study.

In the present study, the multiple linear regression models have also been used to analyse the influence of independent variables on the dependent variables, namely EVA and MVA respectively. The analysis of variance and the Durbin-Watson test has been applied to examine the impact of variables.

MAJOR FINDINGS

EVA is based on the sound economic principle that the firm's economic value would increase only if it would be able to generate surplus greater than its cost of capital. Hence, any company running from this well-built theoretical foundation may be considered as bustling from firm economic fact. In India, only a few corporates are using EVA internally as a performance gauge for refining efficiency that may guide them towards the enhancement of shareholder value. EVA provides desirable management incentives under appropriate conditions. Revealing the influence of EVA for rummaging the financial potency of Indian corporates comprising an industry and the Indian industries comprising a particular sector may be measured as the need of the hour for all such companies that have not started reporting their financial position in terms of EVA. A number of imperative findings of the study are outlined hereunder:

CAPITALISATION AND CAPITAL STRUCTURE

Capital Structure can affect the value of a firm through the earnings available to the shareholders. The fixed financial charges do not vary with the variations in the Earnings Before Interest and Taxes (EBIT) or operating profit. They have to be paid regardless of the amount of EBIT available to pay them. After paying them, the operating profits belong to the ordinary shareholders. The firm should select that financing mix which will help in achieving the objective of the maximisation of shareholder's wealth. The broader conclusions of the capital structure analysis and the statistical hypothesis testing by applying t-test and F-test are reproduced below:

The overall average amount of capital employed among the sampled companies during the period was around Rs. 153.87 crores and with the passage of time, the overall average of capital employed showed an increasing trend. A spurt in the capital employed was found among the biggies which rose from Rs. 185.06 crores to Rs. 3398.07 crores during the study period. Every sub-group showed an annual increasing trend in capital employed.

Large companies had the higher compound rate of growth as compared to the overall compound rate of growth of sampled companies as a whole, while small-medium and converts had lower compound rate of growth. In order to test the significance of the differences in the capital employed, ANOVA had been performed and it was observed that there is a significant difference in the averages of sub-groups.

A fluctuating trend had been found in the average debt to capitalisation over the study period. The overall average debt to total capitalization of the sampled companies for the study period was found to be 0.14. The highest debt to total capitalisation was found in the converts group of companies (0.176), while large group of companies recorded lesser reliance of debt capital (0.065). Unlike the general declining trend found throughout the large group, small-medium group and converts recorded an upward swing since 2001-02. ANOVA result showed that the differences among the average proportions of debt to total capitalisation of the sampled companies were significant.

t-test analysis revealed that the values of the coefficient of correlation between the average capital employed and the ratios of debt to capital employed in the case of 102 sample companies as a group was very much insignificant. It is concluded that the reliance on leverage is independent of the size of the sampled companies. Further, the companies having the proportion of debt to capital employed and average capital employed above and below the median value did not show any significant correlation. The overall analysis of capital structure indicates that contrary to the inclination of converts towards increased debt equity ratio, large and small-medium groups tend to borrow less.

COST OF COMPONENT ANALYSIS

The analysis of cost of components of capital structure revealed that the cost of debt had declined over the years while the cost of equity had exhibited wide variations. The study revealed that the cost of debt did not differ from one sub group to another sub group significantly. The average cost of equity capital in large, small-medium and converts group were found as 20.85 per cent, 17.58 per cent and 13.91 per cent respectively. It was found that distinctive cost of equity patterns did not exist though it varied from group to group.

WACC among different sub-groups did not show any distinctive variation. The average cost of debt as well as the cost of equity were the highest for biggies followed by small-medium segment. Converts enjoyed low cost debt and equity and hence their WACC was the lowest compared to other sub-groups. The debt equity ratio was found to be below the standard norm of 2:1 during the entire study period. This indicates an unfavourable position to the shareholders. A very low ratio observed deduce that the firms have not been able to use low-cost outsiders funds to magnify their earnings.

Year-wise averages of EBIT and Turnover showed an upward swing. In the majority of the years under study inverse relationship was found between Debt-equity and Turnover and between EBIT to Capital employed and debt-equity. The positive relationship observed with respect to Total debt and EBIT and Debt-equity and ROCE favours the proposition that the use of debt upto an optimal level could boost earnings related variables.

EVA ANALYSIS

The beginning of EVA as competing performance matrix may be considered as one of the most earth-shattering financial management innovations of the past decade. As key components of the shareholders value movement, the researchers have stimulated both management interest and academic research. A variant of the long-appreciated concept, EVA is well understood to provide desirable management incentives under appropriate conditions. The select financial variables like Turnover, ROS, ROTA, ROCE, EPS, Market Price, MVA and SVA have been compared with EVA. The very purpose is to observe whether there exists any meaningful association of the select financial measures with EVA.

During the first five years of the study period, 57.84 per cent of the companies in 1996-97, 28.43 per cent in 1997-98, 84.31 per cent in 1998-99, 13.73 per cent in 1999-2000 and 18.63 per cent in 2000-01 have registered negative EVA. Around 10 per cent to 40 per cent of companies during the first five years and around 9 per cent to 25 per cent of the sample companies during the last five years were generating positive EVA, but it had been upto Rs.3 crores. The dual effect of decrease in NOPAT and increase in cost of capital employed may be the cause for reduction in EVA.

Trends in EVA of top ten and last ten (selected for the F.Y. 2005-06) of the sample companies revealed that in four out of ten years, INFOSYS, SATYAM and WIPRO were holding the first three ranks. Trend in NOPAT-based ranking showed that INFOSYS, WIPRO, SATYAM, I-FLEX and TECHM come under the first eleven ranks in eight out of the ten years of the study period indicating their consistent and good performance. A fluctuating trend was found among the companies, ranked on the basis of WACC. INFOSYS hold the first rank with respect to EPS in six out of the ten years of the study and remained among the top 4 in the rest of the years. MVA based ranking revealed that INFOSYS, WIPRO and SATYAM hold the first three ranks in the last four years of the study period. Except WACC all other variables had positive influence on shareholders wealth. Among the biggies, INFOSYS, DIGITALEQP, TECHM, HP and WIPRO remain in the toppers list in most of the wealth related variables. INFOSYS emerges as a leader, as it finds place in rank list pertaining to all parameters barring WACC. HP is the only company in the large category to be listed in the WACC toppers.

Eight corporates under the small-medium group and two under converts group had a positive effect regarding WACC. Company-wise statistical analysis of EVA showed that the number of companies displaying the positive mean EVA were twelve. GTL secured the first position with regard to the mean EVA followed by INFOSYS. Twenty per cent of the sampled companies had their EVA positively skewed and a double over this percentage indicated a positive kurtosis indicating longer tails. Thirty one had registered negative average NOPAT, whereas INFOSYS stood first in the list with higher average. Major proportion of the selected companies (82%) had shown their WACC positively skewed and only 5 per cent of the companies registered the positive values of kurtosis reflecting that the observation cluster more and with longer tails.

The correlation coefficients between EVA and NOPAT (Whole sample) had been observed as negative in three out of ten years. NOPAT and WACC were found to be inversely related in three out of ten years and in the remaining seven years, positive but very low correlation coefficients were found. The correlation coefficients between EVA and NOPAT (Large group) had been observed as negative in four out of ten years of the study period, whereas the correlation coefficients between NOPAT and WACC showed a high negative for four years and a high positive in the rest of the years under study except 1998-99.

Considering the small-medium and converts group of companies, the correlation coefficient between EVA and NOPAT were found to be a high positive in the seven out of ten years of the study period. Three out of ten years in case of small-medium group and in four out of ten years in case of converts showed negative relationship between NOPAT and WACC. The overall analysis showed that an increase in the cost of capital over the earnings resulted wealth reduction in many software companies during the study period.

Paired sample test revealed that there existed no significant differences in the paired samples. The analysis of relationship of EVA with the select financial variables with regard to the whole sample revealed that the first year of the study (1996-97) indicated positive figure whereas the year 2005-06 explained negative relationship among all the other variables excluding MVA. Significant relationship between EVA and select financial variables had been observed during 2005-06. Among the sub-groups only in the small-medium group, though EVA had negative and below moderate relationship with all the variables selected for the study, such relationship was found significant in most of the years. The backward mode of regression analysis exhibited that Market Price, ROCE, ROTA and MVA are the best predictors on EVA. The Durbin-Watson model ruled out any positive auto-correlation between the dependent (EVA) and the independent variables.

Logit loglinear relationship revealed that beta coefficient had maximum covariance among whole sample, large, and small-medium group of companies which showed greater variability whereas cost of debt was found to be maximum in converts group. The minimum covariance observed was cost of debt in case of whole sample, debt to total capitalisation in case of large group, cost of equity in case of small-medium group and equity to total capitalisation in case of converts group stating their consistency.

Discriminant analysis revealed that the three variables namely EPS, Market Price and Turnover were substantially important variables in discriminating between groups. Chi-Square analysis concluded that the differences between the expected and actual figures of EVA were insignificant

MVA ANALYSIS

A research idea has been evolved in this chapter to find out the industry-wise and sector-wise trends in the independent variables that affect MVA. Favourable wealth creation (MVA) was noticed in case of large group of companies whereas in case of small-medium and converts group, wealth reduction had been observed. A significant and high positive relationship between EVA and MVA had been observed during 1996-97, 2001-02 and 2003-04 regarding the whole sample.

A significant and positive relationship was deduced only in two years of the study (2001-02 and 2003-04) among the large group. Insignificant relationship in six years and negative but significant relationship in two years (1997-98 and 1998-99) had been found. A positive relationship was noticed during 1996-97, 2000-01 and 2001-02 with regard to small-medium group. Strong relationship during 2000-01 and negative relationship in seven out of ten years had been observed.

In case of converts group, the above moderate relationship had been found in six out of ten years. Insignificant association between the variables had been observed in the remaining four years of the study. The whole sample result of factor analysis revealed that NOPAT and ROTA had stronger relationships. In case of large group, 3 variables namely MVA, ROS and ROTA and in small-medium EPS, MVA and ROTA and in converts MVA, ROCE and EPS exhibited strong relationships. All the selected variables got selected in all the rotations.

Multiple regression analysis using backward method revealed that there existed positive auto-correlation among the variables. Among the three important variables remained after the least predictors being eliminated, ROCE stood third, SVA second and market price stood as the best predictor. '*t*' test analysis revealed a high positive relationship between MVA and SVA, very low positive relationship between EVA and SVA, and a negative association between EVA and MVA. This showed that MVA had been influenced more by the exogenous factors.

RECOMMENDATIONS

Barring multinational companies, most companies in India till recently paid lip service to the goal of shareholder wealth maximisation. They showed sporadic concern for the shareholders, mainly when they approached the capital market for raising capital. The higher corporate needs for funds and the greater dependence on the capital market have induced firms to become more friendly with shareholders. Institutional investors tend to be more discerning and have the muscle and motivation to nudge companies to pursue shareholder friendly policies. With the abolition of wealth tax on equity shares and other financial assets, there is now an incentive to enhance share prices. An attempt is made here to sketch a few recommendations emanating from the findings of the study to the software companies for effectively competing in the global arena.

Cost of Capital

Cost of capital of a company is the minimum expected rate that a company requires to meet its obligations and sustain itself in the market. In designing the financial policy i.e., the proportion of debt and equity in the capital structure, the firm aims at minimizing the overall cost of capital. The empirical analysis revealed that the cost of debt stood at 0.44 per cent and 0.35 per cent among the large and small-medium group of companies. The overall cost of capital also remained high in these two groups viz, 19.77 per cent and 17.14 per cent respectively. It is suggested that the companies belonging to large and small-medium groups should redesign their capital structure in order to reduce the cost of debt as well as WACC. The companies can have a large portion of debt in its structure, as debt is much cheaper than equity. While augmenting the debt capital, the companies have to keep in mind the standard norm of debt equity ratio.

Debt-Equity ratio is the simple measure of the balance between the finance provided by equity share holders and that desired from external borrowings. It provides the best start for the assessment of capital structure. Debt-Equity ratio (Average) in the study showed fluctuation ranging between 0.083 during 1999-2000 and 0.217 during (1996-97) and was found to be below the standard norm of 2:1 in all the years under study. This shows that the select software companies are low geared. The companies may try to have more low cost borrowed capital which will enable to have wide operations.

When an investor is investing in shares, he is taking higher risk and expects a high return because there is an uncertainty with regard to dividend which he may or may not receive. There is an uncertainty with regard to the movement in share price. If the company does not perform, the investor may not even get his money back. The cost of capital plays a role in deciding upon the dividend policy of the firm. In the present study, wide fluctuation is being noticed regarding the behaviour of cost of capital and hence the software companies are suggested to follow appropriate dividend policies with a view to maximise the wealth of the shareholders as well as the company as a whole.

Awareness on EVA Concept

Maximising shareholder value is superior to any other governing objective that a company might adopt because it will lead managers to make the decisions most likely to increase the company's competitive, organisational and financial strength over time. Enlightened managers and public officials recognise that increase in stock prices reflect improvement in competitiveness – an issue which affects everyone who has stake in the company or economy. Wealth creation is not a zero-sum game where an increment to shareholder value must some how diminish the welfare of other stakeholders. The reverse indeed is true, increments to total welfare can come only from creating wealth. The EVA concept has yet to sink in the minds of shareholders. The companies must view itself as a socially responsive entity and assure wider responsibility to disclose EVA in their annual reports. Applying EVA requries a major change in accounting and financial statements. If necessary, Accounting Standards may also be altered to insist companies to disclose EVA in their annual reports.

Majority of the companies under study have exhibited negative and low positive EVA. Over the period, the average EVA should be an upward moving target with optimistic expectations. The cyclical shocks to EVA will have to be compensated immediately during the coming years. The yearly deviations are to be met. The investors may be suggested to subscribe for or buy the shares of the companies which have greater EVA.

Policy Implication

Corporate governance embraces not only the way in which a company is managed and its dealings with shareholders but also every aspect of its relationship with society. Shareholders and others dealing with a company wanted assurance that it was being well and correctly managed. Value based companies regard value maximisation as the governing corporate objective. They hammer out strategies aimed at overcoming the forces of competition. They develop superior organisational capabilities meant to surmount internal barriers in the process of value creation. Transparency should be demonstrated both within and outside the corporate boundaries. The competent authorities in the country like ICAI, SEBI, RBI and the government should issue wide-ranging guiding principles for the computation of EVA and its practices in financial reporting and accounting disclosures by the corporate world.

The EVA literature suggests that EVA is a trendy tool for measuring the management performance. The main problem with EVA is the calculation of its various elements. Particularly the Net Operating Profit After Tax and the average cost of capital. The fact that several adjustments are to be made in order to convert the GAAP based income to economic income make this performance metric a complex one. Using EVA for capital budgeting decisions has to be augmented with traditional metrics such as Net Present Value, Discounted Cash Flow and Payback period.

Both EVA and NOPAT are single period measures, and negative values of either may represent wise investment for the future, not the destruction of value. No clear advantage to shareholders is seen by looking at EVA, as the accounting return on their investment is the NOPAT. While these investors certainly need to be aware of capital structure, they should be familiar with the opportunity cost of their investments and may not need to incorporate this into the measure of performance. It seems essential to investigate the ability of other measures of short-term performance to reflect long-run value added.

For the performance evaluation by management, desegregations of data used in EVA calculation is a very complex process, and in some cases, may be considered unattainable objective. A recommended approach is to use one metric (EVA) for top-level executives and different metric for middle and lower level managers. Since the use of EVA as a performance measure gained popularity in recent years, continued research in this area is needed.

At present the companies are paying more attention on the profit generated by them, whereas the value added is neglected. But it is well known that in the long run only those companies will survive who will add value. Whether the organisation is profit-oriented or non-profit oriented, they have to keep in mind, the human aspect of operation in their activities. The human aspect explains that while satisfying one's activities, one must also keep in mind the ethics generally accepted by the society at large. Every human activity should be directed towards adding value by their activities and functions. Value addition is the increment in the satisfaction provided by the product or services or activities of an organisation.

EVA should be used with care in valuing and identifying stocks that have the potential to outperform the market. EVA is a reasonable valuation tool for the shares of companies whose prospects can be forecasted with reasonable accuracy. It appears to be crucial in spotting out changes in a company's on going performance that are hidden in EPS numbers.

When any company sells the shares at the premium, MVA will be high which implies great benefits to the shareholders. The question which arises is, how besides anything else can the EVA factor be governed? Growing mergers and acquisitions among the corporates is the proof for creating shareholder's wealth. Shareholders understanding and acceptance of EVA concept is quite essential.

CONCLUSION

The software industry has a strong future regardless of whether its products are as a service, or as a component or in packaged form. The software industry is going through a rapid and significant transition. India's domination in the IT and software sector and its growing reputation as one of the world's best outsourcing destinations have created good basis for future prospects. Wealth creation is a desire to be rich, desire to have control over the aspects that affect financial life, a desire to command respect with the control of money power. Wealth creation includes the decision making processes of a business unit whether the unit grows organically or through acquisition. Wealth creation is not material, it is spiritual by nature with the ability to produce or manifest material wealth. Globalisation, outsourcing and world flattening advances in technology continue to rock the software industry in ways that will significantly alter the way that technologists do business.

Wealth creation is considered imperative for equitable distribution of the same. This creation and distribution process will go towards alleviating the plight of the downtrodden. The IT/ ITES industry has set this process of wealth creation in motion. Wealth creation is the key to financial freedom and building one's wealth requires the right information, planning and making skilful investment choices. The key to creating wealth is adding value. All financial success, especially business success, is based on adding value. It is based on the old saying, "find a need and fill it". Adding value is the way that all fortunes are made. In many studies relating to EVA and MVA, the twin wealth creation measures were established. Even though in the present study, most of the companies have observed negative and low positive EVA, their MVA performance is good. This implies that wealth creation has the direct influence on the market forces. Large companies have exhibited encouraging EVA performance when compared to the other two groups.

Inflationary pressures, higher perceived business risk and market imperfections are the main reason for the higher cost of capital. (*PricewaterhouseCoopers 1999*). While macro-economic conditions and market imperfections are beyond the control of these companies, Indian software companies could try to enhance their business focus, improve investor perception, diversify to reduce revenue volatility, and ensure that they comply with strict reporting norms that encourage corporate transparency as well as increase their investor base. A SWOT analysis of the Indian software industry may reveal strategies for continued predominance of the Indian software industry.

The present study leaves the scope for future research relating to the applicability of Economic Value Added among the Indian Software Companies. With this, the researcher places this piece of research work as an adding-up in the in-attendance literature of the area under discussion and further more there is open-handed compass for future researches in this pasture of EVA.

BIBLIOGRAPHY

BOOKS

Anthony P.D' Costa and E. Sridharan, *India in the Global Software Industry—Innovation, Firm Strategies and Development*, Macmillan India Ltd., Delhi, 2004.

Ashok.H. Chandra Prasad, S. George, *EXIM Dynamics Services and WTO... An Indian Perspective*, Commonwealth Publishers, New Delhi, 110002.

Bardia S.C., *Accounting and Finance for Managers*, RBSA Publishers, Jaipur–302 003.

Bhalla. V.K., *Financial Management and Policy, Text and Cases*, 4th Revised and Enlarged Edition, Anmol Publications Pvt. Ltd, New Delhi-110002 (India).

Bob Vause, The Economist, *Guide to Analysing Companies*, Profile Books Ltd., 58-A, Hatton Garden, London, 2004.

Brigham E. and J. Houston, *Fundamentals of Financial Management*, 8th Edition, Dryden, 1998.

Corporate Finance and Control, *Research Series in Applied Finance*, The ICFAI Journal of Applied Finance, ICFAI Press, 2000.

David, S. Young and Stephen F.O Byrne, *EVA and Value Based Management*, A Practical Guide to Implementation, TATA McGraw–Hill, New Delhi, 2003.

Dolphy D'souza, *Indian Accounting Standards and GAAP*, Ketan Thakkar Snow White Publication Pvt. Ltd, Jer Mehal, 532, Kalbadevi Road, Mumbai-400 002, Vol. 1, 2005.

Falguni C. Shastri, *Capital Structure of Indian Corporate Sector*, Book Enclave, Jaipur, India, 2005.

Hawawini (Gabriel) and Viallet (Claude), *Finance for Executives*, Managing for Value Creation, Thomson Asia Pvt. Ltd., Singapore, 2002.

Nand Kishore Sharma, *Finance and Accounting Issues and Perspectives for 21st Century*, Mangal Deep Publications, Jaipur, India.

Dr. Niranjan Swain, Dr. Chandra Sekhar Mishra, Economic Value Added-concepts and Cases, ICFAI PRESS, 52 Nagarjuna Hills, Hyderabad, India–500082.

Pandey. I.M., *Financial Management*, Vikas Publishing House, New Delhi, 8th Edition, 2002.

Prasanna Chandra, *Finance Sense—Finance for Non-finance Executives*, 3rd Edition, Tata Mc Graw Hill Publishing Co., Ltd., New Delhi.

Ravichandran. N., *Competition in Indian Industries—A Strategic Perspective*, Vikas Publishing House Pvt. Ltd, New Delhi–110014.

Ross, Westfield and Jorden, *Fundamentals of Corporate Finance*, TATA McGraw-Hill, New Delhi, 2002.

Samuel C. Weaver and J. Fred Weston, *Finance and Accounting for Non-Financial Managers*, Tata McGraw–Hill Publishing Company Limited, New Delhi.

Singh.K.P. and M.C.Garg, *Economic Value Added in Indian Coporates*, Deep & Deep Publication Pvt. Ltd., F-159, Rajouri Garden, New Delhi-110027.

Dr. Sonia Agarwal, *Value Added Statement* (Analysis and Interpretation) RBSA Publishers, S.M.S Highway, Jaipur (India).

Vedpuriswar.A.V., *Strategic Financial Management – Achieving Sustainable Competitive Advantage*, Vision Books, New Delhi – 110024.

JOURNALS/ARTICLES/MAGAZINES

Abhi Gyan, *Quest for Excellence ISSN 0970—2385*, Vol. XXIII No. 3, Oct-Dec, 2005.

Abuzar MA Eljelly and Khalid, S.A., *Performance Measures and Wealth Creation in An Emerging Market*, International Journal of Commerce and Management, Indiana, 2001, Vol. 11, p. 54.

Anand Ganpatrao Jumle, *Financial Implications of Risk Management Practices in Small and Medium Software Development Organisations in Pune*, The Journal of Accounting and Finance, Vol. 20, No. 1, Oct. 2005-March 2006, pp. 75-83.

Anand Parthasarathy, *ITES/BPO: Passage to India*, Industrial Survey of India, 2004.

Anand Parthasarathy, *IT Infrastructure—Stray Islands of Progress*, The Hindu Survey of Indian Industry 2007, p. 226.

Anand Parthasarathy, *Software and Services—Opportunities Nearer Home*, The Hindu Survey of Indian Industry 2007, p. 234.

Arnaud Castillo: *Using EVA for Acquisitions*, Acquisitions Monthly, Dec. 98, p. 87.

Bacidore J. Boquist J. Milbourn T and Thakor A, *The Search for the Best Financial Performance Measure*, Financial Analysts Journal, May/June 1997.

Balaji.C.D., *Economic Value Added—The Ideal Performance Metric*, Syndicate—The Journal of Business, 2005, pp. 12-17.

Banarjee, Ashok, *Economic Value Added: A Better Performance Measure*, The Management Accountant, December 1997, pp. 886-888.

Bennett, Linda, *The EVA Yardstick*, Management Review, No. 7, July 1995, p. 47.

Bert Van Wegen and Robert De Hoog, *Measuring the Economic Value by Information Systems*, Journal of Information Technology, Vol. XI, 1996, pp. 247-260.

Bhargava, Sunitha Wadekar, *Software Exports from India? Yes it is for Real*, Business Week, Jan 18, 2003, p. 77.

Bhatnagar. S.C., Shirin Madon, *The Indian Software Industry: Moving Towards Maturity*, Journal of Information Technology, 1997, pp. 227-288.

Blair, A., *EVA Fever*, Management Today, Jan. 1997, pp. 42-45.

Blair, Alistair, *Watching the New Metrics*, Management Today, April 1997, pp. 48-50.

Bonu N. Swami, *Risk and Return Analysis: Case Study of Selected Industries*, Journal of Accounting and Finance, Vol. VIII, No. 1, Apr. 1994, pp. 78-100.

Brian Campbell, *Software Asset Management Helps Reduce Licence Non-compliance as well as the Risk of Software Failure and Corruption*, Express Computer, April, 16, 2007, p. 10.

Carlo Alberto Magni, *Decomposition of Net Final Values: Systematic Value Added and Residual Income*, Bulletin of Economic Research, 2003, pp. 149-174.

Chamboli, P.C., *A Panorama of Capital Structure Planning of Indian Cement Group*, Lok Udyog, 19(9), 1985, pp. 23-30.

Chandrashekaran V, *Business Quality—The Cutting Edge*, Management Review, Jan-March, 1996.

Charu Bahri, *Does India have a Killer IT Product?*, I.T., April 2007, pp. 52-57.

Clinton, B.D. and S.Chen, *Do New Performance Measures Measure up?*, Management Accounting, Oct. 1998, pp. 38-43.

CMIE Industry: *Financial Aggregates and Ratios*, Jan 2006.

CMIE Industry: *Market Size and Shares*, Feb. 2006.

Cyrus A. Ramezani, Luc Soenen and Alan Jung, *Growth, Corporate Profitability and Value Creation*, Financial Analysts Journal, 2002, pp. 56-65.

David Crowther, *Corporate Social Responsibility Increases Shareholder Value"*, ICFAI Reader, July 2004, pp. 21-25.

David F Rico, *ROI of Software Process Improvement–metrics for Project Managers and Software Engineers*, ICFAI Reader, Jan. 2005, pp. 63-68.

David Young, S., *Some Reflections on Accounting Adjustments and Economic Value Added,* Journal of Financial Statement Analysis, Winter, 1999, Vol. 4, p. 7.

De Villers J., *The Distortions in Economic Value Added,* Journal of Economics and Business, Vol. 49, No. 3, May/June, 1997, pp. 285-300.

Deependu Jain, Hemant Daga and Nitin Kakkar, *Theory of Business of Indian Software Industry,* IIMB Management Review, Volume 15, No. 1, March 2003, pp. 61-68.

Dennis G. Uyemura, *EVA: A Top-down Approach to Risk Management,* The Journal of Lending and Credit Risk Management, Feb. 1997, Vol. 79, p. 40.

Dierks Paul A and Ajay Patel, *What is EVA and How Can It Help Your Company,* Management Accounting, No. 5, Nov. 1997, pp. 52-57.

Dillon, R.D and J.E Owers, *EVA as a Financial Metric: Attributes, Utilisation and Relationship to NPV,* Journal of Applied Corporate Finance, 1997, pp. 32-40.

Economic Intelligence Service, *CMIE—Industry Market Size and Shares,* Aug. 2003.

Edger, Norton, *Factors Affecting Capital Structure Decisions,* The Financial Review, 26(3) 1991, pp. 431-446.

Edwards. B, *Survey: Faster, Cheaper, Better,* Ibid, p. 3.

Edwards. B, *Survey: The Place To Be,* The Economist, November 13, 2004, Vol. 373, No. 8401, p. 8.

Edward J. Lusk, Ruth A Pagell and Michael Halperin, *EVA: CFO Opinions—The Hawthorne Effect?* Financial Executives Magazine, March/April 2002, pp. 134-139.

Edward V.McIntyre, *Accounting Choices and EVA,* Business Horizons, Jan-Feb 1999, pp. 66-72.

Ehrbar and G.Hamel, *Debate: Duking It Out Over EVA,* Fortune, Vol. 136, No. 3, 1997, p. 232.

EVA: What Time India?, Chartered Financial Analyst, ICFAI Press, Nov. 1998.

Galen R. Hatfield, *R & D in an EVA World*, Research—Technology Management, pp. 41-47.

Geyskens, Inge, Katrijin Gielens, and Marnik G Dekimpe, *The Market Valuation of Internet Channel Additions*, Journal of Marketing, 66 April 2002, pp. 102-119.

Ghosh. D., P. Gupta, J. Gulati, G.S. Srinivas and A.Agarwal, *India's Software Exports: Prospects and Opportunities*, Exim Dynamics of Services and WTO, pp. 91-100.

Giridharan, P.T., Ph.D. Thesis, 1996, Saurashtra University, Rajkot.

Glasser, James, *How EVA Works Against GATX*, Chief Executive, No. 110, Jan-Feb 1996, pp. 42-43.

Glassman, David, *Contracting for Value: EVA and the Economics of Organisations*, Journal of Applied Corporate Finance, 1997, Vol. 10, No. 2, Summer.

Gopalan.S., *SMITs: From Infancy to Adulthood*, IIMB Management Review, March 2003, pp. 80-83.

Grant J.L. *Foundation of EVA for Investment Managers*, Journal of Portfolio Management, Vol. 23, 1996, pp. 41-48.

Gupta, O.P. and Sehgal Sanjay, *An Empirical Testing of Capital Asset Pricing Model in India*, Finance India, December, 1993, Vol. VII No. 4, pp. 863-874.

Howl, John S., Ji-Chain-Lin, Journal of Financial Research, Vol. XV, Spring 1992.

ICRA—Information Technology—The Indian Software Industry, May 2004.

Indian Journal of Business Papers, Vol. 2 & 3, No. 4 & 5. Dec-June 2002.

Industry: Financial Aggregates and Ratios, Centre for Monitoring Indian Economy, Jan 2005.

Industry: Financial Aggregates and Ratios, Centre for Monitoring Indian Economy, May 2004.

Jakob H. Iverson, Lars Mathiassen, Peter Axel Nielsen, *Managing Risk in Software Process Improvement: An Action Research Approach*, MIS Quarterly, Vol. 28, No. 3, Sep. 2004, pp. 395-433.

Joel Stern, *EVA Disciplines Management*, Business India, June 4, 2006, p. 103.

John C. Groth, Ronald C. Anderson, *The Cost of Capital: Perspectives for Managers*, Management Decision 35/6, 1997, pp. 474-482.

Jordan, J., Lowe, J. and Taylor, P. *Strategy and Financial Policy in UK Small Firms,* Journal of Business Finance and Accounting 25(1), 1998, pp. 1-27.

Joseph C. Hartman, *Technical Note—on the Equivalence of Net Present Value and Market Value Added as Measures of a Project's Economic Worth*, The Engineering Economist, 2000, Vol. 45, No. 2, pp. 158-164.

Journal of Accounting and Finance, Vol. XV, No. 1. March 2001.

Jayachandran, *Indian Software Industry: Structure, Trends and Constraints*, Journal of Services Research, Vol. 1, No. 1-2, Oct. 2001, pp. 73-93.

JTD Journal, XXXIII: No. 3-4, July–Nov. 2003.

Kalpana Sharma, Vandana Sharma, Mitra Joshi, *e-waste Land,* I.T., June 2007, pp. 55-57.

Kambhampati U, *The Software Industry Development: The Case of India*, Progress in Development Studies, 2002, Vol. 2 No. 1 pp. 23-45.

Kapil Sharma, *Economic Value Added in Indian Environment*, Business Perspectives, Vol. 6, No. 2 pp. 127-134.

Karen Spinner, *A New Tool to Measure Performance*, Global Finance, Nov. 1997, Vol. 1, p. 24.

Kiran Karnik, *Software and Services: Riding on Boom, Industrial Survey of India,* 2004.

Kiran Karnik, *Indian Software Exports Head North,* Banking and Finance, May-June 2004, pp. 35-38.

Koppar. A., *SMITs:Growth Issues*, IIMB Management Review, March 2003, pp. 88-89.

Kroll K.M., *EVAs and Creating Value—Is Economic Value Added the Best Way to Keep Capital Costs Covered?*, Industry Week, 1997, Vol. 246, No. 7, pp. 102-109.

Kumar. K., *Growth Issues of Small and Medium Enterprises in the IT Sector (SMITs): An Overview*, IIMB Management Review, March 2003, pp. 70-72.

Lakshminarayanan.N., *Niche is Where the Prospects Lie*, IIMB Management Review, March 2003, pp. 77-79.

Larry M. Prober: *EVA: A Better Financial Reporting Tool*, Pennsylvannia CPA Journal, Fall 2000, Vol. 71, p. 27.

Matthew, Billet T., and Ryngaert, Mike, *Capital Structure, Asset Structure and Equity Takeover Premiums in Cash Tender Offers*, Journal of Corporation Finance, Volume 3, No. 2, April 1997, pp. 145-165.

MC Conville, Daniel J, *All About EVA*, Industry Week 243, No. 8, April 18 1994, pp. 55-58.

Michael D. Johnson, Eugene W. Anderson, Jaesung cha, and Barbara Bryant, *The American Customer Satisfaction Index: Description, Findings and Implications*, Journal of Marketing, 60, October 1996, pp. 7-18.

Milunovich, S and A. Tsuel, *EVA in the Computer Industry*, Journal of Applied Corporate Finance, Vol. 9 No. 1, Spring 1996, pp. 104-115.

MIS Quarterly, *Management Information Systems*, Vol. 27, No. 3, Sep. 2003.

MIS Quarterly, *Management Information Systems*, Volume 27, No. 4, Dec. 2003.

MIS Quarterly, *Management Information Systems*, Vol. 28, No. 2, June 2004.

MIS Quarterly, Vol. 28, No. 3, Sep. 2004, pp. 395-433.

Mohnot, Rajesh, Mohnot Abstract of Doctoral Dissertation, *Capitalisation and Capital Structure in Indian Industries*, Finance India, Vol. XLV No. 2, June 2000, pp. 546-551.

Nancy L.Beneda, *Valuing Operating Assets in Place and Computing Economic Value Added*, The CPA Journal, Nov. 2004, pp. 56-61.

Narasimhan Mandyam, *Bigger is Better*, IIMB Management Review, March 2003, pp. 84-87.

Nicolas Mottis and Jean—Pierre Ponssard, *VBM-The Building Block for EVA Implementation*, European Business Forum (www.ebfonline.com)

Nuelle, Frances, *The Two Faces of EVA*, Chief Executive No. 110, Jan/Feb. 1996, pp. 38-39.

O' Byrne, S.F., *EVA and Shareholder Return*, Financial Practice and Education—Spring/Summer, 1997, pp. 50-54.

O' Hanlon.J and K. Peasnell, *Measure for Measure?*, Accountancy, Feb 1996, pp. 44-46.

Peterson, Pamela p and David R. Peterson, *Company Performance and Measures of Value Added*, Monograph, The Research Foundation of the Institute of Chartered Financial Analysts, 1996.

Prabhakkar Sharma and Santhosh Patnalk, *Advantages Lure Investors*, The Hindu Survey of Indian Industry, 2007, pp. 235-236.

Pradeep Tibrewala, *Use of Accounting or EVA in Corporate Performance Evaluations*, The Accounting World, Dec 2005, pp. 42-49.

Prashant Gupta, *The Indian Software Industry*, Competition in Indian Industries: A Strategic Perspective, pp. 237-264.

Premchander, *India's Software Industries; A Diagnostic Analysis*, 1993.

Prestige Research Abstracts, Vol. 1, No. 1, Jan 2004.

Radhakrishnan. K.G., *Software Exports*, Yojana, Nov. 2004, pp. 15-21.

Raina. S.N., *How Indian Software Companies are Taking on the West: An Insight Into What Goes on in These Companies*, Vision—The Journal of Business Perspective, Vol. 11, No. 1, Jan-March 2007.

Raj Aggarwal, *Using Economic Profit to Assess Performance: A Metric for Modern Firm*, Business Horizon, Feb. 2001, Vol. 44, p. 55.

Ramachandra Reddy B. Yuvaraja Reddy, *Financial Performance Through Market Value Added (MVA) Approach*, The Management Accountant, Jan. 2007, pp. 56-58.

Rao Cherukuri. U., *Capital Project Evaluation and Risk Adjustment Practices in South Korean Companies*, GITAM Journal of Management, Vol. 2, Jan-June 2004, No. 1, pp. 25-43.

Rao, Rajeshwar, K. and R.Sadanandam, *Impact of Capital Structure Decisions*, Finance India, Vol. IX No. 1, March 1995, pp. 64-89.

Reimann. B.C., *Managing for the Shareholder: An Overview of Value—Based Planning*, Planning Review, Jan-Feb, 1988, pp. 10-22.

Rice, Victor, *Why EVA Works for Variety*, Chief Executive, No. 110, Jan/Feb 1996, pp. 40-41.

Robert R. Tumble and Delowell, Angela N, *Connecting CEO Performance to Corporate Performance: Examining Intangible Metrics of Shareholder Value*, Journal of Compensation and Benefits, 2001, Vol. 17, p. 8.

Saint, Daniel K., *Why Economic Value is a Yardstick for Numbers, Not People*, Financial Executive, No. 2 March/April 1995, pp. 9-11.

Sajosps, *South Asian Journal of Socio-Political Studies*, Vol. 6, No. 1, Dec. 2005.

Samuel C. Weaver, *Measuring Economic Value Added: A Survey of the Practices of EVA Proponents*, Journal of Applied Finance—2001, pp. 50-59.

Shinichi Shibayama, *Integrated Value Management: A Multi-faceted Approach to Creating Corporate Value*, The ICFaian Journal of Management Research, Vol. III, No. 1, Jan. 2004, pp. 71-85.

Siddharth A.Pal, *Global Outsourcing—Leveraging India's Strengths*, The Hindu Survey of Indian Industry 2007, pp. 218-220.

Singh, Kumar, Ajay, *Maximising Wealth of Shareholders Through EVA and BPR*, Pranjana, Vol. 2, No. 1, Jan-Jun. 1999.

Sona School of Management, *Journal Global Management Review*, Vol. 1 Issue 2, Feb. 2007.

Srikanth. V., *Marketing Strategies of Software Export Industry—A Study of Select Companies*, GITAM Journal of Management, Vol. 3, July-Dec. 2005, No. 2, pp. 170-176.

Sriram Rajamani, *Software Engineering Growing Smarter by the Day*, I.T., May 2007, pp. 78-80.

Srivastava, Rajendra K. Tasadduq A. Shervani and Liam Fahey, *Market—Based Assets and Shareholder Value: A Framework for Analysis,* Journal of Marketing, 62, Jan. 1998, pp. 2-18.

Stern, Joel M.G. Bennett Stewart III and Donald H. Chew, Jr., *The EVA Financial System,* Journal of Applied Corporate Finance, No. 2, Summer, pp. 32-46.

Stewart, G. Bennett, *The Quest for Value: The EVA Management Guide,* Harper Business, New York, 1990.

Stewart, G. Bennett, *EVA™: Fact and Fantasy,* Journal of Applied Corporate Finance, 1993, pp. 6-19.

Stewart III, Bennett. G, *EVA: Fact and Fantasy,* Journal of Applied Corporate Finance, 1994, No. 2 Summer, pp. 71-84.

Subramanya Sharma, Jai Krishna Ramesh P and Ravikiran.A., *Indian Software Industry: An Operations Perspective,* IIMB Management Review, June 2002, pp. 17-27.

Subramanyam. G.V., *Increasing Distribution will Drive Greater Use of Collaboration in Software Development,* I.T., May 2007, pp. 81-84.

Som Mittal, *Indian SMIT Sector: Poised for Growth,* IIMB Management Review, March 2003, pp. 73-76.

Suresh Babu, Calicut Regional Engineering College and P.K. Jain Professor of Finance, Department of Management Studies, IIT Delhi, Article Published in Indian Management, January/ February, 1999, pp. 46-53.

Syndicate—The Journal of Business, 2005.

The Economic Challenger, No. 9, Issue 34, Jan-March 2007.

The Economist, *Business America's Pain, India's Gain: Outsourcing,* January 11, 2003, Vol. 366, No. 8306, p. 59.

The Economist, *Business: Time to Bring It Back Home? Outsourcing,* March 5, 2005, Vol. 374, No. 8416. p. 70.

The Journal of Accounting and Finance, Vol. 19, No. 2 April-Sep. 2005.

The Journal of Indian Management and Strategy, Vol. 10, No. 4, Oct-Dec. 2005.

The Management Accountant, June 2004, pp. 502-505.

The Most Comprehensive Ranking of Indian's Top Companies, Business World, March 5, 2007.

To EVA or Not to EVA: Is That the Question? Journal of Applied Corporate Finance, Summer, 94.

Tully Shawn, *The Real Key to Creating Wealth*, Fortune 128, No. 6, Sep. 20 1993, pp. 38-50.

Tully. S., *America's Greatest Wealth Creators*, Fortune, Nov. 9, 1998, pp. 193-204.

Valuing Companies: A Star to Sail By, The Economist, Aug. 2nd, 1997, pp. 57-59.

Venkataramana Gajjala, *Role of Information and Communication Technologies in the Enhancing Processes of Entrepreneurship and Globalisation in Indian Software Companies*, The ICFAI Journal of Entrepreneurship Development, Vol. IV, No. 1, 2007.

Viswanadham.N. and Poornima Luthra, *Models for Measuring and Predicting Shareholder Value: A Study of Third Party Software Service Providers*, Sadhana, Vol. 30, April/June 2005, pp. 475-498.

Walbert, Laura, *America's Best Wealth Creators*, Fortune 128, No. 16, Dec. 27, 1993, pp. 64-76.

Walbert, Laura, *The Stern Stewart Performance 1000 Using EVA to Build Market Value*, Journal of Applied Corporate Finance, No. 4, Winter, 1994, pp. 109-112.

Walsham G, *Cross–cultural Software Production and Use: A Structural Analysis*, MIS Quarterly, 2002, Vol. 26, No. 4, pp. 359-380.

Wheatly Mallom, *IT Passage to India Today*, Management Review, 1999.

Xavier Adsera and Pere Vinolas, *FEVA: A Financial and Economic Approach to Valuation*, Financial Analysts Journal, 2003, p. 16.

REPORTS

IBA Bulletin Special Issue, March 2003.

The Indian Banker, March 2006, Vol. 1, No. 3.

NEWSPAPERS

Kiran Karnik, *TCS Remains Top Exporter*, Business Line, June 17, 2005, p. 5.

NASSCOM Seeks Special Courts for Piracy Cases, Business Line, April 27, 2005, p. 10.

IT Capital Spend Very Low in India: NASSCOM, Business Line, April 29, 2005, p. 5.

Rukmini Priyadarshini, *Climbing the Curve*, Business Line, Oct. 10, 2005, p. 1.

Mirza Viquar Ahmed, *The Ever-growing Impact of IT*, Business Line, Aug. 16, 2005, p. 9.

Software Export Growth May Top 35 Per Cent, Business Line, March 30, 2005, p. 5.

Joel Stern, *EVA Disciplines Management*, Business India, June 4, 2006, p. 103.

TCS Retains Top Slot as Software Services Exporter, Business Line, June 28, 2006, p. 13.

Moumita Bakshi Chatterjee, Bharat Kumar, *Escrow Accounts Yet to Make Mark in IT Industry*, Business Line, Oct. 10, 2005, p. 1.

Moumita Bakshi Chatterjee, *A Tough Nut to Crack*, Business Line, Oct. 17, 2005.

Sriram. B., *Where It Hits IT—A Look at Service Tax Implications on the IT Sector, Post-Budget 2006*, Business Line, March 27, 2006, p. 10.

Business Line, Dec. 23, 2004, p. 5; Dec. 26, 2004. p. 9; Dec. 29, 2004. p. 5 & 13; Jan. 4, 2005, p. 5; Jan. 17, 2005, p. 1; Aug. 29, 2005.

WEBSITES

www.eva.com

www.indiainfoline.com

www.capitaline.com

www.bseindia.com

www.investopedia.com

www.iba.org.in.

www.valuebased management.net

www.icraindia.com

Index

□□□